Paul Stiles

# IS THE AMERICAN DREAM KILLING YOU?

## How "the Market" Rules Our Lives

Collins

An Imprint of HarperCollinsPublishers

HarperCollins books may be purchased for educational, business, or sales promotional use. For information, please write to: Special Markets Department, HarperCollins Publishers Inc., 10 East 53rd Street, New York, New York 10022.

Designed by Kathryn Parise

LIBRARY OF CONGRESS CATALOGING-IN-PUBLICATION DATA

Stiles, Paul.
Is the American dream killing you? : how "the market" rules our lives / by Paul Stiles.
p.  cm.
Includes bibliographical references and index.
ISBN 0-06-059378-4
1. Markets—Social aspects. 2. Free enterprise—Social aspects.
3. Capitalism—Social aspects. 4. Economics—Sociological aspects.
I. Title.

HF5470.S75 2005
306.3'42'0973—dc22                                    2005041392

ISBN-13: 978-0-06-059378-0

05 06 07 08 09 DIX/RRD 10 9 8 7 6 5 4 3 2 1

*To My Parents*
*Curtis and Marilyn Stiles*

The gods we worship write their names on our faces; be sure of that. And a man will worship something—have no doubt about that, either. He may think that his tribute is paid in secret in the dark recesses of his heart—but it will out. That which dominates will determine his life and character. Therefore it behooves us to be careful what we worship, for what we are worshipping, we are becoming.

—Ralph Waldo Emerson

# CONTENTS

Contents

# IS THE

# AMERICAN

# DREAM

# KILLING

# YOU?

# PROLOGUE: The Sound of the Alarm

The alarm is ringing.

You jerk awake, tense, aware only of the blare, then fall back in recognition. There is a brief moment of peace, as if your consciousness were confused about what to do next, and then it hits you, arising from your subconscious, where it has lain all evening: The List. All those things you did not complete yesterday, and all those other things you have to get done today. The List is its own infomercial, in full sound and video, complete with snippets of conversation and shots of the office. And stuck on auto replay. Okay, you think: just put your feet on the floor.

That's it: the race is on. In the next hour the entire house fires its engines and rolls to the starting line. Kids up, dog out, showers all around, paper fetched, breakfast on the table . . . You pass your wife in the hallway several times, both of you half-dressed, seeking to check off the next item. Mayhem.

Inevitably you forget something, and today it's the trash. The trash! It dawns on you in the shower. You bolt out, throw on a robe, run out back with your loafers on, and drag the two overflowing cans up to the street just in time to catch the truck. Phew!

Walking back down the driveway, you briefly marvel at those cans. By the end of the week the two of them are always full, and you can't for the life of you figure out why. How does your family consume so much? Yet you do, and millions like you do too. The average American discards nearly a ton of trash every year, which is twice as much as a Western European, and nearly three times as much as a Japanese. Scientists even estimate that if Earth's 6 billion inhabitants consumed as much as the average American, we would need at least four additional planets to keep up.

Back in the house the kids are watching television, and you tell them to shut it off, just as you have to keep them off the Internet. There are only so many murders and copulations to be had before breakfast. Today you even hold back the sports page, since there's nothing but steroids and rape. So you sit there reading it yourself, the List playing in the background, until you look up, startled by what you find. Your young one is reading *The Cheerios Play Book,* in which he's placing the little *O*s in cardboard holes, and your oldest is eating a bowlful of . . . Cheerios. There it is, you think: another cradle-to-grave victory for the General Mills marketing department. You can't win.

The List breaks in, you glance at your watch, and tell your oldest to finish up. You have so much to do today. Your wife does too, and the young one is swept off to day care with hardly a word—did she say good-bye? You drop the bowls in the sink for later—there's no time now—herd your budding teenage daughter to the car, and pull out of the driveway with a brief screech.

Straight ahead, an enormous object expands to fill the windshield: Xanadu. Your new neighbor's megahouse weighs in at ten thousand square feet, easy. It's got a couple of turrets, multiple decks, a three-car garage, an indoor pool (so you've heard), an outdoor pool, and a gazebo with more frill than a wedding dress. From up there, the rest of the neighborhood must look like a tiny hamlet at the foot of the lord's castle. The new American Dream. And they don't even have any kids! A marketing exec, you've heard. After six months, you haven't even said hello.

You look in the rearview mirror: your seventies ranch is looking smaller every year. And in relative terms, it is: since 1975, the average American home has grown steadily in size, while the number of people per house has steadily declined. Go figure. Pretty soon every man really *will* have his own castle.

You step on it now, acutely aware that you are driving away from your office, and finally reach your daughter's school. The flag is snapping in the breeze out front. You are happy she is in private school—she is getting a great education—but you wish she could go to the local junior high. Then your wife wouldn't have to work. After all, you pay your taxes, don't you? But when you went to the open house you couldn't believe it. It was like entering the set of *Road Warrior*. The body art, the nose rings, the tattered clothes, boys with their pants below their hips, the underwear hanging out in emulation of their ex-con heroes—the first thing they do in prison is remove your belt. That girl with HO! on her T-shirt, a diamond in her navel. Hoods over headphones, rap leaking through. Black T-shirts with MEGADEATH on them. All flowing past you in the hallways like sea wreckage, all that is left after the ship goes down.

No way, you couldn't do *that* to her, no matter what it took.

Your daughter leaps out with a quick good-bye, and the car is silent. With the List playing in your mind, you've hardly spoken to her.

Now at least you are headed toward the office. You count the traffic lights until you see the one with the camera, and give it the gas. You hear it's a private company that runs the damn thing, and they get a percentage of every ticket. No wonder the light is so quick. Then it's time for your morning pit stop. The Golden Arches appear, and you head to the drive-thru for your coffee. As you wait at the window, you look inside, where the obesity epidemic is in full view. Thirty percent of American adults are now obese, and McDonald's seems to be their home away from home, on both sides of the counter. The problem is spreading among children, too, but you only see one of those, a kid getting his supersized soda on the way to school. The statue of Ronald looks on.

The entrance ramp is just around the corner, and the long haul to D.C. begins. The traffic is thick this morning, but still moving. You are an expert on every leg of this journey, and its history. Just five years ago, your commute took 45 minutes, but now there are days when it hits an hour and a half. If there is an accident on either side of the road, you've had it. On Fridays in the summer, you can count on two hours. You added this up once, stunned by the result: If you commute one hour each way every working day, and work 48 weeks a year for 30 years, you will have spent 14,400 waking hours in your car by the time you retire. Since you are awake only 16 hours a day, that is 900 waking days in your car, the equivalent of a two-and-a-half-year sentence in solitary confinement. And now that the traffic has added another half hour each way, you've just received another 1.25 years for good behavior.

The rise in commuting time is all because of the sprawl, of course, which has congested the entire area in recent years. When you first started this commute, there were green fields here. Now all you can see is mile after mile of tract homes, broken only by strip malls, all of it designed by an architect in love with military barracks. And yet this is nothing but the beginning: the entire area from Washington to Boston has been slowly congealing into a single megalopolis, a landscape as intricate as any semiconductor, while the green space everywhere has been evaporating at a record rate. Two acres of farmland disappear every minute to development, the fastest such decline in the country's history. The road to your kids' school used to be two lanes; now it is nine lanes wide at one point, if you count the turn lanes.

As the open space has shrunk, so has the patience of the commuters. It used to be people would slow down when they saw your blinker and let you in when you came off the ramp: no more. The commute is tenser than ever. But what can you do about it? You have to worry about road rage, some psycho with a gun. After all, when you have snipers gunning people down from the trunk of their car, as happened right near here, the commute has certainly changed.

As if to reinforce that thought, the prison soon appears ahead, in all its deathly calm. Slits for windows. Slinkies of razor wire. An empty courtyard by the highway's edge. You drove by it for years without giving it a second thought, as if it was a natural part of the landscape, but now it haunts you every morning. Somewhere along the line you learned that the United States has the highest incarceration rate in the world. In the past twenty years, it has increased nearly five hundred percent. There are now 2.1 million Americans behind bars, the equivalent of putting the entire populations of Boston, Seattle, Denver, and Washington, D.C. in prison. God only knows what goes on in there, you think: One out of five is mentally ill. The brick fortress accelerates behind you, and you breathe easier again. A sip of coffee through a plastic lid.

A helicopter is circling over the highway, which reminds you to turn on the traffic report. No major backups, you are happy to learn, so maybe just an hour today. The air quality is Code Red, however, which basically means you are breathing through your tailpipe. Then the new electronic sign over the highway appears, the one that broadcasts the latest Threat Level from Homeland Security. You're lucky: It's only yellow today, a "significant risk of terrorist attack." So it's safer to move around than it is to breathe.

As the neon sign passes overhead, it's like a border crossing. Home lies behind you, Washington lies ahead, and chaos enters your mind, a babble of media images: towers collapsing, a dark hole in the side of the Pentagon, the anthrax strike—the last two dead ahead. Afghanistan, Iraq—the news is all about Iraq. But for all the news, you can't make sense of it all. You know the country was attacked by people who hijacked airplanes and crashed them into our buildings, but you're really not sure why, no one has adequately explained it, these people killing themselves like that, all because they hate the United States? Three thousand people, dead. Silence. You know we invaded Afghanistan to take out the terrorists, which made perfect sense, but didn't we give these same people $3 billion just a few years ago? Then we invaded Iraq, whom we also used to fund, because they were supposedly linked to the terrorists and had weapons of mass destruction that would make the air even worse than it is. But then no weapons of mass destruction were found, and the president admitted that there was no link after all, so what are you supposed to make of that? It sure would be nice to know what you are fighting for, particularly if you may die for it. Forty billion a year on intelligence, and this is the result. If your kid was on the ground there, you would be going out of your mind. Over one thousand so far, gone. No wonder trust in government has plunged. Can't you see the sign over the highway? HOMELAND SECURITY ALERT, LEVEL RED: SEVERE THREAT OF COVER-UP.

A bump jars your thoughts, and you realize you have entered D.C. because the road is so bad. Welcome to the legacy of Marion Barry. Imagine, the capital of the world's superpower, run by a crack user. A great place to launch a war on drugs. And now he's back on the city council. You tense up at the wheel, unconsciously. Somehow, as the density of the buildings increases, the temperature seems to rise. And of course, now is the time when your gas light goes on. You hate stopping here, you feel so exposed, but you pull over to the next pump and do it anyway. As you are paying the cashier, a young black man, it suddenly strikes you: it's people like him who are dying in Iraq. The all-volunteer force, they call it. It sounds so fair and just. But none of the top professionals you know have ever served; nor do their kids. Why don't the rich serve the country anymore?

Back on the road, the huge white dome of the Capitol appears in the distance, as magnificent as ever, but once you look past the architecture, you're not sure what to think anymore, there's just a wrenching feeling, more potholes in the road. In the past few years you've seen your country do things you thought were impossible. Round people up and send them to Cuba with bags on their heads, where they sit indefinitely, without benefit of a lawyer, until a military tribunal decides their fate. Scores of them, trying to commit suicide it's so bad. Or worse, shipping them to other countries, where we know they will be tortured for information, thereby justifying everything they might have done to us. Invading an entire nation on false pretenses, then torturing prisoners in Saddam Hussein's own prison. Numerous unexplained deaths. Unspeakable.

As a lawyer, you cannot believe this is happening, and that people here, in Washington, D.C., bear much of the responsibility for it. The new attorney general even wrote the torture policy. You did not think such things were possible, here in America. This is not the Constitution you studied. Does anyone care anymore? But you also feel that knife twist deep inside you, hear that hollow ring to your own words. What leg do you have to stand on? The fact is, you went to law school with all kinds of ideals, and they all disappeared on the way to partner, when you discovered that the law had become a business, and nothing more. For years you lived off the misery of others: nasty divorces, personal injuries, medical malpractice. You leveraged a society that had turned on itself, where if you burned your lip on some hot coffee you could sue McDonald's for millions. Winning was everything. And when you finally got sick of it, in ways you could not express, you did what you thought was the right thing and took the corporate counsel job, where at least the hours were less, only to find yourself in an even deeper moral swamp, a place with less integrity than the Simpson trial. Oh yes, O.J.: the blood on his socks just wasn't enough.

Several potholes later, you finally turn into your parking garage. You are late, as you frequently are on drop-off days, but there is no way around it. So far no one has said anything, but it adds a tangible layer of stress that you don't need. You enter your office at a full clip, toss your coat on the chair, and look at the clock: you're okay, fifteen minutes until the staff meeting. You sit down in your chair, collect your thoughts, and unfurl the paper you haven't had time to read. The media, you think with a sinking stomach. Celebrity journalists hawking products without telling you, chasing ambulances, always trying to tear down somebody, and not even trying to be evenhanded, the whole thing looking more like entertainment every day. What happened? Something has come between you and the truth, between you and all that exists beyond your own immediate experience, what your own two eyes can tell you. You have to question everything you read.

You look at the clock: time to go. A minute later you are in the CEO's office with the rest of the management team. You are polite, of course, but as assistant corporate counsel, you know too much to respect the man who runs your corporation. You know he is out for himself, that he has formed a small cabal at the top to leverage the entire company for their own personal gain, that he has stocked the board with supporters and presented rosy projections to analysts that you strongly suspect are fraudulent. When you were younger, you would have said something about this, but now you know that what is going on is not only common, but in many ways expected these days, and that if you stick your neck out it will only get cut off. The CEO makes over five hundred times what the average person in the company makes, but this is normal in America today, where the gap between rich and poor has grown steadily for thirty years, and is now the widest in all the rich democracies, on par with the third world. In the world at large, you read in *Forbes,* there are 358 billionaires, whose net worth is greater than that of the poorest two and a half billion people, people who live on less than two dollars a day. How long can this continue?

The meeting drones on, but you can't keep focused on it. The last few years in business have been such an eye-opener. Outside the company there has been an unprecedented number of scandals, so many that you can hardly keep track of them all. Enron, WorldCom, Adelphia, Tyco, Freddie Mac, Andersen, all the major Wall Street banks . . . They involved some of the largest corporations in America, companies that provided the Internet, appliances, electricity, mortgages, phone service, computers, medicine, even the kids' toys. No matter where you go in your house, you run into them. Still, the scandals just revealed what you knew had been going on all along, what everyone in business knew was going on, but no one wanted to admit, because that wasn't part of the game. If your CEO knew what you were thinking, he would be the very first to call you a cynic. Though it took you years to realize it, and to admit it to yourself, the essence of business, and thus the fundamental principle of your professional life, was no different than a con. It was maintaining the appearance of a moral reality while practicing the opposite, and pocketing the difference. Your own CEO was always making statements about his responsibility to the employees and the public while secretly draining the world around him of every cent. He was rich, though, which made him an American success story. He was frequently on television, where the truth about him was never spoken. And while you hoped and prayed that his lies would catch up with him in the end, you also knew that they probably wouldn't. For every CEO who was caught, there were a hundred more still under their rocks. That is how they got to the top in the first place. And even if they were caught, the worst they would get is a slap on the wrist, a function of the weakness of the law, the impotence of government, and the lawyers they could buy, lawyers like you.

After the meeting you go back to your office. As you walk through the company, you acknowledge the people you pass by, but it is nothing but the nod between jousters. Office relationships are like business as a whole: pleasant on the surface, deadly underneath. There was loyalty and teamwork when you first got here, but somehow all that evaporated, replaced by a cycle of hirings and firings, and competition so intense that you always kept one eye forward, another on your back. The only good thing about the stress was that it made the day pass quickly. You had no time to think.

The phone rings. You look at the caller ID and cringe: a 212 area code. You pick up the phone, and your worst fears come true. It is your company's investment bank, calling about their latest scheme, something dreamed up on their computers that is supposed to save you taxes while making your balance sheet look stronger than it really is. All of it very legal, of course, your account manager is quick to point out. You don't know whether to laugh or throw up. Since 9/11, nothing has changed at all. But the CEO has a cozy relationship with them, so you have to listen.

The rest of the day passes quickly, so quickly that it seems, as you step back into your car, that you just got out of it. It's almost six as you pull onto the Beltway, and you groan at the sight of the parking lot ahead of you. Two hours tonight, easy. This kind of traffic does not suddenly clear up. You look in the glove box, but you don't feel like any more books on tape, you don't even want any music, so instead you start thinking about the weekend, even if it is a few days away. You've got a lot to do, things have been piling up. There's two soccer games, and the grass, and the car needs an oil change, and your wife finally found a babysitter, so you're actually going out on Saturday night, though you can't remember where. It doesn't matter. You just want to spend time with her and the family, forget about things. You used to be more community-focused, but all that has changed in the past few years. You don't have a lot of time, first of all, but the world has changed, too. You used to spend a lot more time at church functions, but how can you, when you can't even look at the priests anymore without wondering what they are doing with the altar boys? And you used to volunteer at the United Way, but after the third financial scandal you finally said enough. You don't even donate anymore. Now you just like to take the kids to the park, which is beautiful, but virtually empty, even on the weekends, since everyone is at the mall.

Suddenly you feel a familiar headache coming on. You pop an aspirin, remembering how you swore you weren't going to live like this anymore, when you were down in the Islands. The thought spreads an achingly beautiful panorama across your mind: brilliant white crescent of beach, leaning palms, aqua water. It took you three days just to get all the motion out of your system and relax, but by the end of the week you were ready to trade places with the fishing guide. You even looked at real estate, some bungalow with a view to St. Barts. It all seemed so real, so doable, just chucking it all. What happened?

The pounding in your temples is still there when you arrive home: two hours, door-to-door, as predicted. Your wife and kids are eating dinner, as you asked them to do when you're late. Otherwise the kids stay up too late, and you have no time to yourself. Your daughter is wearing a T-shirt with the picture of a rapper flipping you off. This is art. You tell her to take it off, and ask your wife why she didn't say something. "Because I can't do everything," she says, and you know where that conversation is going, she looks frazzled, so you drop it and get a beer out of the fridge. This one beer is your evening gift. You savor it. It brackets the thirty seconds you spend in your cocoon upon awakening, the antidote to the List. As you crack it open, you notice the cereal bowls from this morning—and yesterday—in the sink. But you don't have the energy.

You sit down and have your dinner, the second half alone. Upstairs your wife is putting the kids in bed. You wish you had had more time with them, but your commute is a lot longer than hers. When you are done, you go to their rooms, but they are already asleep. Then you crawl into bed yourself, next to your wife, who puts aside her laptop. You have a brief conversation about bills, and how the kids are doing, but you don't feel like talking about your day, and you don't particularly want to hear about her office politics, either. So after the practical matters conclude, you both lie there reading next to each other, not saying anything, for half an hour, until one of you finally clicks off the light. Shortly thereafter you feel her hand on your back, but that is the very last thing you want, you can't even imagine it right now, your body feels so completely dead. At the same time you know why, because you are very well informed. Over half of all married couples are too tired when they get home from work to have sex. Over 65 million Americans suffer from the symptoms of stress, including nearly half of all salaried workers. Clearly this must have something to do with the divorce rate, which is hovering at an all-time high, with a third of all marriages dissolving in ten years; and the rate of child abuse, which has tripled in the last twenty-five years; but as the hand sags and retreats, and you slip into sleep, you can only hope that your family doesn't become another statistic.

When you awake, it is sudden, and complete, and much earlier than usual. All is dark around you, but your mind is on fire, as if it has been concentrating for hours. It is a moment of great clarity, without the cobwebs of the List, of your entire life weighing you down, a moment when the questions of the day, and of all preceding days, leap out at you in unison, forming a single question.

Why are things this way?

The question is so enormous it seems impossible to answer. It goes beyond your country to the very times you live in, to modernity itself. It leads you into the very thickets of the system, that ethereal boundary you live in, the invisible source of the way things are, a matrix gone mad. But every once in a while, in rare moments like these, when you have a spell of quiet, and feel the presence of your own soul, you sense the answer. There is a common thread connecting the garbage cans to the megahouse, the corporate crime to the selfish government, the income gap to the terrorism, *The Cheerios Play Book* to the war in Iraq, the aspirin to Wall Street, the television to the prison population, the stress to the sprawl. Staring into the quiet darkness, you sense that there is something *out there* responsible for this daily insanity, this perpetual chaos, this devastating meaninglessness. There is a reason why nothing makes sense, why life's purpose eludes you, why happiness is so fleeting, why you can't trust anyone anymore, and why so many people around the world would like to see you dead, just because you are an American. There is one primary cause behind this entire psychotic system, and that is—

You freeze. No, it can't be!

The alarm is ringing.

# INTRODUCTION: The Economic Beast

The Market as ethereal boundary: a huge glass cylinder surrounds the "market center" at the Tokyo Stock Exchange.

When Americans think about who and what they are, they inevitably turn to their founding documents, the Declaration of Independence and the Constitution of the United States. I did this recently, and came away with a hunch confirmed. Apart from authorizing Congress to regulate commerce and mint money, there is no reference to capitalism, corporations, business, or markets of any kind. One finds it hard to imagine that if we were redrafting these core documents today, the market economy would be so mute. Since our founding, that nebulous power we call "the market" has deeply penetrated our national identity, to the point where it is now difficult to separate the so-called free market from America. Somewhere along the line, the business of America really did become business, a philosophy that would come as news to the Founders, not to mention the Pilgrims. The very idea of democracy no longer stands alone in our minds, but is found within such phrases as *market democracy* and *democratic capitalism,* each conjuring up the image of a company run by co-CEOs. And like that situation, it leads one to wonder who is ultimately in charge, the people or the market, two very different powers indeed.

Since democratic principles and market principles are so utterly different, this transformation reflects no small change in the nature of the American republic. It has redefined who we are in the most fundamental way, and without much debate. It is as if we have amended the Constitution without going through the appropriate process. Our new split personality is simply chalked up to "changing times," the product of "modernity," the natural extension of the "progress" that has created the "industrialized world." Like an aging merchant ship, we find ourselves with the same old hull but a very different crew.

At the same time, we have willingly sailed in this economic direction for good reason. We have long considered the free market to be a natural extension of that core democratic principle, freedom itself. And our faith in the free market as the engine of our economy has been repaid many times over. The free market has been the undeniable source of tremendous material prosperity. It has driven historic advances in technology, conferred unprecedented material advantages upon the public, and made America the world's economic superpower. These are no small achievements. So I suppose it is natural that we would come to the conclusion that the free market is an unlimited good, and always will be, even as it wraps its fingers around our throat.

## The Mystery of Our Time

When one adds up the power of the market in our lives today, it is truly staggering, and far, far greater than we commonly recognize. Since we don't live off the land anymore, our lives now depend on the modern economy, and the market is in control of it. The market is the ultimate judge of all economic life. It determines the fate of all organizations, products, services, and people that it touches. Through this power, it strongly influences what we do, where we do it, how long we do it, and how much we get paid for it. In turn, this greatly impacts the quality of our lives: the home we own, the neighborhood we live in, the education our children receive, our sense of security, our standing in society, our self-esteem, even our health, whether mental, physical, or spiritual. As we go about our daily lives, we tend not to pay too much attention to this economic judge, or to even notice its existence. We operate within the economic system, unconscious of the invisible walls it represents, or the forces at work within it. But the market is a constant presence in our minds, where it appears in the guise of time demands, competitive pressures, social pressures, and survival pressures. It creates the challenges we face and the stress we feel, with all of its physical and emotional repercussions, both good and bad.

Beyond ourselves, the market is the driving force of material progress. Through its incessant demands and timeless rewards, it transforms raw materials, extracted from nature, into an increasingly complex and valuable hierarchy of products, creating the artificial world in which we live. Every widget in the modern world has a market price upon its head. By linking these parts together the market erects vast systems, from telecommunication networks to transportation hubs. Buildings, streets, and cities are all enabled and constrained by its will.

Within society, the market shapes institutions to support itself. Our educational system bends to respond to its needs. Through the media, a voice captive to market forces, it exercises control over much of what we know about the world, while broadcasting its own health on the nightly news: GDP, S&P, Dow. It has tremendous leverage over our politicians, and through them, over the entire operation of government. No matter where you find a dollar, a euro, or a yen, the market is close behind.

Since the market judges all things over time, it has become a force in history, too. By its very presence it has favored some nations over others, and marshaled resources in certain areas of the globe, granting power and privilege here, depressing it there. It treats nations no differently than corporations.

In the modern world, the market has become the template of our lives, the dominant metaphor of our time. We live in a market age, in which our lives are market-driven. We operate on market principles, hold to market values, and breed market culture, in a society shaped by market forces. We believe in the "free market," we put our money in the market, and now, particularly in America, we are handing the future of our society to the market. We are increasingly confident that the market will solve our social problems, make Medicare more affordable, clean up the environment, fix Social Security, reform education. There is nothing, it seems, that the market cannot do, if only given the proper resources.

Bolstered by early returns, we are now in the process of taking the market global. The market economy is the system of choice for providing for the material welfare of mankind, and for good reason: it works. It is the natural solution. These days the sun never sets on the market's empire, which runs 24/7, worldwide. The market has elevated itself above all nations, above the United Nations. It is vastly more powerful than the United States, with all its financial, political, and military might. Meanwhile, no one can control it. We cannot question it, nor even see it. If we disobey its principles, we simply suffer the consequences, without appeal. That is the way the market works.

But the most amazing fact of all about the market—indeed, the most astonishing fact I know—is how little we know about it. What, exactly, *is* the market? Ask your neighbor this question, and he will likely answer "the stock market," which is a bit like saying your local car dealer is General Motors. Ask someone who should really know, like an economist, and you may hear that the market is "the organized exchange of commodities between buyers and sellers within a specific geographic area and during a given period of time." But how, as we shall see, this same power can run your life, harm your health, fragment your family, dumb down society, destroy the environment, incite global conflict, and displace God Himself is not a story his field is set up to tell. The truth is, America has now handed its destiny to a faceless power we know very little about and find hard to explain. What the market really represents is a profound mystery, an enormous hole in the body of modern thought, one large enough to swallow us all.

## Mr. Market

In order to shed some light on this mystery, let's begin by looking at how people talk about the market, as opposed to how they consciously define it. If we search the Internet using "the market is," we come upon a host of results that fall into three main categories. The first of these are phrases that describe the market as action, such as:

"The market is stable."

"The market is slowly turning its back."

"The market is about to turn the corner."

"The market is coming back."

"The market is in rapid evolution."

"The market is on the threshold of a new phase."

"The market is shrinking."

"The market is fragmented."

"The market is falling apart."

The second category of results refers to the market as a mind, to include characteristics of personality and intelligence:

"The market is fragmented and does not yet share a common language or identity."

"The market is getting smarter."

"The market is overly optimistic."

"The market is celebrating."

"The market is emotionally reactive to short-term events, but over the long term generally gets it right."

"The market is very unforgiving."

"The market is racist and sexist and possibly homophobic."

"The market is blindly committed to profit above all else."

"The market is always right."

"The market is still gripped with geopolitical problems."

"The market is watching CNN."

If we now broaden our query, we find several other aspects of mind. For example, the market has desires, as evinced by the following two queries:

Query: "The market wants"

"What the market wants the market gets."

"The market wants results."

"What the market wants is hope."

"This market wants you!"

"Let's see if the market wants democracy."

"Produce what the market wants."

"Deliver solutions your market wants."

Query: *"The market likes"*

"The market likes new varieties."

"The market likes gridlock and government inaction."

"The market likes to throw you tricky moves when you're off your guard."

"The market likes bad news much more than it likes uncertainty."

"The market likes divided government."

"The market likes repentant sinners."

"The market likes the deal we did."

"The market likes to look to the future."

"The market likes to catch people off guard."

There is also much evidence of what is known as "market sentiment," here expressed in terms of love, hate, worry, and fear:

Query: *"The market [emotion]"*

"The market hates uncertainty."

"The market hates surprises."

"The market hates indecision."

"The market loves to talk China."

"The market loves wellness and energy drinks."

"The market loves comfort—stable growth, stable low inflation, strong profit margins."

"The market loves to prove the cocky wrong and usually waits until they're at their cockiest to inflict the most sudden and crushing blows."

"The market loves to take money from impatient traders."

"The market loves to humble us, and does so quite effectively."

"The market worries about the very short term."

"The market worries about colder than average weather."

"The market worries about growing geopolitical tensions."

"The market fears uncertainty like Superman fears kryptonite."
"At midweek the market's fears over inflation and interest rates came
   to a boil."

So what are we to make of all this? Well, as the above makes clear, people commonly personify the market. The market is given emotion, desires, personality, and intelligence. It is very much alive. The stock market has even been called "Mr. Market," a term attributed to both value investor Benjamin Graham and billionaire Warren Buffett. This idea is used as an investment strategy, in which one is supposed to think of Mr. Market as a rather manic-depressive individual, and to invest accordingly. No one is suggesting that the market is really a person, of course, but it certainly begs the question of what is lying behind the metaphor. As economist Walter Williams joked in *Capitalism Magazine,* "Who is this guy we call the market?" [1]

Coincident with this personification is the idea of the market as a "higher power." Certainly Mr. Market is not an individual like you or me. The market is part of society, and acts *upon us* from that higher perch. This facet of the market has resulted in its capitalization, in the same way that Nature was commonly capitalized up through the nineteenth century. [2] For example, in *Meanings of the Market: The Free Market in Western Culture* (2002), a book that takes an anthropological look at its subject, "the Market" is used throughout. [3] Other times one finds editors clearly struggling over the proper case, upper or lower. In 1997, *The Atlantic Monthly* published a widely discussed cover story by George Soros entitled "The Capitalist Threat." The cover announced, "One of the world's most prominent financiers warns that leaving social decisions to 'the market' poses a danger to society itself." Here the quotation marks neuter the market, thereby raising the question: how can such a nonentity pose a threat to human society? Two years later, having apparently rethought the matter, *The Atlantic* published an insightful article entitled "The Market as God." As the bull market was nearing its apex, Mr. Market had become our deity.

In addition to how we talk about the market, we have also chosen to symbolize it in revealing ways. The classic examples are the bull and bear of the securities industry, which are used to indicate a general rise and fall of prices over time. Such images are far from accidental; why not represent the market as a honeybee, or a butterfly? Instead, they reveal what we really think about the market's true nature. The market is a beast, raw, primitive, aggressive, tough, brawny, dangerous. Gordon Gekko, the financier in the movie *Wall Street*, takes his name from a reptile for a reason. "To most traders and investors," a commodities trader opines, "the market is a dangerous and undependable animal. Their mottoes are: 'Don't count on it' and 'Get it before it gets you.'"[4] While that may or may not be true, the market is certainly full of bull, as anyone who believed their Wall Street research during the boom can attest, and this is more than most of us can bear, but these are additional meanings whose implications are more legal than symbolic.

The Market as moving quantity: the NASDAQ's MarketSite Broadcast Center.

The most common symbol of the market, and one that is easy to overlook because it is so obvious, is quantity, the very numbers that flicker on trading screens around the globe, and find their way onto price tags at the mall. Every market price, the price of a particular class of goods, reflects a judgment of the market, its determination of what that commodity is worth. They are visual symbols of the market's discrete decisions. Over time they move like brain waves, as presented in countless charts and graphs. Indeed, the waves produced by the mind of the human, as revealed by an EEG, and those

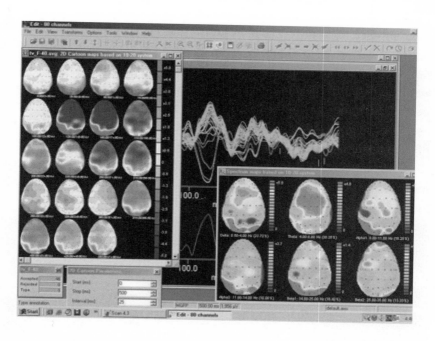

The Market as mind. TOP: The analysis of brain waves (the "eggs" are human heads). BOTTOM: The analysis of "market waves."

produced by the market, as seen on a trading screen, not only look the same, but are analyzed with some of the same techniques. The difference is that while the human mind may engage in moral reasoning, the market is as amoral as they come. When buying a barrel of oil, a trader does not consider whether it will cause global warming. He is only interested in the price per barrel. Likewise, the market forces inspired by billions of consumer purchases operate purely in the service of a bloodless mechanism.

Market prices are also connected in profound ways, revealing a deep economic structure, a neural network that we can depict, at least partly, with more complex information maps. An example is *SmartMoney*'s "Map of the Market," as shown below.

The Market as financial matrix: Smartmoney's interactive "Map of the Market" (http://www.smartmoney .com/marketmap/). The map shows the performance of the top companies in the U.S. stock market, updated every fifteen minutes. Each tile represents a single company, its size being proportional to its market capitalization. The color of the tile reflects the change in the company's stock price over a set time period: red is declining, green is increasing, black is flat. The stronger the color, the stronger the price movement. Companies are further arranged in eleven major industry sectors. Neighborhoods within each sector contain similarly performing companies. By scrolling over a company, one can access another level of quantitative data.

What such maps reveal is how deeply ordered the market's thinking really is. It is a financial version of The Matrix, an ethereal boundary that undergirds society.

So these are various ways in which the human mind thinks of the market: as a higher power, one that is often personified, has animal instincts, and makes quantitative judgments. This is not necessarily how we choose to *define* the market, however, creating a schizophrenic, left brain/right brain divide in our minds, one that pits our modern penchant for inert technicalities against an ancient desire for metaphoric understanding, to see the cosmos as alive. The market has fallen through the gap. We don't know how to define the market, because we cannot bridge science and religion, economics and art. Instead we are left with a profusion of alternatives. Falling back on the Internet, the same query we used before, "the market is," trawls up the following:

> "The market is a mathematical hypothesis."
> "The market is what defines the value of a thing."
> "The market is the new religion."
> "The market is a force of nature."
> "The market is the mother of invention."
> "The market is a simple interaction of atomistic individuals."
> "The market is the lap of the gods. And what a god the market is.
>     So caring. So nice."
> "The market is an impersonal mechanism for bringing together
>     producers and consumers."
> "The market is the sum of all voluntary human action."
> " 'The market' is where supply meets demand."

All of these statements are true in their own way. But their fragmentation suggests that we have still not hit the proverbial nail upon its head—a frightening point, when you think about how much power that nail has, how deeply it is driven into all of us, and how sharply it has divided the world in the past. Since the market is such a vital part of modern life, the uncertainty surrounding its nature has bred all kinds of political conflict over how it operates and what role it should play in our lives, from clashes between political factions within America to situations as extreme as the Cold War, an entire era when the future of mankind hinged on the reassuring notion of Mutually Assured Destruction. More recently, we have had violent demonstrations over globalization, terrorists have struck down the most well-known symbol of the global market, the World Trade Center, and an unprecedented wave of corporate scandals has spread across America. Far from being put to bed, as so many in the post–Cold War era predicted, the market debate is alive and well. So the most pressing question, today as yesterday, still remains: what is the nature of the market?

## What Is the Market?

If you were to make the statement "the market is running our lives," or "the market is the most powerful force in America today," many people would undoubtedly stand up and second the motion. But when it comes to explaining how this can be, we have fallen down on the job. We recognize that there are many market-related facets deeply entwined with modern life. Market principles, market forces, market values, market culture, marketplaces, and market prices are just some of them. But what we have not done is the obvious. We have not assembled all of these diverse facets into a single unified paradigm, the Market, with a capital *M*.

Why is this important? Because this paradigm is not just a passive model, it is the dominant power in modern life.

To explain what I mean, consider the Lenape Indians. The Lenape, you may remember, were the less-than-savvy traders who sold the island of Manhattan to the Dutch in 1626 for goods supposedly worth twenty-four dollars. They lived in an era in which the dominant power in their lives was Nature, as it had been throughout most of human history. Nature was their source of survival, providing them with food, clothing, and shelter. Now fast-forward to the present and imagine those same Indians standing in the concrete canyons of modern Manhattan. Here Nature no longer holds sway. The forest that once covered the island has been leveled. People don't spend their time worrying about the rain, or the heat, or the change of seasons, or even the rise and fall of the sun. Indeed, they can't even see the stars anymore. They live in a world that is in many ways hermetically sealed from Nature, a world of air-conditioned spaces, supermarkets, and brand-name attire, of cars and aircraft, malls and movie theaters, skyscrapers, highways and apartments, and twenty-four-hour lighting. The entire environment is different. So the question is, what is the power that governs the lives of today's New Yorker?

The answer, of course, is the Market. The Market has replaced Nature as the dominant power in modern life. You might even consider it a modern version of Nature. It is the power that runs the economy, and hence commands the economic environment we live in. While we are all still mortal, our most common day-to-day concern is no longer what Nature is going to do to us next, but what the Market has up its sleeve.

The fascination, and challenge, of exploring the nature of the Market is that it quickly leads to the loftiest questions, those normally reserved for philosophers, theologians, and systems theorists. Since it exists in the economic realm, the Market is not a physical principle, like gravity. We cannot go out, drop an apple from a tree, and prove its existence. Yet we know that a higher power must be ruling our economy, because we cannot explain it otherwise. The market price of a commodity, for instance, is beyond the control of any individual or corporation. It is purely the product of the Market. So if the Market did not exist, there could be no commodity pricing, and the entire market economy would collapse. Just as clearly, the Market must be an active agent in our lives. Something must be judging us with the market price, and selecting the winners and losers. And since our lives are market-driven, as anyone today would be hard-pressed to deny, then what is doing the driving?

Such logical arguments provide us with a new definition of the Market. The Market is active, in that it operates upon us; its nature is purely economic; and it is a single principle, one found everywhere people trade. The Market is *the active economic principle.* This principle manifests itself through all the facets of the market paradigm: market forces, market values, market culture, etc. In fact, the scope of this influence suggests that we should recast the Market's animal symbolism as well. The Market is an octopus. It has many tentacles wrapped around our society, and is squeezing for all it is worth.

As a power operating within society, this definition of the Market takes us away from purely economic considerations, and far from conventional economics. At the same time it better explains everyday life, which is, after all, the acid test. Today we all feel a diversity of market pressures—time demands, competitive pressures, social pressures, financial pressures, and sheer survival pressures—all of which exist to make the economy more productive, the Market's raison d'être. It may well be, in some abstract sense, that the economy is moved by supply and demand, but that is not what gets each of us out of bed in the morning. Instead, we all know that there is a decisive economic principle at work in our lives, and if we do not obey it, we will suffer the consequences. The octopus squeezes everyone.

As an idea, the Market becomes even more compelling when placed in the context of modern systems theory. One of the critical insights in this field has been that parts and wholes, the basic elements of a system, have their own independent existences. This means that while each of us is part of an economic system, there must also be an independent whole. This is the Market. Note, therefore, that the Market is not synonymous with *the economy*. The economy is the entire system, parts *and* whole at once.

This is a critical distinction, for it redraws the economic map. It divides the economy into two levels, individuals and the Market, and creates a key relationship between them. When buyers and sellers trade, they impact the market price of what they trade. At the same time, the market price influences their behavior. It is this feedback loop that makes the market economy "self-adjusting" or "self-governing," its very essence.

In turn, this idea fills an enormous hole in economic thought. Since the founding of economic science, the economy has been treated solely as the product of individual actors. This is the bottom-up view of the system. But the modern definition of a system also requires a top-down influence, the other half of the feedback loop. This is the role of the Market. Indeed, it is what brings the Market to life.

While systems theory brings a welcome legitimacy to the idea of a feedback loop in society, we should note that this is hardly a novel concept. While each of us shapes our society in some way, we are all undeniably shaped by it as well, from our accent to our worldview. Each man makes his small contribution, but is subject to the whole. Thus, as an idea, the Market only captures dynamics that, while new to free-market theory, have long been common sense.

By bringing the Market into this book, we are going to halt our longstanding tradition of looking at society with one eye, and open the other. For the first time, we are going to look at society from the Market's point of view. This is a powerful approach, for it will allow us to cut through the apparent complexities of the world around us, and see the higher cause lurking behind them all. It only requires that we adopt the perspective of a higher power bent on making us more productive—regardless of the repercussions.

Remember that the Market is not "the collective will of the people." While a human being is defined by his ability to distinguish between good and evil, to the Market good and evil are nothing but profit and loss—a very different standard. The Market may represent one side of human life— the collective judgment of people *acting as traders*—but it is not the voice of mankind.

The Market as Beast: the bull and the bear sparring over time.

Most important, we must remember that when we refer to the Market as a "higher power," we are not insinuating that there is anything supernatural about it. The Market is the economic system, as a whole, operating upon us, as individuals. It is as natural as they come. On the other hand, the current template of the system is not sufficient to explain it. Whether it is the bull, the bear, the lizard, or the (capitalist) pig, human beings have long detected an animal spirit lodged within our modern version of Nature. It is the amoral spirit of prices. The system is just the bones of a Beast.

# 1. Burnout

"In general, you will find the forms and dispositions of mankind to correspond with the nature of the country." —Hippocrates

CHANG (speaking of Shangri-La): It is quite common here to live to a very ripe old age. Climate, diet, mountain water *you* might say. But we like to think it is the absence of struggle in the way we live. In your countries, on the other hand, how often do you hear the expression "he worried himself to death" or this thing or that killed him?

CONWAY: Oh, very often.

CHANG: And very true. Your lives are therefore as a rule shorter. Not so much by natural death as by . . . indirect suicide.

—Frank Capra's *Lost Horizon* (1937)

For over a decade now the World Bank, the World Health Organization, and the Harvard School of Public Health have engaged in a landmark study of disease throughout the world involving over a hundred researchers. Known as *The Global Burden of Disease,* this ongoing, multivolume project is particularly remarkable for the way it measures the health of societies. Since illnesses like depression generally make you miserable rather than kill you, mortality statistics fail to assess their impact on a population. To correct this, the researchers created a single measure, known as Disability Adjusted Life Years, that measures lost years of healthy life through death *or* disability.

This approach considerably changes the public health picture. *The Global Burden of Disease* reveals that the burden of mental illness on health and productivity has been vastly underestimated. While psychiatric conditions are responsible for just over 1 percent of deaths, they are nearly 11 percent of the disease burden. Of the ten leading causes of disability worldwide in 1990, five were psychiatric conditions: unipolar depression, alcohol use, bipolar affective disorder (manic depression), schizophrenia, and obsessive-compulsive disorder. Unipolar depression alone is responsible for more than one in every ten years of life lived with a disability worldwide, second only to heart disease. As a whole, mental illness ranks higher than even cancer or HIV in the global priority list. Most striking of all, the disease burden for mental illness is highest in what the researchers called "the Established Market Economies." The report projects that by 2020, fully 15 percent of all illnesses in the Established Market Economies will be mental illnesses. Part of this increase will come from success in wiping out other forms of illness; part of it will come from the persistent inability of the market economies to conquer their mental health problems, a failure for which there is currently no explanation.[1]

This report raises the question, why is it that mental illness is so common, and so persistent, in market economies? Is the Market driving us all crazy? Yet as obvious as that question is, you will look a long time before you find anyone investigating it. Instead, a paper by a World Health Organization team asks, "Why does the burden of mental disorders persist in established market economies? There are four possibilities: the burden estimates are wrong; there are no effective treatments; people do not receive treatment; or people do not receive effective treatments."[2] Here no one even considers the obvious answer: something about market economies is *causing* mental illness.

One reason we fail even to consider such a connection is that it has become politically incorrect to criticize the Market, particularly in America, where the Market has become wedded to our national image. To associate the Market with mental illness is like saying Uncle Sam is on Prozac. Another reason is that the Market lies deep. It is a prime mover behind the world around us, but there may be several steps in the chain reaction before the symptoms appear. So it is that your organization may post a list entitled "Ten Steps to Prevent Workplace Violence," but none of them refer to moderating market pressures. Yet another reason is that we have long assumed that the Market is good for public health. After all, people's health is, in general, much better in industrialized countries than it is in developing countries. However, such assumptions only reveal our innate *marketism,* our bias toward the Market:

> It is true that to achieve the high levels of population health enjoyed today in the West, particularly the very low rates of infant and neonatal mortality, substantial economic wealth has been a necessary precondition. But there have also been many, many other factors necessarily involved, of a social, political, ideological, and cultural nature, to convert the wealth generated by the processes of economic growth into increased population health for all. Economic growth is an intrinsically disruptive process. The history of almost all successful economies of the West shows that, in the absence of a sufficient political response at both national, state, and local government levels, this disruption will result in deprivations, disease, and death.[3]

What we see here is the danger of confusing the Market, which is part of society, with society itself, and all the higher values it contains. As the same author concludes, "in almost every historical case, the first and most direct effect of rapid economic growth has been a negative impact on population health," the classic example being the Industrial Revolution.

At the same time, the Market clearly does a tremendous amount of good for our health and well-being. It is, after all, the material supply system that supports our entire society. So what exactly is the connection between the Market and human health?

## The Hypermarket

In the past few decades, the market experience has greatly changed. The temperature of our society has been rising, year after year. There is no single thermometer to directly measure this rise, but numerous different gauges, their readings confirmed by a great deal of everyday experience.

One of these is the pace of life. Here the title of James Gleick's book on the subject says it all: *Faster: The Acceleration of Just About Everything.* Such acceleration is not just the pace at which we move, it is the number of things we do in a day, and the many ways in which we order our lives to maximize them. Our communications have been stripped down from thoughtful letters to e-mail burst transmissions, without even a salutation. Over half of Americans now skip lunch at work. We are a people, as Gleick points out, who wear out the "close door" button on the elevator just to save us those five seconds.[4]

Another indicator of our rising social temperature is working hours. Throughout the nineties we saw a spate of books dealing with the increase in working hours, led by Juliet Schor's *The Overworked American,* which concluded in 1991 that American working hours had increased steadily for twenty years. Contrary to our prejudices about the past, Americans worked even harder than medieval peasants. While some (such as Gleick) have questioned her findings, Schor is still humming the same tune today. Her latest calculations are that from 1973 to 2000, the average American worker added five weeks of work per year to her schedule, a finding supported by other researchers.[5] Indeed, this figure could well be understated, as the pace of technological change has swamped the statisticians. One Wall Street economist recently noted:

> In financial services, the Labor Department tells us that the average workweek has been unchanged, at 35.5 hours, since 1988. That's patently absurd. Courtesy of a profusion of portable information appliances (laptops, cell phones, personal digital assistants, etc.), along with near ubiquitous connectivity (hard-wired and now increasingly wireless), most information workers can toil around the clock. The official data don't come close to capturing this cultural shift. As a result, we are woefully underestimating the time actually spent on the job.[6]

Concurrent with increased working hours, of course, is a decrease in leisure time. Americans currently have the least leisure time of any industrialized nation. We get three fewer vacation weeks a year than do workers in Western Europe. This situation has spawned a new term, *time poverty,* and a new national movement, Take Back Your Time Day, advertised as "a call to action for all of us who believe that the aim of society is to benefit its people, not to maximize profits."[7]

The evidence suggests that our society has also become a great deal more competitive in the past few decades, both in business and socially. When competitive pressures get too high, people start feeling threatened, and the bonds between them break. Trust plunges, ethics declines, and community spirit flags. In the nineties, corporate loyalty died, and we found ourselves bowling alone. In the past few years, we have experienced an unprecedented wave of corruption in all sectors of the economy. This decline has bled into society at large, from cheating in schools to corruption in newsrooms to the use of performance-enhancing drugs among professional athletes. We have experienced, as the title of one bestseller put it, *The Death of Right and Wrong*.

In terms of social competition, another gauge is how far people are willing to go financially to keep up with the Joneses. Here two compelling indicators are the personal savings rate and credit-card debt. Since the early 1980s, the personal savings rate among Americans has fallen sharply, as people have chosen to spend nearly all that they earn. It now hovers between 3 percent and 4 percent, less than half of what it averaged in the eighties, and significantly less than other industrialized countries. From 1980 to 2001, for instance, Japan averaged 13 percent, Germany 12 percent, and France 15 percent.[8] The problem is even starker when one considers how the savings rate is spread over the population. In 1999, the lowest third of Americans had no savings, and the middle third had less than three thousand dollars in savings.[9] It appears that those least capable of keeping up with the Joneses are spending every last cent to do so.

Even more remarkable, the plunge of the U.S. savings rate took place during the greatest bull market in American history. At a time when personal incomes were rising, consumption was rising even more, as if it were feeding upon itself. Part of the impetus was supplied by credit-card companies, which in 1995 alone sent out seventeen preapproved credit-card solicitations to every American between eighteen and sixty-four.[10] Between 1989 and 2001, credit-card debt in America almost tripled, from $238 billion to $692 billion, with the average American family experiencing a 53 percent increase.[11] Naturally, the end result of this national spendathon has been the rise in a third indicator, personal bankruptcies, now at an all-time high. Between 1989 and 2001, the number of people filing for bankruptcy jumped 125 percent.

We have all felt the environment in which we live changing, too, as the well-known rat race continues to evolve, fueled by new technologies like lap-tops, cell phones, and PDAs. Society is not just faster, but noisier, more congested, and never out of reach; more artificial, and less natural. Many have fled to the suburbs, but for most the promises of telecommuting have not been realized, so the new *market environment* cannot be avoided. In northern Virginia, for instance, the morning backup into Washington, D.C. is now well over twenty miles long, Monday through Friday—twice what it was in 1999.[12] The complexity of the market environment has also translated into increasingly complex lives. The number of keys we carry, of devices we use and program, of appointments we keep, of all the myriad details that compose a modern life, create a psychological pressure all their own. If you add up the e-mail, voice mail, snail mail, and memos handled by an average worker, from the receptionist to the CEO, it is now over two hundred per day.[13]

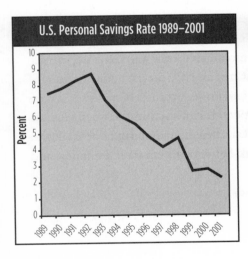

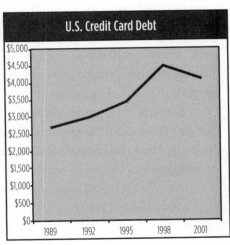

Finally, as the winner-take-all society has broken out, we have all taken on more personal risk in our lives. The corporate safety net has gradually eroded, and the larger social safety net with it. Job security is a thing of the past, and for 45 million Americans, so is health-care insurance. For many, sheer survival has increasingly become an issue.

All of these trends may appear to paint a very complex picture, particularly as they touch virtually every aspect of our society. But if we look at them now from the Market's perspective, the reason for our rising social temperature becomes obvious. The Market is simply trying to boost productivity, its raison d'être. In order to do that, the Market has selected the technologies that accelerate the pace of life, thereby producing more value in the same period of time. This has changed the entire environment in which we live, fomenting the legendary rat race. As the pace of life has increased, time demands and competitive pressures have increased, intensifying survival pressures. This has encouraged people to work harder, to spend more (even at their own risk), and to do anything to win. The Market has thus inspired a kind of social vortex into which our entire society has fallen: a *hypermarket.*

From the Market's standpoint, this hypermarket has been a tremendous success. From 1950 to 2000, the American economy enjoyed unprecedented growth. But when it comes to the health of the average American, there is a very different story to tell, one found on the dashboard of any sports car. In a high-performance vehicle, the tachometer is the instrument that measures the revolutions per minute of the engine. As the RPMs rise, the needle eventually hits a point where it crosses into a zone of red, known as the red line. This is the point where the RPMs are so great that the engine begins to damage itself. The stress is just too much for the parts. A hypermarket has the same effect on a population. When an efficient economy accelerates past the red line, it puts an entire society under a dangerous load of stress. In fact, the word *stress,* as applied to people, comes from the word *stress* as applied to metals. The result is physical, mental, and spiritual breakdown. Stress is thus the critical missing link between the market economy and human health.

## Stressed Out

According to psychologists, stress is caused by "any circumstances that threaten or are perceived to threaten one's well-being and thereby tax one's coping abilities. The threat may be to one's immediate physical safety, long-range security, self-esteem, reputation, or peace of mind." [14] Such stress stems directly from all the market pressures we have just described. In effect, it is our response to the Market's efforts to make the economy more productive. And to some extent, that response is natural and healthy. It is only the hypermarket that pushes us over the edge.

In a hypermarket, credit-card debt, unpaid bills, collection agencies, foreclosures, personal bankruptcies, and all the other problems associated with living on the financial edge breed intense survival stress. As the economy becomes more efficient, selection pressures increase, and the price of failure increases, both in the workplace and society. Schadenfreude rules. The accelerating pace of life puts increasing time demands on people, both at work and at home. The very scope and intensity of all forms of advertising breed social stress, as one is led to believe that one is never good enough, or high enough in the pecking order. The good life, and one's self-esteem, is always one brand, one product, one neighborhood, or one social club away.

The pace of technological change is also a source of stress, a platitude that we nevertheless fail to appreciate over time, as it is occurring every day. Consider the reflection of one man in his sixties:

> I was born in 1936. At that time there were no jet planes and commercial plane traffic was effectively non-existent. There were no computers, no space satellites, no microwave ovens, no electric typewriters, no Xerox machines, no tape recorders. There were no stereo music systems nor compact disks. There was no television in 1936. No space travel, no atomic bomb, no hydrogen bomb, no "guided missiles," as they were first called, no "smart" bombs. There were no fluorescent lights, no washing machines nor dryers, no Cuisinarts, no VCRs. There was no air conditioning. Nor were there freeways, shopping centers, or malls. There were no suburbs as we know them. There was no Express Mail, no fax, no telephone touch dialing, no birth-control pill. There were no credit cards, no synthetic fibres. There were no antibiotics, no artificial organs, no pesticides or herbicides. . . . During my lifetime all of this changed.[15]

The cause of stress here is the growing dependency on things you cannot understand, fix, or control, a "technostress" that affects people's attitudes, thoughts, behaviors, and physiology.[16] How many of us have felt stressed out by computer malfunction?

The deepest element of hypermarket stress is perhaps the least obvious: a lack of trust. Trust is an enormous stress reliever. If you trust the people around you, then you will open up to them, and it is this human bond that is the most effective means of reducing stress. If, however, competitive pressures drive people apart, if people lose faith in their institutions and their fellowman, if corruption becomes endemic, then the result is increasing levels of stress in all social dealings.

As a physiological response, stress goes back to the dawn of man. It is the original fight-or-flight response, crafted to ensure human survival. As the brain becomes aware of a perceived threat, it sets off an alarm that gears up the nervous system, turns up the flow of hormones, sharpens the senses, quickens the pulse, tenses the muscles, and shallows the breathing. Emotionally we may feel anger, fear, anxiety, annoyance, apprehension, grief, guilt, rage, sadness, envy, shame, disgust, elation, and gloom.

Here the hypermarket is a particularly insidious problem. The fight-or-flight response was designed for physical threats from predators, which are typically brief, if you survive them. But the Market does not walk away the way that lion did on the Serengeti. This means that the modern body is kept at a constant state of activation, increasing the wear and tear upon it.

The first person to voice concern over this problem was Hans Selye, the man who coined the term *stress*, and the father of the field. In the 1950s, Selye came up with a simple theory, called "the general adaptation syndrome," that is basically the bell curve of stress. The theory proposes that there are three stages to the physiological response to stress: the flight-or-fight response, which he called the alarm reaction, when the body arouses itself; the stage of resistance, in which the level of alertness remains essentially stable; and finally a stage of exhaustion, in which the body is worn out by its own efforts, causing a host of physical problems. What Selye warned about stress is thus a particular application of Aristotle's "moderation in all things."

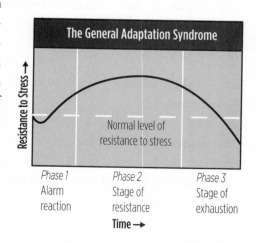

Unfortunately, Aristotle's advice is difficult to follow in a hypermarket. The forces that stress us out today are so all-encompassing, and so powerful, that one is tempted to laugh, or at least groan, at the thought of doing battle with them. How do you keep yourself immune from the very system you live in, when it is the most powerful mankind has ever seen? Here, not surprisingly, the greatest challenge arises from the epicenter of the Market's activity: work.

Depending on your survey, anywhere from a quarter to a half of all Americans say that their job is extremely stressful, and three-quarters say that it is more stressful than a generation ago. One study even finds that "increased stress is driving workers to tears, insomnia and illness, with unrealistic goals and rudeness from clients and colleagues a major contributor. As a result, workers are turning on each other." [17] Overall, more than 65 million Americans suffer from the symptoms of stress. [18]

The toll this has taken is clearly enormous, yet not known in its entirety. Under chronic stress, the body's entire stress apparatus (the brain, heart, lungs, vessels, and muscles) is adversely affected, as is the power of the immune system. Chronic stress is like a virus, traveling the pathways of body and mind and causing pathology wherever it happens to land. Stress has been linked to an amazing variety of diseases, both mental and physical, including depression, anxiety, eating problems (weight gain, weight loss, anorexia, and bulimia), headaches, sleep disturbances, heart disease, stroke, susceptibility to infections, immune disorders, cancer, gastrointestinal problems (irritable bowel syndrome, peptic ulcers, and inflammatory bowel disease), diabetes, muscular and joint pain, sexual and reproductive dysfunction, loss of memory, inability to concentrate, allergies, skin disorders, unexplained hair loss, and periodontal disease.

Stress even defines its own personality type, the famous Type A. First described in 1974, Type A behavior, or "hurry sickness," stems from trying to accomplish as much as possible in the shortest period of time. This creates a person who is hard-driving, competitive, controlling, manipulative, and hot-tempered. Because they push themselves so hard, Type As easily become impatient, irritable, and potentially hostile or angry. [19] Not surprisingly, being Type A magnifies one's susceptibility to many stress-related problems. Researchers have speculated that fast-paced cities attract Type A individuals, who then sustain and promote their preferred way of life.

What makes stress most insidious is the same problem that has disguised the role of the Market in our lives: the path between cause and effect is difficult to trace. Stress reverberates throughout the entire biological system, the way the Market reverberates throughout the entire social system: at a deep level, and without leaving a calling card behind. Since there are many other causes of stress-related illnesses in addition to stress, it is not always clear who the culprit is.

Heart disease, for instance, is the top killer in America. There are many causes of it, but many of them are stress-related. Stress causes angina, while acute stress can trigger heart attacks. The emotional effects of stress alter heart rhythms and increase the risk of serious arrhythmias. Stress thickens blood, increasing the chance of a clot. Stress may raise cholesterol levels. Chronic stress may reduce estrogen levels in women, which impact cardiac health. Stress can release enough immune-system proteins to damage heart cells. Stress can cause high blood pressure. Then there is the indirect impact of stress. People deal with stress by adopting unhealthy eating habits, such as high-fat and high-salt diets, and they abuse substances, from alcohol and to-bacco to drugs, all of which can impact the heart.

This is just one example of the many pathways stress can take to a single disease. So how much heart disease is attributable to stress? It is impossible to say. But Dr. Meyer Friedman, who first described the Type A personality, believes that the number one cause of premature heart disease in the United States is time pressures.[20] Other researchers have found a significant correlation between rates of heart disease and the pace of life in 36 cities, with New York as the fastest highway to a heart attack.[21] And how many other illnesses are the result of stress? It is also impossible to say. What seems clear, however, is that the toll is a lot more than we currently recognize, that it is beyond the statistics we keep, and that it is growing. The word *stress* didn't even enter the popular lexicon until after 1950. Since then it has become its own field of study, while stress reduction has become its own industry, involving pharmaceutical companies, booksellers, masseuses, yoga instructors, and, of course, doctors. Multiple sources indicate that stress is now responsible for approximately three-quarters of all visits to primary-care physicians—a stunning figure. According to the National Institute for Occupational Safety and Health, in the past four years alone the number of employees who have called in sick because of stress has tripled.[22] In 2002 the market for antidepressants and antianxiety drugs alone was $17.2 billion.

## The Aftershocks

We cannot deal with all the repercussions of market stress here, but it is worthwhile to explore a few primary examples:

*Depression.* Depression is the top mental health disorder in the Western world. In America, the National Institutes of Health estimates that major depression will strike an estimated 16 percent of Americans in their lives, or approximately 35 million people.[23] That is one in every six people you see. In any given year, around 14 million of us have it.

Depression is a social problem that has been growing for a long time. In 1994, the Harvard Medical Health Letter reported that "twelve independent studies covering 43,000 people in several countries have found an overall rise in the rate of depression during the twentieth century."[24] Other studies have found ten times more major depression in older people than younger people.[25] Clearly, the problem is environmental; human genes don't change that fast. And as we saw in the beginning of this chapter, with the latest *Global Burden of Disease* study, the environmental cause is linked to market economies, where depression rates are much higher than elsewhere. This connection has also been made by diverse other studies since the late eighties, as best summarized in Robert Lane's *The Loss of Happiness in Market Democracies.*[26] The question is why.

Once again, market dynamics provide us with a strong explanation. When competition becomes too intense, it separates people. Your neighbor becomes your adversary. Your society may start making market sense, but it stops making moral sense. You lose your connection to other people, and to anything larger than yourself. This cuts the very bonds that give life meaning. Bonds between an individual and his family, his neighbors, his community, his country, and even his God all erode and break. The result is a life that feels meaningless, triggering depression. In short, the more intense the market experience, the more meaningless life will become, and the more depressed the population will be. Depression is thus a psychological response to an unbalanced society, one in which the market system is pressuring people to lead a meaningless existence—to serve the Market at their own expense.

Based on this interpretation, we would expect that as the market experience intensifies, traditional values will fracture, giving birth to a "Me Generation" and, ultimately, radical individualism. As this takes place, human bonds of all kinds will break, causing a spike in depression. Older people, who formed their worldviews in an earlier time, will be less susceptible to it than younger people. Among the very young, those who are least capable of handling their sudden injection into the market environment, depression will be most pronounced, leading to a rise in suicide rates. All of this, unfortunately, has already come to pass in America; we have just failed to trace it back to its primary source.

If the hypermarket breeds depression, we would also expect to find higher rates of depression where market forces are more intense than usual. This also turns out to be the case. One study that examined the impact of work stress on twenty-six top Wall Street brokers found that 38 percent met the criteria for subclinical depression, and 23 percent had major depression—four times the national average.[27]

In contrast, consider the ten thousand Old Amish people living in Lancaster County, Pennsylvania. These people have intentionally isolated themselves from the hypermarket. They use no electricity and no automobiles. Their community is intensely religious and tight-knit. When an Amish family needs to build a barn, the entire community turns out to lend a hand. After a monumental twenty-year study of the mental health of the Amish, researcher Janice Egeland discovered that their rate of unipolar (nonmanic) depression was a tenth of that in nearby Baltimore—or roughly what it was in the U.S. two generations ago. In fact, among less technologically advanced cultures of all kinds, depression is virtually nonexistent.[28]

As bad as it is, depression is by no means the end of the trail. It is itself the beginning of an entire series of negative chain reactions in people's lives, from broken relationships to suicide. As we move further along this chain, the fingerprints of the Market become fainter and fainter, but the hypermarket is still the primary cause.

*Burnout.* Another word in the modern lexicon is *burnout.* This caustic term describes a human being who has essentially shut down on the job. The first occurrence of this term was in 1974, when it was used to describe frazzled health-care workers whose long hours under life-or-death pressure caused emotional and physical exhaustion. In the years since, however, it has come to be applied to diverse representatives of the Market Age.

Burnout is not the same as fatigue or depression, although the symptoms may coincide. It is essentially the arc of a good person who makes the mistake of thinking that his job will provide his life with meaning. Those who are most in danger of burnout are the so-called "best and brightest," people who are high achievers, idealistic, and committed. Instead of backing off when they face frustration and a lack of fulfillment, they redouble their efforts, increasing their stress load, and commencing a spiral that ends in exhaustion, cynicism, and despair.

Burnout is facilitated by one of the Market's great lies. The Market is always broadcasting, through its omnipresent media, that the meaning in life is found in the economy, typically through financial success. This tremendous fraud, which has led so many to their deaths, survives on marketing alone, and fails to stand up to the slightest inspection. The Market cannot provide any meaning to life, simply because that is neither its role nor its nature. The Market is nothing but a practical tool, a system designed for putting a roof over our head, food on the table, and clothes on our back—and that's it. The market system can no more provide life with meaning than can the transportation system. Work can certainly be meaningful for noneconomic reasons, such as when it calls forth your creativity, but the more it serves a purely financial end, the more meaning is drained from it.

Burnout results from looking for meaning in such inherently empty work. As the victim accelerates toward the Market's mirage, he only cuts off his ability to find what he is looking for.

*Rage.* In recent years, the term *rage* has been applied to many aspects of life: road rage, air rage, desk rage (hostility at work), tech rage (screaming at your computer, however justified), even rink rage (violence at your kid's hockey game). Of course, rage is not a new phenomenon, but like many repercussions of the hypermarket, a change in degree, not kind, has taken place. As market pressures have increased, and stress levels risen, we have seen rage become a widespread descriptor of modern life.

Road rage is the type of rage that has captured the most attention, driven by media coverage of the most extreme incidents. In northern Virginia, a road rage battle ends in the death of a violinist from the National Symphony

Orchestra, when his car crashes into a concrete barrier. "In the stressed-out area where we live, it doesn't take much for people to go off," says the defendant's lawyer.[29] In San Jose, a man who is rear-ended bounds from his car, snatches the dog from the lap of the woman who hit him, and tosses it into oncoming traffic. In Long Island, two men start dueling during their morning commute, pull off the road, and fight in the pouring rain; one stabs the other to death. In North Carolina, a woman is taking her two kids to elementary school when she encounters traffic. Suddenly she snaps, pulls the car off the road, and starts driving down the sidewalk and across people's lawns. A traffic cop stops her at an intersection. "I don't have freakin' time for this!" the woman screams, and hits the gas, dragging the cop a few feet before he falls free. The woman is chased at seventy-five miles an hour to the elementary school, where she drops off the kids as she is arrested for assaulting a police officer with a deadly weapon.[30]

Are such incidents increasing? We don't know for sure. Like virtually all types of rage, analysis of the issue is hindered by a lack of data. There are challenges in defining what "road rage" is, and no formal reporting system for accumulating reliable nationwide statistics. Most events go unreported, because they end with an insulting gesture rather than death. In any case, road rage fatalities, which are subject to measure, are low when compared with overall road fatalities. An investigation into incidents of road rage between January 1990 and August 1996, for instance, uncovered reports of 10,037 incidents, resulting in 218 fatalities. Total traffic deaths are currently around 40,000 per year. However, fatalities do not tell the story, as they are obviously the extreme. An analysis of cell-phone calls to police from roadways in the San Diego area, for instance, revealed that 16 percent of calls were for road rage incidents. And according to a 1997 American Automobile Association report, nearly 90 percent of motorists had experienced road rage incidents during the previous twelve months, while 60 percent admitted to losing their temper behind the wheel.

Road rage has a sister problem that is better known, and far more deadly: aggressive driving. In 1998, *USA Today* analyzed 50,000 traffic accident reports over a ten-year period and found that aggressive driving was responsible for one in five crashes with injuries, killing 1,500 people a year, and injuring 800,000.[31] While the overall rate of aggressive driving incidents with injuries was constant during that period (a statistic influenced by other factors, such as seat-belt use), crashes involving speeding rose 48 percent. "Our reading of the literature is that aggressive driving may be as large a risk factor for accidents as driving under the influence of alcohol," concluded Edward Blanchard, a psychology professor at the State University of New York at Albany.[32]

Lying behind both road rage and aggressive driving is the same set of market issues, beginning with time pressures. "No one gets angry when they see an empty stretch of highway," says one auto-industry consultant. "They get angry when they see a 5-mile backup and they're late for work." Not surprisingly, congestion is far and away the top environmental cause of aggressive driving and road rage, according to one study of media reports.[33] "People get frustrated with traffic," says a spokeswoman for the New York Department of Transportation. "Nowadays everyone is in a hurry. They schedule more than they can handle. They're trying to make up time."[34]

This is a problem that is not getting any better soon. As the market environment has evolved, it has congealed around us. Over the past decade, the number of miles driven has risen 35 percent while the number of miles of new roads built has increased just 1 percent.[35] In 1970 there were 89 million cars in America; by 1998 we topped 150 million, driven by the twin spikes of population and the doubling of women in the workforce.[36] This Type A driving is further encouraged by heightened competitive pressures, turning the rat race into the road race. As *Washington Post* columnist "Dr. Gridlock" explains, some of his region's Beltway Duels arise from "the me-first attitude of a metropolitan area where there is such a premium on ambition and careers."[37]

In addition to the roadways, there are many other venues in life where stress manifests itself in angry behavior: the home, the office, the school, airplanes, etc. In recent years both academia and the media have divided our entire society into these rage zones, full of domestic violence, school shootings, workplace violence, air rage, etc. Many of

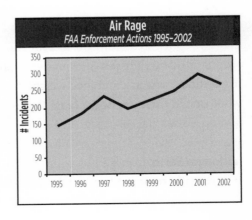

them are enormous topics of study, due unfortunately to their attendant national tragedies. And there are numerous interrelationships between them, creating a vast web. The title of one report on desk rage screams: "23% of American Workers Have Been Driven to Tears as a Result of Workplace Stress, with 10% Working in an Atmosphere Where Physical Violence Has Occurred; Overall, 29% of Workers Have Yelled at Co-workers Themselves." [38]

What is this, however, but the precursor to workplace violence? It is like the connection between aggressive driving and road rage: one thing leads to another. We have even successfully linked numerous rage zones together, showing how they interact on the same level. For instance, several studies have shown that frustration from commuting impacts mood and behavior both at home and at work. [39] "When people commute for an hour a day, just think about how much blood pressure is being raised, how many teeth being gnashed, how many interpersonal relationships are being damaged," says Jerry Deffenbacher, who has studied aggressive driving for twenty years. "It's the wear and tear, the sandpaper on the soul." Likewise, after a forty-year study of eight hundred men, we know that hostility, in and of itself, is a better predictor of heart disease than cholesterol, blood pressure, smoking, or weight. [40] What we have not done, however, is put our finger on the common source of our modern rage or its many physical and behavioral symptoms: the insanity of life in a hypermarket.

## The Obesity Epidemic

We are currently experiencing an unprecedented rise in obesity across the breadth of our population. The Centers for Disease Control reports that nearly two-thirds of all Americans are overweight (i.e., having a body-mass index, which compares weight to height, greater than twenty-five), while one in three are obese (a BMI greater than thirty). Since 1980, obesity among adults has doubled, while the number of overweight adolescents has tripled. America now has the dubious distinction of being the fattest nation on Earth.

I recently returned from a trip to Disney World, where the magnitude of this problem was apparent as never before. The park was full of fat people.

During one performance, I counted eight clearly obese people in a row of eighteen in front of me. In a cafeteria, there was a table of high-school girls, of which four in ten were obese. At one point, as I waited to board a train with my family, an enormous woman got stuck in the turnstile ahead of us. They had to physically remove the turnstile to let her pass. Many like her were so fat that they could not walk themselves around the park, so they rented scooters normally allotted to the physically handicapped, which I suppose they were. One could also clearly see the link between obese parents and obese children, as many of the former were towing the latter.

Overweight (which is now used as a noun) is a complex health issue. Contributing factors, according to the U.S. surgeon general, include genes, metabolism, behavior, environment, culture, and socioeconomic status. The question, therefore, is which of these factors have changed in the past twenty years or so to create the epidemic. Clearly, the genes and metabolisms of Americans have not, so the primary cause appears to be in the environmental, cultural, and socioeconomic variables, creating a change in eating behavior. In other words, the cause lies outside the individual, as reflected in this telling finding from researchers at the University of North Carolina: "Adolescent obesity increases significantly among second- and third-generation immigrants to the United States."[41]

The Market's fingerprints are all over this phenomenon, beginning with market stress. One of the ways people react to stress is by eating. Eating is actually a natural part of the body's response to a stressful situation. When the brain triggers a stress response, it releases the stress hormone cortisol into the bloodstream. Cortisol directs the body to move excess calories to the abdomen, where they get deposited as fat. This improves the liver's access to fat, which can be quickly transformed into energy. Once the fat is deposited, it actually triggers a reduction in the stress response. The body is essentially telling the brain that it has been refueled. However, chronic stress, which is not natural, warps this process, creating a cycle of eating and fat deposits that lead to obesity.[42] In one survey, for instance, 26 percent of people reported that they responded to stress at work by eating chocolate.[43]

Exercise, of course, is the natural balancing force to energy intake, but here the Market has had its say as well. The Market has always focused on the creation of laborsaving devices. Ironically, this has never produced free time—quite the opposite. But what it has produced is a sedentary society, one hermetically sealed from natural exercise. According to the CDC, 70 percent of American adults are not regularly active during their leisure time, and 40 percent are not active at all.[44] This issue arises from the entire market environment: the transportation system, based on automobiles and roads; the elevators in the cities; the ordered cubicles in the offices, where only keyboards get a work-out; the commute in the subway, where you couldn't move if you tried. Ironically, one of the great causes of stress, the pace of life, only serves to make the problem worse. People who are pressed for time don't always take the time for exercise. And when they eat, they often go to places that have been designed for speed: fast-food restaurants.

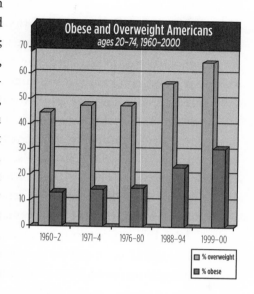

Fast-food restaurants are the tip of an enormous industrial chain, a chain whose every link has been beaten upon the Market's anvil. Apart from the convenience of fast food, the success of the industry requires that people like what they're eating. Because of the magnitude of consumer demand, the fast-food industry has expended tremendous resources creating a product that appeals to consumers. Behind every Whopper is not only an enormous supply chain, and massive advertising budgets, but laboratories full of scientists bent on reducing the human appetite to its biological elements, and crafting chemical solutions that will trigger the appropriate reaction. Since the aroma of food accounts for 90 percent of its flavor, fast-food companies rely heavily on flavor companies, which concoct the smell of perfumes and charbroiled burgers alike. Other scientists examine the color of food and how it affects taste. There are even machines that analyze the "mouthfeel" of food and categorize it according to its bounce, creep, breaking point, density, crunchiness, chewiness, gumminess, lumpiness, rubberiness, springiness, slipperiness, smoothness, softness, wetness, juiciness, spreadability, spring-back, and tackiness. In this way the fast-food companies can engineer products that people will buy, as published in the pages of *Food Product Design* and *Food Engineering*.[45]

All of this may sound like free-market theory is working well to serve the public, when in fact it isn't. In all the vast apparatus of the fast-food industry, no thought has been given to create food that is good for people. Instead, the entire mechanism has been focused on getting people to buy food that is laden with fat, sugar, and calories, regardless of its impact on them. And the success of the industry shows the flaw in free-market theory, the idea that a system designed to give people what they want is inherently a moral system. In a simpler world it may be, but once science reaches a point where the Market is exploiting the nature of the body at levels beneath consciousness, all to sell a Quarter Pounder, the Market has overwhelmed the consumer.

While the Market has been subtracting the nutrition from fast food (and many other processed foods), it has been trying to get us to eat more of it as well. Another crop of scientists has determined that the human stomach is a natural binge eater. In Paleolithic times, it behooved us to eat up when given the chance. Consequently, the way to sell people more food is to give them bigger portions. This insight has led to the supersizing of America, from the Big Mac to the Big Gulp. The way to expand the market, in other words, is a simple matter of fattening every individual.[46] The final step was to open up 24/7 Binge Centers so that one could drop by for fifteen hundred calories whenever the impulse grabbed you. The irony of the obesity epidemic is that, having embraced the principle of excess, from megahouses to Cigarette boats, the American public has itself become a physical symbol of the hypermarket.

There is one last market explanation for the obesity epidemic that has not, to my knowledge, been explicitly made, although it has been made for its related condition, depression, as well as two other eating disorders, bulimia and anorexia. That is social competition. The social competition theory of depression holds that depression is a response to a loss of status, or to an unsuccessful attempt to gain status. It is a kind of implosion of self-esteem. Since being fat is both unattractive and unhealthy, the same dynamic would appear to explain at least some obesity. There are many reasons why low self-esteem might exist in an individual, but one of the more common is a sense of social failure. In a hypermarket fueled by the keeping-up-with-the-Joneses phenomenon—a phenomenon independent of income level—there will always be millions of people who do not feel that they have kept up, particularly at the lower socioeconomic rungs. It may well be that some people get fat because they hear the Market constantly telling them that they aren't good enough.

Like depression, obesity is just a beginning, not an end. It has been linked to numerous health problems, many of them serious, causing an estimated 300,000 adult deaths in the United States each year. As the problem worsens, U.S. surgeon general David Satcher warns that "overweight and obesity may soon cause as much preventable disease and death as cigarette smoking [and] could wipe out some of the gains we've made in areas such as heart disease, several forms of cancer, and other chronic health problems." Clearly, the impact of this development on our already burdened health-care system will be huge. The total cost of all overweight was estimated at $117 billion in 2000.[47] How it will impact the rest of society remains to be seen, but there are signs that the Market is already responding. Government agencies are relaxing their weight and fitness guidelines; restaurants are widening their seats; new vacation resorts for the obese have opened up, as have clothing stores that cater to the extra large; the very sizes of American clothing are being revised.

From the perspective of the individual, obesity is a matter of personal responsibility, and thus, it reflects a lack of will and self-discipline. People cannot get fat without deciding to eat. This is a perfectly legitimate, bottom-up viewpoint, but also incomplete, as evinced by the obesity statistics themselves, which are rising more or less uniformly among all sectors of the population. What is causing this general fattening of the American population? Obesity is also part of the vast, interrelated network of problems that define life in established market economies. While malnutrition is a problem in underdeveloped nations, overnutrition is a problem in advanced ones—a revealing symmetry. Lying beneath both ideas is the top-down view, the degree to which the Market shapes the world we live in. As one physiologist concludes, obesity is "a normal response to the American environment."[48] According to the secretary of health and human services, Tommy Thompson, "Our modern environment has allowed these conditions to increase at alarming rates and become a growing health problem for our nation."[49] These opinions echo those of the father of all medicine, Hippocrates, who noted in 400 BC: "in general, you will find the forms and dispositions of mankind to correspond with the nature of the country." [50]

## The Bottom Line

While the United States spends more per person on health care than any other nation (approximately $5,440 per person annually, 15 percent of our entire GDP[51]), it does not have anywhere near the healthiest society. "As a country, we make up about 4 percent of the world's total population," writes one physician, "yet we expend almost half of all the money spent on medical care. We should be pretty healthy. Yet I have always been amazed at how poorly the United States ranks in health when compared with other countries. When I began medical school in 1970 we stood about 15th in . . . the ranking of countries by life expectancy or infant mortality. Twenty years later we were about 20th, and in recent years we have plunged even further to around 25th, behind almost all rich countries and a few poor ones. For the richest and most powerful country in the world's history, this is a disgrace." [52] If one looks at life expectancy alone, the U.S. was twenty-seventh on the list in 2000. If one factors in disability, the picture worsens. During the 1990s, the U.S. was second from the bottom among OECD countries. While the average American male can expect about fifty-eight years of disability-free life, the average Japanese male can enjoy *fifteen years more*.[53] We have all heard the legendary stories of how long Japanese salarymen work, so why doesn't their health suffer as much as ours? One suggestion from an American physician who has studied the matter extensively: "Japan is a more cooperative society and far more egalitarian than the U.S." [54] In other words, we are paying a health penalty for excessive self-interest, the hallmark of the market state. What breeds stress, and the health problems that go along with it, is not just hard work, but going it alone in an intensely competitive, dog-eat-dog environment.

John Komlos, an economist at the University of Munich, has used a more novel approach to track our decline: height, which increases in good times and contracts in bad. When one compares the stature of Americans relative to Europeans, the results are striking:

Within the course of the 20th century the American population went through a metamorphosis from being the tallest in the world, to being among the most overweight. The American height advantage over Western and Northern Europeans was between 3–9 cm in the middle of the 19th century. Americans were also underweight. However, today the exact opposite is the case as the Dutch, Swedes, and Norwegians are the tallest, and the Danes, British, and Germans—even the East-Germans—are also taller, towering over the Americans by as much as 3–7 cm.[55]

So why is America faring so badly relative to other countries? Komlos and several other respected voices have concluded that income inequality is to blame.[56] However, income inequality is just another result of a hypermarket, in which social bonds break and selfishness becomes the norm. In effect, the entire top tier of society becomes a cabal exploiting the rest, a phenomenon no different than the cabal at Enron. Thus, income inequality is correlative, not causative. The primary cause is the hypermarket, which not only causes both mental and physical illnesses, but undermines the health-care system necessary to treat them.

The U.S. health-care system is patently skewed toward the rich. The rich can get better health care in the United States than anywhere else on Earth. Meanwhile the health-care standard for the poorest 5 percent of Americans is equivalent to that of West Africa. Furthermore, 40 million Americans have no health-care insurance, while 60 million lack insurance at some point during the year.[57] The reason for all this is that we have let the Market rule the health-care system. As a result, the Market has prioritized the rich over the poor, skewing its resources in one direction. While we preach that all men are created equal, there is no philosophy of equality underlying the U.S. health-care system, no sense that all people have a right to life, nor any laws to enforce it, even though providing for the health of its citizens is arguably the single most important responsibility of any government. In the hands of the Market, the American health-care system has become, inevitably, a branch of social Darwinism, where those at the economic bottom—or even the middle—live at mortal risk. It is winner-take-all health care.

Surprisingly, however, the nature of the health-care system is not the dominant factor in the health of a population. The more important factor

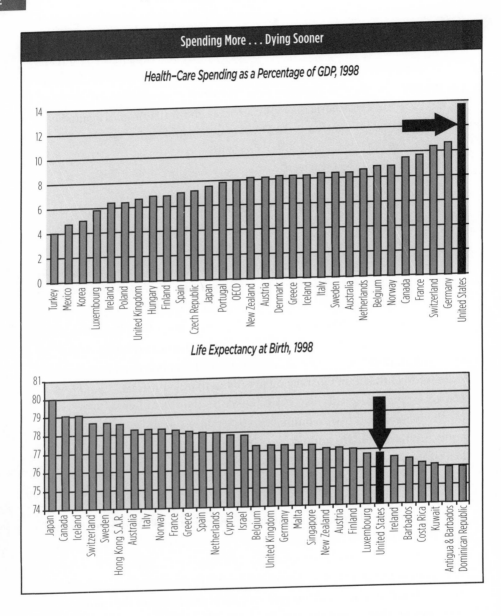

is how many people get sick to begin with. And here the Market is playing a critical role. Human health is inextricably bound to the human mind, and in the modern world, the human mind is inextricably bound to the Market. By unbridling the Market, Americans have placed their minds in the hands of an excessive system that is taking an unseen toll on their physical and mental health. As we have seen, under intensifying stress people get angry, they eat, they get depressed, they drive faster, and they burn out, causing a chain reaction of diverse, interrelated problems that reverberate throughout the society. Research links stress to depression, and stress to obesity, and depression to obesity, creating a seamless whole, a round-robin that argues against any scientific reductionism, while calling for a holistic understanding of the human being.

The human spirit can be enabled or disabled by its relationship with the Market. As the Market liberates our spirit to pursue its happiness, that freedom becomes a powerful, and highly productive, energy; as the Market bears down upon the spirit with intense pressure, the spirit flags, resulting in a host of pathologies. For better or worse, the Market is tied into us at a spiritual level, an idea that is anathema to Western economics and medicine alike. The power of the Market to penetrate the human senses, using advanced sciences, coupled with the saturation of market-controlled media, where each commercial is the tip of an enormous advertising firm, means that the average person is now surrounded by highly sophisticated forces operating upon mind, body, and spirit at a level where he is not even conscious of them—forces that aren't just trying to get you to buy something, but are projecting, in total, their own belief system.

There are many other significant repercussions of the hypermarket that we do not have space to address here. For example, when people are stressed out they abuse alcohol, a well-known and well-documented form of self-medication.[58] We are all aware of what an enormous toll this takes on our society, so I have chosen not to elaborate on it. Suffice it to say that the dollar cost runs into the hundreds of millions every year, while the human cost is unquantifiable. Here the chain reaction is especially broad, as the damage spreads out to encompass one's health, family, company, and community.

Certainly not all social problems are caused by market stress, and some of it is unavoidable. There will always be winners and losers in the market, so to some extent, that is just the way life is. On the other hand, the important question is how much pathology is *entirely unnecessary*. How much anger, stress, heart disease, obesity, depression, alcoholism, burnout, and a million other illnesses are being caused by overwork, little vacation, false notions of happiness, intense social pressure, or a simple lack of savings? How many people drink because of a profound, unexplainable feeling of meaningless in their lives? If the Market only exists to put a roof over our head, clothes on our back, and food on the table, how much of this profound social devastation is simply *pointless*?

John Sidgmore was not someone you would have considered a victim of the Market. A professionally successful Washington entrepreneur, and one of the best known in the region, Sidgmore had led UUNet technologies from a small company to the dominant carrier in Internet traffic, a public company with $4 billion in sales in 1999. In 2002 he gained national prominence when he took over as CEO of WorldCom, where he helped federal investigators uncover an $11 billion accounting fraud, the largest in U.S. history. In the months that followed, Sidgmore waged a multifront war as he sought to keep the company afloat while fending off the critics on his board, a battle he lost that December, when he was replaced.

Twelve months later John Sidgmore suddenly died, age fifty-two, a third of his life unlived. The medical explanation was kidney shutdown due to acute pancreatitis. His associates noted that WorldCom's troubles had taken a heavy toll on Sidgmore. "He ran himself into the ground," said a fellow investor. Another friend and venture capitalist explained, "I don't think he fully understood that when the world came crashing down on the company the position it would put him in or the stress it would put on him." He left a wife and one son.[59]

# 2. Meltdown

America's Family: The Bradys (1970–74) vs. The Osbournes (2001–present).

t is 1950, and the Market is not happy. From the summit of the economic system, it stares down upon America with a jaundiced eye. America's most important resource, its labor force, is incredibly unproductive, for one simple reason: Most women aren't employed. Homemakers work, of course, but they don't get paid for it, which means they add nothing to the GDP. And without a salary, the Market has no control over them at all. The Market cannot fire them, promote them, or move them to where it needs them most. They are basically off the economic grid. What an enormous opportunity cost!

The Market ponders the situation like a general analyzing his battle plan. The primary objective is to take the woman, who is commonly a mother, out of the home and put her into an office. Standing in the way are several defenses that must be overcome. At the deepest level, mothers are attached to their children. They stay at home to take care of them. This is an incredibly strong human bond, perhaps the strongest of them all. But clearly, this bond has to be weakened, otherwise the Market will never put mothers to work from nine to five every day. Surrounding and protecting this core bond is a host of other values that also need to be undermined, the traditional values supporting the nuclear family. How is the Market going to do this?

As we look back now from 2005, the answer is clear. The Market used its classic pressures, supplemented by a great deal of advertising. It convinced people that they needed to buy certain things in order to keep up with the Joneses, to feel successful, and to lead a decent life. Their very self-esteem was at stake. And as the resulting vortex of consumption took shape, it sucked women right out of the house:

> Vested as it was in the trappings of a consumer economy, to sustain the household at what the Bureau of Labor Statistics called "a modest but adequate" level increasingly required women's wage work. As blue-collar workers and a growing corps of bureaucrats moved into postwar sub-urban communities, household needs expanded dramatically. Homes and cars, refrigerators and washing machines, telephones and multiple televisions required higher incomes. Keeping children at school be-yond the age of sixteen and sending them to college meant foregoing their income, and sometimes paying tuition as well. Higher real wages of male breadwinners could pay for some of these, but as the level of consumer aspiration rose, wives sought to aid husbands in the quest for the good life. The two-income family emerged. In 1950, wives earned wages in only 21.6 percent of all families. By 1960, 30.5 percent of wives worked for wages. And that figure would continue to increase.[1]

As this change unfolded, its purely economic merits became apparent to government policy makers. A sign of the times occurred in 1955, when the White House held a conference on "Effective Uses of Women-power." Two years later, another conference on "Work in the Lives of Married Women" brought together economists, business leaders, and government representa-tives to chart a new social course. James Mitchell of the Labor Department noted that the U.S. could not "continue to advance our standard of living without the integration of women in greater numbers into the work force." A few years later, President Kennedy called a Commission on the Status of Women that reiterated the same theme.[2]

Concomitant with this social revolution was the crafting of an entirely new ideology to support it. And here the Market took its cue from Nature.

Natural selection works on the principle of variation. At any one time, there are always slight variations among individuals. Nature rewards the most productive variations, and evolution takes place. In the evolution of society, some variations are ideas. In order to transform the nuclear family, the Market thus rewarded those ideas that broke with tradition. In this way, it crafted an entire strategy aimed at overthrowing the nuclear family, the strategy of *market feminism:*

### The Strategy of Market Feminism

• Stress need for women to liberate themselves from traditional values. Depict the current existence of the housewife as a negative. The housewife is little more than a slave, exploited by her male masters. She performs mundane chores in virtual isolation. In contrast, depict professional life as exciting and glamorous, the route to self-empowerment. This will lead the mother to choose career over family.

• Focus women on individual self-interest. Deny that they need men. Depict men as selfish, power-centered sexists holding women back for their own gain. Deny that they go to work to support their wives and family. Female independence from husbands/family will lead to greater dependence on corporations/industry.

• Equate career success with a woman's personal value. Depict success as a mother as worthless. Workplace will be seen as source of feminine progress.

• Undermine value of nuclear family. Position it as one option among many. As the family structure weakens, deny that the past was better.

• Discredit importance of motherhood. Position it as a myth created by men and clergy to subordinate women. Deny that women have any more responsibility to raise kids than men do. Claim that fathers can do it equally well.

• Undermine importance of early bonding between mother and child. Stress quality of time over quantity of time spent with child. Deny that working moms spend less quality time with kids. Attribute family problems to stress, not time. Create studies challenging need for mother to bond with children. Reduce amount of bonding time as fallback position. Accuse foes of trying to make women feel guilty about their independence. Use science to label guilt as "separation anxiety." Provide pharmaceutical cure.

• Take children out of hands of mothers. Deny that latchkey kids suffer. Sell alternative to maternal care in marketplace, i.e., day-care centers. Position it as improvement over motherhood: a great learning environment, expanded social interactions, a new extended family. Encourage corporations to provide programs attracting mothers to workplace, including corporate day care. Lobby government for tax incentives for mothers to utilize day care, indirectly taxing homemakers. Build day-care industry across country. Franchise model most effective.

• Overcome resistance by recruiting key supporters and suppressing debate. Critical nodes include the media, social scientists, corporate leaders, politicians. Some suggested titles: *Remaking Motherhood; The Way We Never Were; The Myths of the First Three Years.* As social damage becomes apparent, attribute to numerous unrelated causes.

• Once critical mass of women in workplace is reached, declare that we can never go back. Continue institutionalization of corporate and governmental programs and services, including a permanent lobbying effort, along with change in family economics. This will create insurmountable barrier to reversal.

• Above all, detach issue from moral truth and make it purely political. Resulting battle will disguise what is really happening.

This market feminism represented a significant corruption of the original feminist ideal. During the early twentieth century, *protecting* mothers from having to work had been a core part of the feminist platform. This *moral* feminism eventually evolved into ensuring the right for all women to gain equal opportunity in the workplace, should they *choose* to enter it, a noble goal that has continued to the present and greatly changed society for the better. In contrast, *market* feminists were not out to provide women with a choice. They wanted all women to work, period, whether they liked it or not. Whatever their motives, their radical ideas were consequently supported by, and used by, the Market for one simple reason: they increased productivity.

The combination of market pressures and market feminism proved to be highly effective. As more and more women poured into the workforce, working patterns changed. Women first stopped quitting work after marriage. Then they returned to work as soon as their youngest child was in school. Then they started returning to work soon after having a child. In 1950, when a third of all women were working, only half of them were full-time. By 1975, nearly 50 percent were working, and more than 70 percent were full-time.[3] Today about two-thirds of American women work.

As expected, this mobilization of the female was a tremendous boon to productivity. Not only was the overall labor force expanded, but just as important, the surge of women into the workforce created thousands of new businesses. Between 1950 and 2000, the role of the traditional homemaker was effectively industrialized. As one demographic survey put it, "A new generation of time-pressured consumers spent money to create thriving new markets for take-out food, home cleaning, and other substitutes for housekeeping."[4]

Consider the cooking function. Without the time she once had to shop at the grocery store and run the kitchen, the working woman began to increasingly depend on someone else's food preparation. In 1955, the portion of the food dollar spent away from home was 25 percent. Today it is double that. Half of these meals are dinner, 11 percent breakfast, the rest lunch.[5] At the same time, the number of meals eaten at home is part of a trend toward what branders have labeled the "home meal replacement," or HMR. The HMR is not just fast food taken back to the house, although clearly that is one common option, but is more often higher-quality fare that is closer to the traditional meal, such as that served up by Boston Market and many ethnic take-out restaurants. Grocery stores have also gotten into this act, first with TV dinners, then quick-preparation meals, and now with an expanding selection of ready-to-eat meals. With all this has come a huge change in cooking demographics, as many young women have never learned to cook, or have forgotten how, thereby ensuring that the HMR industry will be around for a long time to come.[6]

Cleaning has also become a major industry, with its own specialized niches: home cleaning, carpet cleaning, window washing. By 1996, about 9.4 million households in the U.S. were using professional cleaning services, and many more had formed informal relationships with individuals that were less formal, and therefore beyond the reach of statistics. In 1994, 17 percent of householders said they paid someone to do the cleaning.[7] While some household services include doing the wash, the dry-cleaning industry has also greatly benefited from the introduction of women into the workforce, particularly as it pertains to their professional attire. There are currently around thirty thousand commercial dry-cleaning businesses in the United States.

The Market's greatest coup was the day-care industry, which has tripled in size since 1970. It now has over 500,000 outlets in America, serves 12 million preschoolers, and adds $36 billion a year to the GDP. Corporate child-care programs alone have spun off over $100 million worth of day-care subsidiaries. Over twenty top corporations now invest in a fund that distributes $136 million a year to day-care centers in local communities.[8]

Even relatively infrequent parental tasks have become major businesses. Chuck E. Cheese, for instance, is a corporation that specializes in entertaining children, with birthday parties a specialty. It has over 450 outlets in forty-seven states and four countries, trades on the New York Stock Exchange, and has a $1.3 billion market capitalization.

This industrialization of the homemaker role was propelled by a great feedback loop in the economy. As women entered the workforce, they needed entirely new businesses to perform their previous jobs. And as these businesses sprang up, they attracted more women into the workforce. So it is today that you find mostly women in the day-care business, where the Market harnesses their maternal instincts. Meanwhile, they have put their own kids in day care.

As time demands have increased, even men have seen their traditional roles industrialized. They have turned to their own portfolio of house-painters, lawn cutters, and oil changers. Even routine tasks, like installing a dimmer switch or changing a tire, are increasingly handed off to specialists, as practical know-how has atrophied.

Finally, let us not forget the enormous economic benefits that followed the breakup of the extended family in previous generations. There are now more assisted living and elder-care facilities in the United States than dry cleaners. One might say that the breakup of the extended family was the Market's dry run for taking on the family itself.

Now here is the irony of all this, the truth that many recognize but few want to face, because it is so damning. Today survey after survey shows that *the majority of working mothers wish they could return home*. A recent *Redbook* survey, for instance, finds that:

- 35 percent of mothers who work full-time said they envy stay-at-home mothers, while only 15 percent of the latter said they envy working mothers.
- 65 percent of the stay-at-home mothers said they're pleased with the choice they've made.
- Only 27 percent of full-time working mothers said they work because they want to and find it fulfilling. Fifty-seven percent endorsed the statement "I would quit my job this instant if we didn't need the money."[9]

The reason for this turnaround? The claims of the market feminists have simply turned out to be fraudulent. The majority of women have found the working world to be far less than it was cracked up to be, as a result of their separation from their children, the stress and guilt involved in the dual-income family, and a deep dissatisfaction with the nature of the workplace itself:

Women brought up under the influence of postwar feminism still carry the traditional expectations of their mothers and grandmothers; they want to have a personal life, a family, and a community role. They find themselves in a male work system, where work comes before personal life and personal success is equated with work success, and before long they're judging themselves by their boss's standards—attendance, long hours, productivity, and ability to suppress their feelings. By the time they hit their professional stride in their thirties or forties, they're fed up or empty or both, so they reclaim their values by cutting back, quitting altogether, or making a career change.[10]

Unfortunately, most working women who desire to be homemakers today face a stark new reality. As prices have adjusted to dual-income standards, two incomes have become a middle-class necessity. An American middle-class family used to routinely enjoy pensions, full health-care coverage, good public schools, and reasonable credit-card interest rates. But today, with public schools in decline, they face the prospect of either paying for private school or taking on a huge debt burden for a house in a good school district; paying for their own health insurance; paying for their own retirement plan; and slipping into the credit-card spiral when the ends don't meet. In fact, in adjusted dollars, the two-income family today makes 75 percent more money than a single-income family in 1973, but has eight hundred dollars *less* discretionary income.[11]

So now, with the benefit of hindsight, an accurate balance sheet has finally emerged from our national accounting department. Over the past fifty years, the Market has scored a brilliant strategic victory. Having lured women into the workplace under the pretense of liberation, fueling a tremendous postwar economic boom, it has succeeded in cutting off their retreat. It turns out that the claims of the market feminists were built on productive lies, lies the Market seized on and promoted, with horrific irony, to control rather than to liberate. Today's true feminist hero has come full circle: she is the woman who, facing intense pressures to work full-time, refuses to submit and stays at home with her baby.

## The Marital Bond

The industrialization of the homemaker was only the opening salvo in the Market's attack on the family structure. The nuclear family is defined by two critical bonds: the marital bond between husband and wife, and the parental bond between parents and children. In a functional family, these bonds are moral, not productive. They are forms of love. But love is not a market principle, which means that the organization of the nuclear family was simply not as productive as it could be. Once the two-income family left the front door open, the Market thus invaded the home and attacked the traditional bonds within it, triggering what sociologists call "family breakdown," a pathology that, like the impact of stress on the body, has caused a chain reaction of damage throughout our society.

Family breakdown begins with the impact of the dual-income family on marriage. The dual-income family is a recipe for stress. Instead of one stressed-out person arriving home from work each night, there are two, both carrying the load of the hypermarket. Meanwhile, a new cause of stress has arisen between them. In a single-income family, all the homemaker duties are accomplished by the stay-at-home spouse. But in the dual-income family, you have two people who need to perform three jobs, as the homemaker responsibilities have not gone away. Life no longer adds up.

Women are under the most stress here because they are torn between their traditional role in the home and their new role in the office, a problem greatly compounded by having children. A working mother is barely out of the delivery room in America before she is pressured to return to the workplace. Compared with other industrialized countries, our unbridled economy has abysmal parental leave policies. This creates a deep conflict. If the new mother opts to go back to work, she sacrifices part of her relationship with her child during its key formative years. If she stays at home, she hurts herself economically and professionally. She also becomes more dependent on her husband, a very real risk in a country where almost half of all marriages end in divorce, and where the economic damage of those divorces falls disproportionately upon women.[12] To alleviate work pressures, working mothers are now timing their pregnancies around deadlines, such as tax season for accountants, a practice the *Wall Street Journal* calls a "stress-relieving adaptation to the pressures of modern life." [13]

| Mandated Parental Leave Policies for Selected Industrialized Countries[14] | | | |
|---|---|---|---|
| *Country* | *Weeks of Leave* | *% of Pay* | *Recipient* |
| Sweden | 12–52 | 90% for 38 weeks | Mother or Father |
| Germany | 52 | 100% for 14–18 weeks | Mother or Father |
| Austria | 16–52 | 100% for 20 weeks | Mother |
| Italy | 22–48 | 80% for 22 weeks | Mother |
| Chile | 18 | 100% for 18 weeks | Mother |
| Canada | 17–41 | 60% for 15 weeks | Mother |
| USA | 12 | 0 | Mother or Father |

This dual-earner stress naturally increases the chances of what psychologists call "negative mood spillover," i.e. taking your stress out on your spouse. Researchers have even linked certain job characteristics directly to marital tension, be they workload, travel, or job insecurity, many of which have increased in recent years. Women are particularly vulnerable to stress and suffer from depression twice as often as men, a problem that does not help relationships. If one of the spouses (typically the male) is a Type A, the Market's own "hurry disease," erosion is even more likely, as most research shows an association between Type A behavior and marital dissatisfaction.[15]

At the same time, the hypermarket has a propensity for undercutting solutions, as the very time demands that cause stress reduce the time couples have to bond. This problem is particularly acute among those who perform shift work at different hours than their spouse—roughly half of all young parents—or those with significant travel requirements.[16] Likewise, the fatigue involved with the market treadmill neuters the oldest form of marital stress reduction: sex. By the late seventies, there were so many cases of couples not having sex, particularly young couples, that a new term, *inhibited sexual desire*, was coined to describe it. By the end of the eighties, ISD had emerged as the most common sexual complaint, affecting 20 percent to 50 percent of the general population at one time or another, with the most common cases being two-career couples.[17] Informally, it became known as "yuppie disease." It remains the leading sexual problem today.

In extreme cases, chronic marital stress leads to violence. As far back as 1981, researchers found a direct correlation between eighteen different sources of stress (most of it work-related) and spouse abuse.[18] Not surprisingly, men seeking treatment for husband-to-wife violence also report higher frequencies of work-related stress than do nonviolent men.[19] In America, domestic violence is more common than all other forms of violence com-

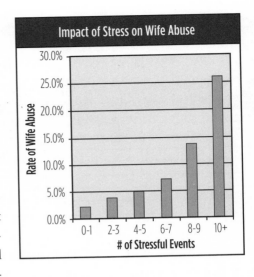

bined. In 1995, for instance, there were 18 million incidents of domestic violence classified as an assault.[20]

All of these market-driven problems inevitably lead to one thing: divorce. And after a half-century in the hypermarket, the United States has the highest divorce rate of any country in the world.[21] 20% of couples divorce within five years, 33% within ten, and almost half eventually.[22] It wasn't always this way. Since 1958, at the onset of our great economic expansion, the divorce rate has doubled, though in recent years it has leveled off. In 2002, the divorce rate was roughly half the marriage rate; approximately 1.2 million Americans divorced that year.

From this point on, the chain reaction of market-driven damage reaches its terminus in the affected spouse. According to the U.S. Centers for Disease Control, "Compared to married individuals, divorced persons exhibit lower levels of psychological well-being, more health problems, greater risk of mortality, more social isolation, less satisfying sex lives, more negative life events, greater levels of depression and alcohol use, and lower levels of happiness and self-acceptance."[23] Divorce leads to financial hardship for many; if the father moves out and the mother does not remarry, household income drops an average of 40 percent the first year. Such hardship can even create long-term dependence on government assistance programs.[24] However, we have traveled far enough from the epicenter of the problem that the unbridled market is rarely identified as the cause of any of this damage.

As these changes have taken place, the Market has further succeeded in changing our cultural values. When the institution of marriage becomes increasingly linked to social problems, such as domestic violence and divorce, it takes on great emotional and financial risk, encouraging people not to get married. Marriage itself appears to be the problem, rather than yet another social institution under siege by the Market. At the same time, the Market is broadcasting the idea that one should prioritize one's professional goals above all else, a pressure that is especially acute during the early years of professional life, when one is building a career. The end result is an increasing proportion of people who postpone marriage, a trend that has been growing since the midsixties. For example, from 1965 to 1998 the percent of unmarried women more than doubled in the twenty- to twenty-four-years age group (from 33 percent to 73 percent) and more than tripled in twenty-five- to twenty-nine-year-olds (from 13 percent to 45 percent).[25] This, in turn, has led to increased levels of cohabitation, which has in the past half century nearly offset the decline in time Americans spend married. Discrediting the institution of marriage further encourages people to have children outside it. In 2002, an astonishing one-third of all births in America were to unmarried women, a figure that increasingly cuts across racial lines.[26] It was less than 5 percent in 1950. This change has occurred in the face of conclusive evidence that the single-parent family disadvantages children. According to the Centers for Disease Control and other blue-chip organizations, children in a single-parent family are more likely to have behavior problems, lower grades, drop out of high school, and not attend college; to suffer from depression and unemployment, abuse drugs and alcohol, attempt suicide, and have an arrest record; to become single parents themselves, and also to divorce.[27]

The decline in the institution of marriage is most pronounced, as one might expect, in areas where market pressures are most intense: cities. And here we find, as we also might expect, that market forces do not discriminate. As a comprehensive study by the CDC confirms, all forms of "union formation" are depressed by city life, regardless of race or ethnicity:

> First marriage is more likely in non-metropolitan areas and less likely in central cities [i.e. not including suburbs]. The transition from cohabitation to marriage is less likely in central cities. Cohabitation disruption and first marriage disruption are more likely in central cities. Post-

marital cohabitation is less likely in central cities. Remarriage is much less likely in central cities and more likely in non-metropolitan areas. The overall pattern suggests that central cities have lower rates of union formation and higher rates of cohabitation and marriage disruption than suburbs or non-metropolitan areas.[28]

What makes these statistics all the more striking is that metropolitan areas would otherwise appear to be the ideal place to find a mate, given their high population density. Clearly, there is something about city life that is deleterious to lasting love.

As we saw with market feminism, the Market is quite skilled at creating an ideology to justify itself. So it should not surprise us that as the institution of marriage has weakened, market feminism has adopted an antimarriage platform. This attitude is couched in terms of self-liberation, in which one should free oneself from marriage—and seek satisfaction in one's professional career. Here we see a deep connection revealed, one that we will delve into later on: When one listens closely to the ideology known as "modern liberalism," one hears the Market's laugh.

## The Wall Street Marriage

As the Market has eroded the traditional idea of marriage, it has simultaneously redefined it along more productive lines. With every passing day, marriage becomes more of a contractual issue, begun with prenuptial agreements and ended, in nearly half of all cases, with divorce lawyers. In the middle there is the idea that marriage is another market contract, an exchange of goods and services between buyers and sellers, each out for themselves. The true marital bond has slowly been transformed into a Wall Street relationship. So in the end, the Market now offers us one of two productive choices in life: stay a single professional, or create a small brokerage firm.

The role of the Market in marriage is as old as the dowry, of course, but it is also true that the deeper the market belief system penetrates society, the more people are likely to view marriage as another market relationship. Indeed, the term *marriage market* has now become a technical term used by sociologists to describe the trading activity surrounding the marital bond.

As a study of the economic factors influencing marriage in the nineties concluded:

> Overall, the evidence suggests that, although men's earnings continue to be somewhat more important than women's in family formation, the role of economic factors in women's and men's family formation decisions is remarkably similar. Both men and women with better educations, job prospects, and earnings are more likely to marry because both are attractive commodities in a marriage market that seems to rely less on notions of role complementarity and more on economies of scale, reduction of economic risk, and income maximization.[29]

This change reflects a trend that has been going on in market economies for a long time. From the 1860s to the early part of the twentieth century, sociologists Henry Maine, Ferdinand Tönnies, and Max Weber all noted an increasing shift in "progressive societies" from human relationships based on ties of family, community, and friendship to individualistic "conflict of wills" in competitive urban capitalism, based on rational interest.[30] Today the marriage market is even supported by its own NASDAQ, the online dating services, which match buyers and sellers with increasing efficiency. The purpose of the transaction, from either side, is clear, at least according to one sociologist: "A person enters the marriage market if he expects his marital income to exceed his single income."[31] The same philosophy is also on public display in reality TV shows, where "the quest for money is more honorable than the pursuit of love, which as almost every variation on 'The Bachelor' has shown, is actually a grab for fame and fortune dressed up as romance."[32]

Economic realities are, of course, practical realities in marriage, to a certain extent. One needs money for food, clothing, shelter, tuition, transportation, etc. Either one or both spouses must take responsibility for it. But what defines a true market marriage is not mere practicality. It is the nature of the relationship itself. As psychologists have noted, the qualities the Market rewards, such as the ability to look out for oneself, and opportunism, are deadly when carried over into intimate relationships, as such qualities are fundamentally based on a lack of trust.[33] The market marriage is not a traditional relationship, but an exchange of value. It is not till death do us part, but another contract that lasts only as long as both parties continue to get what they want. Instead of a love-based union, one's spouse becomes another material possession, breeding such perversions as the "trophy wife." When the husband gets bored with such a wife, or she merely gets too old, he replaces her with a newer model. Likewise, to the nonworking market wife, the trophy husband becomes little more than a wallet, the source of her own possessions and social position. In market couples where both spouses work, their value to each other becomes a dangerously shifting matter of relative salary. The more a relationship is defined in such terms, the more it becomes sensitive to changing market conditions. You might even say the Market is in charge of it.

## The Parental Bond

At the same time that the Market was eroding the marital bond and changing the nature of marriage, it was eroding the parental bond, too, creating yet another chain of damage. Here the repercussions are equally diverse, especially poignant, and particularly deadly to society, as they will be felt for years to come.

Like marriage, the stress on the parental bond begins with the two-income family. The time crunch caused by two people doing three jobs greatly reduces the time parents spend with their children, particularly the mother, a problem magnified by increasing working hours. In study after study, the vast majority of parents commonly complain that they are not getting enough time with their kids. When it comes to teens, such absentee parenting is particularly harmful, as it occurs at a time when they have an enormous need for a strong relationship.

Kids also suffer from their parents' stress, which leaves their caretakers emotionally unavailable. This incites feelings of abandonment and causes uneven parenting. As one study determined:

> Parents who are under high economic strain are liable to be preoccupied and minimally involved in the parenting role until serious or flagrant child misbehavior jars them into action. Such transgressions are likely to demand a harsh response, so that the pattern of parenting displayed is inconsistent and explosive, vacillating between noninvolvement and harsh reactions.[34]

According to Ann Crouter, professor of human development at Penn State University, "Parents who experience more pressure at work feel more overloaded in general and are more prone to arguing with their children. In turn, their kids feel less good about themselves."[35] This is particularly true when parents are undergoing marital strain at the same time. As an extensive study of Iowa farmers in an economic downturn showed, economic stress results in a chain reaction of emotional distress, marital conflict, and disruptive parenting. In extreme cases, the result is child abuse, ranging from neglect to psychological trauma to physical violence. Kids have that unerring ability to pop a stress balloon.

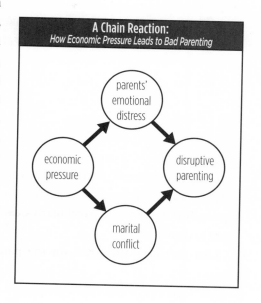

**A Chain Reaction:**
*How Economic Pressure Leads to Bad Parenting*

Divorce, of course, also disrupts the parental bond, and as the hypermarket has driven up the divorce rate, the impact on children has been substantial. According to the U.S. Centers for Disease Control, children of divorce score lower on self-concept, social competence, conduct, psychological adjustment, and long-term health. Even when a divorced mother does remarry, studies show that these adverse outcomes persist.[36]

As the parental bond has come under pressure, it has also changed, like the marital bond. With spouses acting as economic agents, the two-income family has lifted the roof off the family shelter and left it wide open to the Market. Childhood has consequently become an extension of the economy. This is particularly apparent in upper-class suburbia, where one finds highly competitive parents with stressful jobs and high time demands outside of the home transferring their own achievement pressures onto their kids, from the earliest age.

Consider what a clinical psychologist who treats high-school students in Washington, D.C. finds in her young patients:

Here's the recipe for success these kids have learned: Get high SAT's and a high GPA so you can go to this college so you will get this kind of job (and perhaps find a partner with a comparable job) so you will make a lot of money and live happily ever after. The part that's never spoken—and would be disavowed if put into words—is that money will make you happy. . . . There are even parents who transmit the message that college acceptance is so crucial that the end matters more than the means. When their children cheat on the SAT and get caught, both children and parents are outraged when there are real and serious consequences. Sometimes what I hear is almost eerie: young men and women who seem incapable of separating their own aspirations from those their parents hold for them. There are Americans who no longer make a distinction between needs and wants, even between expectations and entitlements. I have heard young men in my office express anxiety about their earning potential, especially in the eyes of their future mates. And I sometimes have to wonder whether their concern is not neurotic, but rooted in present-day American reality. . . . They have internalized a particularly insidious message—that unless a person reaches the top of the remuneration hierarchy, life will hardly be worth living.[37]

So much for "the best years of your life."

This type of market pressure, on those least prepared to deal with it, inevitably breeds pathology. Many kids conclude that their parents are more invested in their "star qualities" than in who they really are. They develop stress-related symptoms like insomnia, stomachaches, headaches, anxiety, and depression. And they turn to the well-known list of destructive behaviors in an effort to kill the pain: drugs, sex, alcohol.[38] In extreme cases, they even attempt suicide. Internationally, the United States now leads the industrialized world in childhood suicide (ages five to fourteen). Our youth suicide rate has more than doubled since 1950. Suicide is now the third leading cause of death for young people aged fifteen to twenty-four.

Just as the erosion of the marital bond ultimately undermined the value of marriage itself, the greatest success of the Market's crusade against the parental bond has been to undermine the value of having children at all. In his survey of the American family between 1960 and 1990, one of the great authorities on family breakdown, David Popenoe, noted that:

there has been a weakening of child-centeredness in American society and culture. Family as a cultural value has diminished. The past few decades have witnessed, for the first time in America history, the rise of adult-only communities, the massive voting down of local funds for education, and a growth in the attitude of "no children allowed." Both in the political process and in the market place, children's issues have been ignored.[39]

This is the inevitable result of a hypermarket. Children are by their very nature highly unproductive. They are a negative balance sheet, absorbing huge amounts of capital with no hope of return to the investor. To parents, they are an unending demand that they take their attention off their job and themselves. They require a philosophy of giving rather than taking, selflessness instead of selfishness. It is no wonder, then, that the Market's capital, New York, has been called "a city for adults."

Here the birth rate harbors another telling clue. While there are many factors affecting this statistic, one association is clear: in modern, industrialized countries, countries with established market economies, the birth rate has been falling. In 2002, the birth rate in America was the lowest since national data became available.[40] In certain parts of Europe, such as Italy, the birth rate is actually negative. So much for the extended Italian family: today the entire country is shrinking.

# The American Hatchery and Conditioning Center

The Market's damage chain has been greatly extended by the central dilemma posed by the two-income family: who is going to take care of the kids? To some people, the answer has become: let them take care of themselves. This is the solution known as self-care, a minor epidemic in America, where around 3 million six- to twelve-year-olds are left home unsupervised each year. Interestingly, more of these come from high-income families than low-income families.[41] The danger here is the obvious damage children can do when left alone, such as burn the house down with them in it.

For the majority of people, however, the solution is not self-care but day care. For decades now, millions of Americans have been participating in an enormous and far-reaching social experiment: they have industrialized the process of raising preschool children. Today 12 million preschoolers, or 63 percent of the preschool population, are in regular child care outside the home, over half of these for thirty-five hours a week. Children under five now spend much more time with nonrelatives each week (thirty-five hours) than with their own family members (twenty-three hours). Day-care centers have thus become the primary molding force behind millions of young Americans in their most critical years. A day-care program that takes care of a child from six months to six years of age, for instance, has over eight thousand hours to leave its mark.[42]

Not surprisingly, this trend has come with the full support of corporate America, which recognizes the importance of attracting and retaining female employees, as well as lowering absenteeism. In addition to numerous on-site child-care programs, nearly three hundred American companies have pumping rooms where mothers use breast pumps so they can send milk to day-care centers. Aetna estimates that its company-funded corporate lactation consultant saves an estimated $1,435 and three days of sick leave per working mother. Eli Lilly prepares take-home dinners four nights a week, helping mothers and others work late. None of these programs, of course, recommends that a woman spend much time at home taking care of her child. But they certainly do improve productivity, and have become an integral part of business strategy. Also not surprisingly, government has followed suit. The federal government now provides more than twice as much assistance, through tax exemptions and credits, to those who use commercial day care vs. those who don't.[43]

So what is the downside of all this? Research clearly shows that the first few years of life are a critical time for all of us. The mind of the child is forming in ways that will stay with him the rest of his life. The attachment process between mother and child is critical in this period. The product of several million years of natural evolution, this bond impacts the emotional, intellectual, and even physical development of the child. The damage involved in breaking this bond is exemplified by a study of eighteen thousand Romanian orphans adopted by couples in the U.S. Having been deprived of their mothers from infancy, 78 percent of these children developed physical, emotional, cognitive, and psychological problems.[44]

The day-care business attempts to act as a surrogate for this bond, and cannot. The low ratio of caregivers to children means that children in day care do not receive the attention they would at home. The high turnover of day-care workers means that a child's primary caregiver frequently changes. From a child's standpoint, this is akin to frequently losing its mother, an unexplained loss that can be traumatic. The daily change between home and day-care center means that the child loses the stability of a single maternal relationship. Given these issues, it is not surprising that researchers have discovered that levels of cortisol, the stress hormone, rise during the day among children in a day-care setting.[45] Add to this the problem of low-quality facilities, in an industry beset with regulatory challenges, and the disease risk associated with pooling large numbers of diaper-dependent infants: Inner-ear problems, severe diarrhea, respiratory illnesses, hepatitis A, and SIDS are all health risks that climb in a day-care setting, in which a common solution is the overprescription of antibiotics.

What is especially striking about the placement of children in this industrialized setting is that it breeds the very attitudes upon which the Market depends, as well as several other related pathologies. As the maternal bond erodes, the selfish child emerges. Studies have shown that day-care kids are more aggressive, want their own way, lack mercy, concern, or respect for others, and become manipulative. They are more likely to push, hit, kick, threaten, swear, and argue. Without the inner bond, they look without, replacing standards of right and wrong with what is fashionable or unfashionable—a hallmark of materialism. Others become alienated and suffer from anomie, two other well-known problems in industrialized society. "The adolescent rage and nihilism that expresses itself in what society regards as the meaningless violence of school shootings," finds one researcher, "may very well have its roots in the undeveloped conscience that results when the normal parent-child relationship is disrupted."[46]

Does this mean that day care necessarily produces bad outcomes in all cases? No, nor do all mothers do their job equally well, either. But of course we are looking at the general truth, and the evidence is in. As Burton White, the former director of the Harvard Preschool Project, concluded, "After more than thirty years of research on how children develop well, I would not think of putting an infant or toddler of my own into any substitute care program on a full-time basis, especially a center-based program."

Millions of Americans either aren't listening, however, or are being forced by market pressures to act against their better judgment. A 1995 study shows that 44 percent of American infants under one year old are in nonparental care thirty-one hours a week. And the ugly fact is that many of those who compose these statistics have the financial means to opt for an alternative solution. Contrary to popular belief, the greatest population of day-care children comes from families with an annual income over seventy-five thousand dollars a year. The highest number of stay-at-home mothers is actually in the twenty-thousand- to twenty-four-thousand-dollar category.[47] Thus to some extent the day-care revolution has been a matter of convenience, a decision made by parents (men and women equally) who have prioritized their market-related desires above their children. On the other hand, this decision making has been encouraged by a day-care lobby composed of liberal social scientists, market feminists, and business interests bent on legitimizing the day-care alternative, backed by the hypermarket. One sees in their arguments a consistent flaw: whether they are trying to lessen mother's guilt, improve business productivity, or promote ideology, the last thing on anyone's mind appears to be the children.

Whatever the reasons, the end result is that we have taken a huge leap toward making the dehumanized horror of *Brave New World* an actual reality, as extreme as that may sound. In Aldous Huxley's futuristic novel, the director of the Central London Hatchery and Conditioning Centre, where babies are fertilized and indoctrinated, reflects on what he considers to be the barbarous practices of the past: "For you must remember that in those days of gross viviparous reproduction, children were always brought up by their parents and not in State Conditioning Centres."[48] Looking forward, how long will it be before some geneticist suggests that the way to combat declining birth rates in industrialized countries is to have day-care centers take on an expanded reproductive role? Now that would be a great business.

## Rockdale County

In order to understand the cumulative impact of the hypermarket on the American family, consider Rockdale County, Georgia, a middle- to upper-middle-class suburb of Atlanta profiled on PBS. In 1996, a syphilis outbreak afflicting two hundred teenagers in that town brought to light a secret teen world of drugs and group sex. Teens were meeting at other kids' houses and at motels for orgies after school. Participants ranged in age from thirteen to nineteen. Some of the youths had up to sixty-five partners. When public health investigators dug beneath the symptoms, what they discovered was a problem deeply embedded in the family. As one expert said after watching the *Frontline* documentary, "While on the surface this is a program about sex and sexual promiscuity, what is far more disturbing than that is the tremendous disconnect that exists between the children of Rockdale County and their families. Over and over again, throughout the program, we see parents who are either clueless or blatantly unconcerned about their children. We see parents who have replaced caring and personal involvement with the purchase of material goods."[49] The group sex club, it turned out, had become a surrogate family for kids bereft of emotional attachment.

The *Frontline* investigation generated tremendous interest when it aired in 1999, not just because of what had happened, but where: Rockdale was Anywhere USA. The girls involved were even described by the Georgia director of public health as "almost cherubic in some of their characteristics." As one public health official commented, "What is so disturbing about the program is not that we are witnessing a rare event in the United States, but rather an event that is quite common." These excerpts from letters to PBS epitomize public reaction to the program:[50]

"What I don't understand is when did this all start? I'm only 19. I did a lot of stuff when I was in high school, I lost my virginity, I drank. My friends did the same. But nothing like these kids. They are out of control. I knew of maybe one or two kids when I was in high school who acted like the kids in the program. But now they seem to be everywhere."

"I think that what is terribly missing is a relationship with God, and a closeness with the family."

"Why do you think these girls behaved that way? They wanted attention, they wanted someone to love them back. To feel it. Not with new sneakers, CD players and Sega. They wanted someone to notice."

"We have been conditioned to accept work weeks of 60 or even 70 hours as 'normal'. Is it any wonder then that parents lack the energy/time to put into the work of raising children and young adults? Is it any surprise that children raised in such an atmosphere would value 'things' above relationships and perhaps even come to regard their bodies as a thing?"

"This problem exists because we as a society let it. We have continually lowered the bar, from the way we dress to the absence of manners in our culture. Nothing is WRONG. No black or white, just gray. To me what's frightening is that if it weren't for the syphilis no one EVER would have known."

Reactions to the program from within Rockdale were very different. Here is Dr. Kathleen Toomey, director of the Georgia Division of Public Health, describing the briefing she gave the townspeople on the syphilis outbreak:

And I remember when I put up the slide that showed that interaction, the sex partners, and the partners of the partners, it looked like a ball of yarn. There was actually a gasp from the audience and this total disbelief that this could have happened in their community. And there ensued a discussion, and with me there was a minister who was involved with the youth ministry, other local public servants, the police, others, talking about how this could have happened. And it was so extraordinary to me that these parents started looking for externally who to blame. "This caused this—TV has caused that—external groups have caused this—" But few of them, none of them that I can recall, ever looked to themselves. And the minister turned to me and said, "They don't see. It's them. It's the parents. They have done this. The kids don't talk to them." [51]

The deeper question, of course, is not why the parents couldn't fault themselves, but why they weren't talking to their own kids. Why the lack of basic parental love? The answer was suggested by one of the health investigators on the case:

People like to be part of the middle class, preferably of the upper middle class. One of the ways in which you achieve that goal is by working hard, by making long hours, by investing all your time and energy and insuring that you can buy a house that is in a neighborhood that you think is safe. . . . As a consequence of all that very little time is left over for emotions. *It's almost like material aspects have begun running people's lives.*[52]

In the spring of 1999, while the PBS special was being filmed and a month after the Columbine massacre, Thomas Solomon, a fifteen-year-old sophomore at Rockdale's Heritage High, entered his school with a .22-caliber rifle and a handgun and shot six students. There were no warning signs. While Solomon was apparently distraught over a breakup with his girlfriend, both his friends and administrators described him as utterly normal.[53]

## Outing the Market

As the nuclear family has broken down, much analysis has been directed upon it, but the primary cause of the breakdown has remained a great mystery. "It is strange," one political economist notes, "the richer and the more educated our country has become, the weaker our family units seem to become."[54] What is astounding about such comments is that we fail to connect the "getting richer" to the "family breakdown," just as we fail, as we saw in the previous chapter, to connect "market economy" to "mental health problems." One might even say we refuse to consider such connections. We implicitly assume that a roaring economy is good for society, no matter how loud it is. Even when the massive movement of women into the workplace is clearly central to family breakdown, virtually no one points the finger at the economic force behind this movement. It is as if the Market were above reproach.

When the Market is mentioned as a cause, it is often in the form of various pseudonyms. One hears social problems vaguely attributed to "economic pressures," or "industrialization," or "urbanization," or "modern life," or "progress." Most of the time the idea of unbridled capitalism is simply overlooked in favor of the symptoms it has bred. Part of this oversight is due to the deep reality of the Market. One finds it hard to imagine a parent standing up in Rockdale, or anywhere else, and blaming unbridled capitalism for their kid's syphilis. The Market remains an enigma, quiet, secretive, yet enormously powerful, the hidden substrate of society. We may recognize it as the power that rules modern life, but we don't typically explain our lives with it.

Once we recognize the Market for what it is, however, and look at the world from its perspective, all becomes clear, and one might even say obvious. In the past half century, a hypermarket has driven the breakdown of the American family. Increasing competitive pressures, increasing time demands, and increasing social pressures have taken a tremendous toll on the American psyche. Stress levels have risen to the saturation point. Many have shed their traditional values in favor of market values. Human bonds, whether marital or parental, have frayed and broken. Women have been alternately pulled and pushed into the workplace, triggering the collapse of the family structure. The result has been social fragmentation and decline.

All of this has occurred for a single reason. The Market hammers organizations of all kinds upon a single template, the family included. It seeks to atomize us all into particles of pure self-interest, turning society into a huge pinball game; to break down allegiances to anything higher than the self, be it the company or the team or the family. Productivity is maximized when every individual is a free agent struggling to survive on his own, with the Market's ax dangling over his neck. The unbridled Market is thus as antifamily as they come. This is not to say that the excesses of the Market have been the only cause of the many social problems we have studied. Clearly, they have not. But the Market is the only force powerful enough to pull the American family apart and cause all the social repercussions that have ensued.

Naturally, not everyone subscribes to the idea that the nuclear family should be dismantled. Market feminism grew out of urban areas, and is the product of the intense market pressures there. Those outside these urban blast furnaces have rejected this philosophy, creating a political schism based fundamentally on where one lives. One result is the so-called mommy wars, in which the forces of market feminism have clashed with those supporting the traditional nuclear family. Lost in the din of battle is the essential truth. The decline of the nuclear family is not social progress. It is the eradication of the core unit of society by unbridled market forces. We all come from a family, after all. Who wants to grow up in a brokerage firm?

The most amazing part of this meltdown is that it should have happened at all. The ability of the Market to overcome the most important human bonds, the natural bonds between man and woman, and between parents and children, and to subvert traditions that have arisen out of millions of years of biological and social evolution, in a short fifty years, is stark testimony to the power of the Market in modern life. That power has now placed us in a position where we are serving the Market from birth, rather than having it serve us. As Joseph Campbell noted over twenty years ago, "Man should not be in the service of society, society should be in the service of man. When man is in the service of society, you have a monster state, and that's what is threatening the world at this minute."[55]

# 3. The Bubble

Product Placement: Nicole Kidman in *The Stepford Wives*, 2004.

While the Market has replaced Nature as the dominant principle in our lives, it also exerts far more control over our lives than Nature ever did. The artificial world we live in may be analogous to the natural world, as a physical phenomenon, but there is nothing in the natural world that is analogous, say, to television. While mankind once sought truth and meaning in Nature, now the Market actively broadcasts its own version. This has created an alternate reality for us to live in, a world apart from Nature, and separate from the truth it represents: the Bubble.

The Bubble arises from commercial media, which is inherently in the control of the Market. The Market thus enjoys the same power as a totalitarian regime, and pursues the same objectives as well. With the media in its palm, it can influence how people think, thereby controlling their behavior. The Market is not interested in broadcasting the truth, but in increasing demand and spreading the values that make society more productive. So from this perspective, commercial media is a form of propaganda. We may not want to think of it this way, because it sounds ugly and cynical, yet who among us would counsel our kids to believe advertisers, to accept the news as unbiased, or to emulate the behavior of celebrities? What we have yet to come to grips with, because it is a difficult truth to face, is the magnitude of the false reality that surrounds us.

## Saturation

The design of the Bubble is quite straightforward. It is based on the strategy of saturation. The Market has focused on building multiple channels linking producers to consumers, and filling those channels with market messages. Today there are innumerable ways in which the Market can reach us: television, e-mail, voice mail, snail mail, cell phones, radio, fax machines, landlines, newspapers, magazines, movies, billboards, CDs, books, and many other media small and large, from the advertisement printed out on your checkout slip to the T-shirt you are wearing to the Goodyear blimp sailing overhead. It is impossible to avoid them all. This communication infrastructure represents an enormous expenditure. From 1984 through 1992, for instance, the cable television industry spent more than $15 billion wiring America, and billions more on program development—the largest private construction project since World War II.

This saturation strategy has been wildly successful, particularly in the area of television. The average American now watches more than four hours of television per day—a staggering figure. That is roughly a quarter of all waking hours. The only category that tops it is work. At this rate, a person who lives to be seventy-five years old will spend over

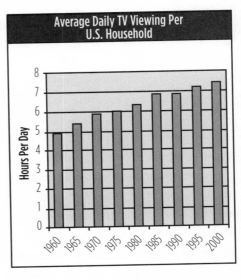

Average Daily TV Viewing Per U.S. Household

*twelve years* watching television. The grip of the tube is even greater among children, indicating a rising influence among future generations. By 2001, 21 percent of American nine-year-olds were watching more than five hours of television each weekday—the highest percentage in the developed world.[1] In terms of household use, the box is now broadcasting over seven hours a day. This rise has even taken place over and above the objections of physicians. For example, the American Academy of Pediatrics notes, "The first 2 years of life are especially important in the growth and development of your child's brain. During this time, children need good, positive interaction with other children and adults. Too much television can negatively affect early brain development." Consequently, the AAP does not recommend any television at all for children age two or younger. Currently, however, 43 percent of American children under two watch TV every day, and a quarter have a TV in their bedroom.

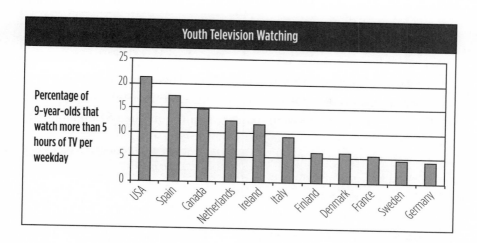

The Market has also greatly expanded its advertising network in recent years, with awe-inspiring results. It has managed to overcome traditional concerns about the public interest and its most vulnerable populations, such as youth, and penetrate all manner of public space, from the bottom of golf holes to the inside doors of restroom stalls. There are even mobile billboards now that do nothing but drive around our cities all day long. When one adds up all the logos, labels, announcements, and various other commercial messages that surround us, they total some sixteen thousand ads daily.[2]

As this saturation strategy has unfolded, our cultural space has necessarily retreated, an example being the branding of stadiums with corporate names. In 1988, the total contract value of these "naming rights" arrangements was only $25 million. Today there are sixty-six deals worth $3.6 billion. More than half of all professional baseball, football, basketball, and hockey teams in America now play on a field named, or renamed, for a corporation, usually one that has nothing to do with sports at all. In San Diego, the pet-food chain Petco bought the rights to Padres Stadium, now Petco Park. Their business logic was simple: "Continually seeing our name," said a company spokesman, "we hope will make our name click with people, and say, 'I want to shop here.' " The cumulative effect of these deals has been to publicly subordinate one of our most common cultural touchstones to the Market. Instead of going to a Fenway Park or a Yankee Stadium, one goes to Ameriquest Field, a stadium named after a mortgage company. Since such "naming rights" are contractual, and only as stable as the company behind them, they are further likely to come and go as quickly as the modern corporation, making them as transitory as they are meaningless. In Philadelphia, for instance, the CoreStates Center has already been renamed the First Union Center, and then re-renamed the Wachovia Center, to reflect mergers and acquisitions. In other cases, name changes are forced by damaging revelations about the corporate parent, whether it is Enron Field in Houston, now named Minute Maid Park for the orange-juice manufacturer, or the Adelphia

| Renaming Baseball |
| --- |
| **bold** = *named after corporation* |
| **Ameriquest Field** |
| *Angel Stadium* |
| **Bank One Ballpark** |
| **Busch Stadium** |
| **Citizens Bank Park** |
| **Comerica Park** |
| **Coors Field** |
| *Dodger Stadium* |
| *Fenway Park* |
| **Great American Ballpark** |
| *Jacobs Field* |
| *Kauffman Stadium* |
| *Metrodome* |
| **Miller Park** |
| **Minute Maid Park** |
| **Net Associates Coliseum** |
| *Olympic Stadium* |
| *Oriole Park* |
| **Petco Park** |
| **PNC Park** |
| **ProPlayer Stadium** |
| **Safeco Field** |
| **SBC Park** |
| *Shea Stadium* |
| *Skydome* |
| **Tropicana Field** |
| *Turner Field* |
| **U.S. Cellular Field** |
| *Wrigley Field* |
| *Yankee Stadium* |

Coliseum in Tennessee, which dropped the *Adelphia* after its namesake went bankrupt and its senior management was indicted on racketeering charges.[3]

The end result of this renaming phenomenon is to publicly subordinate culture to the Market. Instead of the sporting event being the end, it becomes the means through which advertisers can reach consumers, an inversion loudly proclaimed by every ticket stub, radio announcer, and television broadcast. Nor is there any reason to expect that the Market will decide to declare a ceasefire on the culture at this point. Instead, if one goes to the new Citizens Bank Park in Philadelphia, one is met in the parking lot by "ballpark bankers" who will drive you to the stadium, only too happy to discuss how you can open a new account.[4]

Lately the Market has evolved its saturation strategy in two new directions. The first is targeting children. Here the idea is simple: Get 'em while they're young. In Maryland, for instance, the Petco pet-store chain offers local schools field trips to its stores. Likewise, regional supermarket chains are leading field trips down their aisles. In Chicago, an entire company, the Field Trip Factory, has been set up to facilitate such arrangements for corporate America. The National Theater for Children works in the other direction, bringing corporate-sponsored messages into elementary and middle schools. As its head of sales and marketing explains, "school is the place where marketers can find kids in an uncluttered environment."[5] Part of the reason marketers are so successful in this arena: schools are strapped for cash. Advertising in child-oriented media has soared to several billion dollars per year, but our schools can't afford field trips.

Outside of school, the entertainment industry takes over. In 2003, the number one hit single was "Get Rich or Die Tryin'" by the rapper 50 Cent—hardly a subtle message. A wider academic study of teen pop lyrics reveals that the dominant subjects today are romantic love and consumption. An entire line of books targeting girls from ages twelve to eighteen, the "Gossip Girl" series, revolves around shopping. Young readers are taken from one brand to another: Barneys, Burberry, Takashimaya, Christian Louboutin, Prada, as if traveling to exotic countries. One of the titles, *All I Want Is Everything,* has appeared on several bestseller lists. Educators say that the popularity of the series is linked to the success of TV shows that also celebrate consumption, like *Sex and the City.*[6] In the latter case, the

HBO Web site even offered directions on where to buy the main characters' possessions.

Another new approach in the Bubble is to collapse the barrier between advertising and programming. In this way, all market media can be broadcasting market messages all the time. The most obvious way this is done is through "product placement," i.e. putting products into movies and television programs. The rapidity with which the Market has been able to penetrate programming in this way has been stunning. It was only in 1998 that Hollywood was satirizing the phoniness of product placement in *The Truman Show*. Now, only six years later, product placement has become de rigueur, an essential part of movie financing. The James Bond film *The World Is Not Enough* was a two-hour catalog featuring a BMW car, an HP handheld, Brioni suits, a Motorola cell phone, a Fujitsu laptop, an Omega watch, Samsonite luggage, Bollinger champagne, Church's shoes, Calvin Klein sunglasses, and Heineken beer. As if to show how far this inversion of priorities can go, we have already reached the point where the entire purpose of a feature film is advertising:

> "The Last Ride," which appears tonight on USA, is a brazen commercial for Pontiac that is souped up to look sort of like a car-chase movie. The network has made no pretense about this, hyping its achievement as an "unprecedented integrated marketing opportunity." You can't skip the ads without missing the movie. Sure enough, gleaming cars with fantastic handling are never far from view, or earshot, as roaring engines and singing brakes dominate the soundtrack. During a scene at a car show, no less, a woman in leather even recites the mantra of Pontiac's new sports car: "Zero to 60 in 5.3 seconds!"[7]

The Market is also moving in the other direction, by bringing programming into advertising. This so-called advertainment is exemplified by a recent "webisode" of *Seinfeld* done for American Express. In this five-minute Internet commercial, Seinfeld is walking through New York with Superman when someone steals his DVD player. Superman springs into action and collars the crook, but damages the DVD player. Never fear—Seinfeld bought it on his AmEx card, so it's covered. Viewers are then prompted to apply for one themselves.[8]

# The Message

Once the Market has found a way to reach us, the question is what to tell us. Here the most obvious point should be that the many speakers that broadcast the Market's voice do not exist to tell us the truth, the whole truth, and nothing but the truth, so help them God, or to connect us to reality at all. Rather, as most media are market-driven, and as all the sponsors of those media, i.e. advertisers, are market-driven, the entire Bubble is, in one way or another, broadcasting the Market's message, in some cases faintly, in others with a resonant blare.

This message exists on two different levels, which are commonly united. The first, and most commonly recognizable, is the commercial level, which includes messages pertaining to both products and brands. These commercial messages serve to increase the sales of a particular corporation, and are typically contained in advertisements. They are also the most overt message, as the product is identified, and often the brand behind it as well. When we look at these ads, their purpose quickly boils down to "buy this." That is not to say that these ads are ineffective. Innumerable people have been involved in creating and distributing them, a sophisticated, high-tech apparatus aimed at making a quick impression on us without our even knowing. Nor are they necessarily harmless. The danger here is the outright lie, such as the infamous Volvo case, in which the roof of a Volvo was artificially reinforced to keep a truck from crushing it in a commercial. But in general, commercial messages are not of great concern, on an individual basis, because they are overt appeals limited to certain products.

The second level of message, and the one we are more concerned with here, is the one that promotes the entire economic system itself. These market messages are much deeper than product, brand, and corporation, and are contained not only in commercial advertisement, but in the content and programming supported by it. Their sponsor is never identified, yet all roads ultimately do lead to Rome.

Market messages are manifestations of an entire philosophy aimed at increasing the productivity of the economic system. This market philosophy includes messages about how to live, about the good life, about how to be happy, about what values you should hold, about what is normal and abnormal, acceptable and unacceptable. This philosophy is not immediately apparent, and therefore far more insidious than the overt message. We can certainly become conscious of it, but we typically absorb it peripherally, without focusing our attention on it, or even knowing it is there. It enters our mind at a subliminal level, where it affects our values, our norms, and our expectations. It is the clear walls of the Bubble.

As an example, consider two recent car ads. One reads: "GM introduces the 24 hour test drive. Drive it around the clock. Not just around the block." Another ad, from Toyota, reads: "The new Echo. 43 MPG. Translation: 34 trips to the mall." Overtly, each of these ads is selling a particular product and promoting a brand. Covertly, they are both broadcasting one of the Market's essential messages: shop constantly. The former message is obvious, the latter is not, unless you pause to think about it. Just by staring up at you from a major magazine or two, "shop constantly" becomes an expression of the norms of the culture you are in, whether you agree with it or not. You are *expected* to do it.

The Market crafts many other related messages that directly drive consumption. One is that new things are better than old things; clearly, the retail sector does not benefit from the garage sale. Another is that more things are better. You will not find a television commercial advocating that you cut back and lead a simpler life. Still another is that bigger is better, whether it is the ten-thousand-square-foot house, a larger diamond, or the car capable of going four times the speed limit. Here the power of the Market's message is so great that it convinces people to buy what they cannot even use.

One of the most subtle of market messages these days is heard from metropolitan media. "It's the classic misguided fantasy of big-city dwellers everywhere," declares a *New York Times* book review, "to flee the crowds, the astronomical rents, the impossible traffic, the crime, the take-out dinners in plastic containers and set down roots in some bucolic locale where the meals are home-cooked and life is never anything but Simple and Good."[9] In other words, you can't escape the rat race, so stay put—and keep consuming. Meanwhile, millions of people (myself included) have actually found that the opposite is true, once you drop your market values. This same author adds: "In a culture that becomes more media-saturated with each passing decade, where every new generation lives less through unmediated experience and more through images created with the hand of stylists, surfaces do mean everything."

All of us are bombarded by market messages like these every day, messages that have one and only one goal, from the Market's perspective: to make the economy more productive. They are the voice of the system. And inevitably, they have an impact upon us. Just as one's personality is shaped by family, friends, profession, and country, so too is it shaped by the 24/7 barrage from the Bubble. If you turn an anthropologist's eye on our surroundings, the evidence is everywhere. Some brands, like Xerox, aspirin, cellophane, nylon, thermos, and escalator, have worked their way deeply into our lexicon. Others have so deeply penetrated our minds that people are tattooing them on their bodies, such as the man I saw at a hotel pool with a hand-size Adidas logo on his back. People are even naming their children after their favorite brands. In the year 2000, the Social Security Administration reported the following names among girls: Lexus (353), Armani (298), Chanel (269), Infiniti (250), Loreal (21). Boys included Armani again (273), Cartier (22), Dior (7), Timberland (6), and Guinness (5).[10] Nevertheless, this trend is still preferable to what Jon Blake Cusack, a self-described engineering geek from Holland, Michigan, called his namesake son: Jon Blake Cusack 2.0. Let us hope there are no upgrades.

Amazingly, however, free-market theorists still maintain that our commercial media do not influence how we think—as if all those advertising dollars were spent for nothing. Admitting otherwise would, of course, call the unbridled Market into question. A few years ago I ran into a college classmate of mine who would have set these armchair theorists straight. She worked for a well-known magazine in New York that was a prospective client of my company. What was truly odd about this woman was that, as we sat having lunch, I began to feel that I was on the set of a television drama. Whenever a topic would arise that was rooted in the real world, she would deflect it into the Bubble. So, for instance, everything was wonderful, in a very game-show way, no matter what. Even the report of a death would be met with a smile and a look of "oh no!" At any moment, I expected her to start singing "Don't Worry—Be Happy." She spoke of Sarah Jessica Parker, the star of *Sex and the City,* as if she were a close friend, particularly since she admired her wardrobe. She made several references to brands in our conversation, not as the objects of her desire, necessarily, but as reservoirs of cultural meaning, things of real importance, as if these would naturally be common touchstones for us. It seemed to me that her persona did not come from within, but was manufactured to match an ideal without, an ideal that had been crafted by a lot of scriptwriters, sponsored by advertisers. It was remarkable, how all that had happened without the Market's influence. . . .

## The American Brand

Today what we know about our country comes more from the Bubble than it does from anywhere else, including our own two eyes. Like all Bubble messages, however, the point of the American message is not to tell us the truth about our country. Rather, it is to sell the American consumer something, via one of the classic marketing appeals: making the buyer feel good about himself. The result is that we are constantly being fed messages that boost our national self-image, one of the most powerful, and unrecognized, dynamics in the Bubble.

As a result, it has become increasingly difficult to discern American reality, or even what America means. In effect, America has become the Bubble's leading brand, one that is jointly owned and marketed by thousands of corporations. In my local White Pages, for instance, one finds the following: Ameri-Maid, Ameri-Star Homes, America West Airlines, American Airlines, American Arbor Care, American Auto Exchange, American Automation, American Background Check, American Bearing and Power Transmission, American Blimp Corp., American Boat Center, American Builder Services, American Burglar and Fire Alarm, American Bus Sales, American Business Systems, American Cab, American Capitol Contracting, American Cedar and Millwork, American Cheer and Dance, American Coffee Company, American Craftworks Collections, American Credit Company, and American Cycle Performance, all of which represent merely the ABCs of American branding, so to speak. D through Z requires well over a hundred more discrete entries. Then there are the many derivative forms. Under *All American*, for instance, one finds All American Ambulance, All American Cleaning Service, All American Custom Embroidery, All American Eagle Extermination, All American Electric, All American HVAC, All American

Plumbing, All American Services, All American Sports Bar, All American Tree & Landscaping Service, and All American Well and Pump Service. Moving further afield, one finds that "Liberty" is a gas station, "Freedom" a fence company, and "Red Hot and Blue" a ribs joint. This national branding is further supported on television by a deluge of advertising images that try to rub off the perceived virtues of America onto material goods. Take the Chevrolet ads, "An American Revolution" in red, white, and blue. (Can we have ribs with that?)

Made in the Middle East.

From one perspective, all this may reflect a laudable patriotism; from another, one can easily imagine a conference room full of suits deciding that the best way to sell their product is to link it to the Founding Fathers. After all, do you think that the enormous ad agency that serves General Motors was suddenly overwhelmed with patriotic fervor?

Since we now grow up in this perpetual ad campaign for America Inc., one can certainly understand how one could make the mistake of thinking that the Market is America. And since so many corporations serve to benefit from boosting the value of our national brand, it has become quite a challenge to discover who we really are, to see ourselves in perspective—a critical necessity in a globalizing world. Here there are numerous examples, but one will suffice.

In ways large and small, both directly and indirectly, we are told, essentially from birth, that America is "the greatest country on Earth." The question is, what is the metric we use to measure this? There are many commonly applied standards: education, GDP, military strength, political power, cultural influence, historic achievements. But while many of these are open to interpretation, the larger point is that none of them ultimately matters, *as they all pertain to the system.* When measuring the success of a nation, the only metric that ultimately matters is the quality of life its citizens enjoy, the crowning result of all other factors. And here even the CIA's *World Factbook* indicates that the global winner is Norway, not America. Thus, Norway is actually the greatest country on Earth, *if you prioritize the individual.* But you will look long and hard before you hear the Bubble preaching that message, at least in America.

## The Power of the Bubble

From the standpoint of a corporation, the Bubble is an opportunity, a powerful tool for increasing profits. The power of this tool goes well beyond the obvious, however. When harnessed by a major industry, the Bubble can invert the very nature of free-market theory, such that supply drives demand. Here one of the most compelling examples comes from the marketing of pharmaceuticals.

If anything should be insulated from the influence of the Bubble, it is drug prescriptions. Here common sense, as well as all medical wisdom, dictates that drugs are not brands, subject to a prestige effect, but potent and potentially deadly chemicals that should be dispensed by certified people on the basis of rigorous science. And for many years it was predominantly this way. But in the past decade the drug companies have taken a new tack in America: direct-to-consumer marketing. So it is that we have all seen a new breed of ad on television, the drug ad, and been introduced to a new range of powerful pharmaceuticals, with names carefully chosen by linguistic experts for how they resonate in the human mind. Among antidepressants, for instance, "Prozac" was chosen because the sounds *p, z,* and *k* all score highly for the qualities "active" and "daring." Its cousin, "Zoloft," breaks down to *zo,* which means "life" in Greek, and *loft,* which elevates the concept. "Paxil" contains the sounds *z* and *k* like Prozac, along with "crackling, buzzing sounds [that] may subliminally suggest activity to back up the sequence ac, which suggests the word action." [11]

The ultimate purpose of these new consumer appeals is to skirt the physician and stimulate demand directly from the consumer, i.e. the patient, the person who is typically not qualified to judge what drug he needs, using marketing methods normally used for cars and toothpaste. This is patently immoral. Let us say that you are suffering from depression. Clearly it takes a physician to diagnose this problem and to prescribe the right medicine to treat it. If you have seen an ad for Prozac, in which people appear to be happy because they have taken this drug, this should have no bearing whatsoever on what your doctor prescribes. And yet the pharmaceutical companies have been tremendously successful in raising consumer awareness about certain classes of drugs, putting pressure on physicians to prescribe them. The power of this marketing message is such that when the "new models" hit the showroom floor, they often replace existing drugs without adding any value, while costing more. The painkillers Celebrex and Vioxx, for instance, were heavily promoted when they came out, sparking worldwide sales of $5.6 billion. Yet these designer drugs don't accomplish much more than their Wal-Mart sister, Motrin, which costs sixty times less. Another example is the allergy drug Claritin, another heavily promoted product with multibillion-dollar revenues. Amazingly, a study found that two-thirds of those taking it didn't even suffer from allergies. [12]

The most compelling evidence for the pharma marketing engine is antidepressants. As Dr. David Healy noted in *Let Them Eat Prozac,* when pharmaceutical companies develop a drug to treat a specific condition, they end up marketing the illness, not just the pills. And since depressive illness is a psychiatric condition, where diagnoses are based on "professional opinion," as opposed to physical evidence, this marketing can be unusually influential. The result has been that as more antidepressant drugs have been developed and marketed, there has been an explosive increase in the diagnoses of depressive illness. [13]

The most lucrative slice of the antidepressant market, young people, exemplifies the arc of this phenomenon. Because of the emotional vulnerability of youth and the unprecedented social pressures teens now face, the youthful demographic represents a compelling market opportunity. Major pharmaceutical companies like Wyeth, Pfizer, GlaxoSmithKline, and Eli Lilly have responded by sponsoring such events as National Depression Screening Day at campuses, hospitals, and high schools around the country, where they hand out literature like "Safeguarding Your Student from Suicide," a pamphlet underwritten by Wyeth. The latter implores school administrators to have medical personnel "who can prescribe 'newer' antidepressants." Such efforts have been very successful, from a financial point of view. When the University of Kansas studied its records from 1989 to 2001, it discovered that the percentage of students taking psychiatric medication rose from 10 percent to 25 percent. Ninety-five percent of counseling directors at 283 U.S. colleges have confirmed this same trend.[14]

Within the youth demographic, the fastest-growing market has been preschoolers. A study of 2 million children in the U.S. between 1998 and 2002 found that the number of children younger than five prescribed antidepressants doubled during that time. This is surprising, as it would appear that this group is the one that would have the least medical need for the drugs. "Depression in a 3- or 4-year-old?" says pediatrician Lawrence Diller, the author of Running on Ritalin. "What is that? I can't see any reason for it. Every doctor who's ever prescribed a psychiatric drug to any kid is doing a balancing act between the needs of the kid and the needs of the system."[15]

The pharma marketing engine is even trying to expand the market for antidepressants beyond depression itself. In Canada, Eli Lilly has sponsored a study to determine whether Prozac can be used to treat PMS in twelve- to seventeen-year-old girls. The study was viewed as a means of "creating a new market for the drug company and a new therapy for girls." The girls recruited for the study were asked to fill out a survey that questions them about their menstrual cycles and then invites them to a clinic to discuss "the full range of available treatment options."[16]

As the marketing and sale of antidepressants has overwhelmed the need for them, the inevitable has happened, as an editorial from *The New York Times* reveals:

> Antidepressant drugs are being widely administered to children and adolescents despite increasing concern that the benefits have been oversold and some potentially dangerous side effects minimized. . . . What seems most astonishing is the skimpy evidence that these drugs work at

all in most young patients. . . . Many leading psychiatrists are convinced that the drugs have value in young people, based on what they deem positive results from some studies. But a critical evaluation by Australian researchers in a recent British Medical Journal article concludes that the authors of the largest published studies "have exaggerated the benefits, downplayed the harms, or both," possibly because of financial ties to the pharmaceutical industry.[17]

This alarm was rung by the FDA's decision to issue a public health advisory linking antidepressants to suicidal behavior in children and adolescents, the drug Paxil in particular. In a letter to physicians, Wyeth Pharmaceuticals also indicated that clinical studies on its antidepressant Effexor XR had found an increased incidence of "hostility and suicide-related adverse events, such as suicidal ideation and self-harm."[18]

So now the market economy has come full circle. You walk into your campus clinic, a young kid, mildly depressed, with no idea how pharmaceutical companies work, or the market economy they represent. You simply trust the system, its immediate representatives being your campus medical personnel. They do not tell you to go talk to your parents about what is bothering you. That makes no one a penny. Instead, they reach for the prescription pad, the accepted solution. As a result, you receive a drug like Paxil that, instead of alleviating your symptoms, actually makes them worse. So you continue to take this drug, hoping it will make you feel better, only to find that you are growing more deeply despondent, to the point where your parents get an urgent call from school authorities saying that their kid has tried to kill himself. That is the power of the Bubble.

## Dumbing Down the News

In order to build the phony walls of the Bubble, the Market concurrently follows a related strategy: it destroys the sources of truth, the Bubble's mortal enemy. Society has many such sources, but the cornerstone is journalism, our source of the news. Here the decline has been appropriately charted by some of that profession's own senior members. They include Leonard Downie, the executive editor of *The Washington Post,* and Robert Kaiser, a senior correspondent there, whose *The News About the News: American Journalism in Peril* is a monument to the power of the hypermarket.[19]

According to these and other voices, journalism began its long decline in the 1960s and accelerated in the mideighties. As the power of the Market rose, meaning and substance was gradually subtracted from the news, and replaced by various forms of entertainment and sensationalism: murders, car accidents, fires, etc. Between 1993 and 1996, when the murder rate was dropping, the number of minutes network evening news programs spent covering homicide actually tripled, even after excluding O. J. Simpson stories.[20] Like every other American institution, journalism has also become infected with the celebrity culture, where image trumps truth. Celebrity journalists are paid like Hollywood stars, and even replaced by them, as when ABC used Leonardo DiCaprio to interview Bill Clinton. As image has trumped substance, the "infomercial" has arrived to blur the line between news and advertising, such as Barbara Walters's secret pitch for Campbell's soup, which was interwoven into her talk show on ABC ("Didn't we grow up . . . eating Campbell's soup?" Walters asks her colleagues, to a chorus of "M'm! M'm! Good!"). Under fire, ABC claimed that Walters was acting as an entertainer at that point, not a journalist, which is precisely the point. Corporate owners have also put pressure on their news organizations to do stories of direct financial benefit, such as when WCBS-TV in New York was paid $300,000 to run a Web-site ad for eye surgery, then did a feature on the same procedure in its news program, using the same doctor and patient featured in the ad.[21] In such a corrupt environment as this, the integrity of journalists has inevitably suffered, with several high-profile cases of outright lying and plagiarism, from Stephen Glass at *The New Republic* to Jayson Blair at *The New York Times* to Jack Kelley at *USA Today*.

"Certainly, journalistic business organizations have stopped believing [in public service] to a very large measure," admits CBS News anchor Dan Rather. "And we stopped believing that the public cares. At one time [we believed] if you don't sort of radiate with a sense that what you're doing has to do with public service you're going to pay a price. Now the fear is that if you do that, you will pay a price."[22]

When shown one of his own news broadcasts from 1981, Rather noted twenty years later that the show could not even be done any longer. His management would tell him, "Dan, you cannot lead with El Salvador and take the broadcast through an inside Washington power struggle and go to a piece about Poland. . . . There was a time when you could do that, 1981 was the time. But if you do it today, you die, and we die." [23] Even so, lowering standards hasn't helped much: Between 1981 and 2001, the three network newscasts lost about 40 percent of their audience. The drop has been greatest among the young. In 1991, 48 percent of people in their twenties read a newspaper; by 2002, that had fallen to 25 percent. [24]

Not surprisingly, as NBC anchor Tom Brokaw explains, his profession has fallen in social value as well. "Curiously, the people who are coming to us are smarter than they've ever been, well-educated. They're children of television and they really want to come work here. And a lot of them, unfortunately, don't give a shit about the news. They want to do magazines or they want to do talk shows." [25]

The result of all this has been to gut journalism of its essential requirement: integrity. As Downie and Kaiser conclude, most newspapers "have shrunk their reporting staffs, along with the space they devote to news, to increase their owners' profits. Most owners and publishers have forced their editors to focus more on the bottom line than on good journalism. Papers have tried to attract readers and advertisers with light features and stories that please advertisers . . . and by de-emphasizing serious reporting on business, government, the country and the world." Here the Market's endgame also becomes apparent. As the Market has dismantled the profession of journalism, it has concurrently converted it to the Bubble.

## The Market's Veil

The most pernicious aspect of the Bubble is how it changes the definition of terms. When you change the meaning of a word, you don't just alter the dictionary, you alter the way you think about something. The mind is handed a new meaning, while cutting off access to the old. If you think that success is inherently financial, for instance, what does that say about other forms of success? They don't exist. It is as if the Market has dropped a veil over your mind.

The Market's veil begins with the ur-term, *free market. Free market* was originally defined in a political context. It meant that people were free to own property, to start their own business, or to own a stake in other businesses. This is the essential idea behind capitalism: "an economic system in which investment in and ownership of the means of production, distribution, and exchange of wealth is made and maintained chiefly by private individuals and corporations." The operating definition of *free market* today, however, is an "anything goes" market. It is a place where you can do whatever you can get away with. The "free market" has thus been redefined as a market free from morality. And you wonder where Enron came from?

Another lexical sleight of hand surrounds the term *progress. Progress* was actually once defined in spiritual terms, an idea that began with Judaism and later became central to Christianity. Progress was the ascent of man, the moral purpose in history, the divine purpose in the world, the whole purpose of creation. As the Market's veil has fallen, however, progress has fallen under the same confusion that makes it impossible for us to distinguish between a moral success and a financial success. What kind of success is progress? We don't even ask anymore. We simply assume that *material* progress is progress itself—a deadly assumption:

> Of what avail is any amount of well-being if, at the same time, we steadily render the world more vulgar, uglier, noisier, and drearier and if men lose the moral and spiritual foundations of their existence? Man simply does not live by radio, automobiles, and refrigerators alone, but by the whole unpurchasable world beyond the market and turnover figures, the world of dignity, beauty, poetry, grace, chivalry, love, and friendship, the world of community, variety of life, freedom, and fullness of personality. Circumstances which debar man from such a life or make it difficult for him stand irrevocably convicted, for they destroy the essence of his nature.[26]

The redefinition of progress as purely material has another important effect: it makes the Market look great. The Market is, after all, the ultimate source of material progress. So as the veil has fallen, we have become increasingly impressed with the Market and increasingly reluctant to criticize it.

Indeed, in our effort to enhance the reputation of the Market, we have changed its very name, as economist John Kenneth Galbraith has noted:

> It is my purpose in these comments to urge that in the larger world of social thought and action we must allow for a serious element of what, in a professionally cautious way, we may call innocent fraud. It is innocent because most who employ it are without conscious guilt. It is fraud because it is quietly in the service of special interest. One begins with "capitalism," a word [that] has gone largely out of fashion. The approved reference now is to the "market system." This has the effect of minimizing, indeed, deleting, the role of money, wealth, in the direction of the economic and social system; it breaks with long and adverse connotation going back to Marx. Instead of the owners of capital in control or those with the delegated authority there from, we have the admirably impersonal role of market forces. It would be hard to think of a change in terminology more in the interest of those to whom money accords power. They have now a functional anonymity. Most of those resorting to the new designation, economists in particular, are innocent as to the effect. At most they see a new, bland descriptive terminology. Money and wealth are not singled out for attention; they no longer accord a special power. They do. Thus the term "innocent fraud." [27]

Ironically, the very term *innocent* that Galbraith uses here has also been redefined in our Market Age. In Latin, *innoceo* meant "one who would not hurt another." Now the word is associated with naïveté, as if hurting others were just the way of the world.

The not-so-innocent fraud of redefinition is not just restricted to the Market's name, but extends to its reputation as well. As the veil falls, the fingerprints of the Market are mysteriously wiped clean from the crime scene, as one can see in this example from the health sphere:

> One of the most unfortunate consequences of the Washington consensus policies of structural adjustment imposed on less advanced economies has been a weakening of essential state capacity to collect reliable vital statistics covering the most marginal sections of the

population—child workers, low-paid workers, black market workers, migrants, refugees, and remote rural communities. These are the very people who are paying the principal health price for the global market economy's "successful" growth rates, achieved through shareholder capital's ceaseless search for the lowest labor, production, and fiscal costs. Thus, overzealous application of free market policies can even un-intentionally commit "the perfect crime," removing the epidemiological evidence of the health problems it creates.[28]

These examples of the Market's veil are only those that pertain to the Market itself. When you drop beneath that macro level, you find the market redefining terms everywhere, in far more places than we have space to re-count. Consider this example drawn from the broadcasting industry:

Public service and public interest are familiar phrases to those who follow U.S. broadcasting policy, yet clear and useful definitions of these terms have proven elusive over time. In the early 1900s, America's edu-cational broadcasters built their definition of service on the foundation of comprehensive, pluralistic programming. However, commercial op-erators soon developed their own definition of public service, based on the ability of a given station to reach large numbers of consumers with advertising-supported messages. A wide range of evidence demon-strates that for-profit broadcasters have used a variety of rhetorical and political strategies to maintain the primacy of their definition; further, contemporary broadcast policy demonstrates the degree to which their views have become naturalized. Those who wish for a return to tradi-tional public service broadcasting values in the United States must work at the level of rhetoric and semantics to create effective definitions of their own.[29]

The Market's veil is also contained in the way our language empowers the system over the individual, something we accept without thinking. Consider what happens when an individual and a corporation part company. If the in-dividual instigates the separation, he "quits." But if the corporation instigates the separation, the individual is "fired"—a much stronger term. Unlike the British, we don't even have the softer option of being "sacked." Inherent in this linguistic imbalance is the idea that the corporation is always justified in taking a forceful action against the individual, while the employee is, at best, a quitter—a negative term denoting weakness. We just can't imagine that the corporation could deserve rejection, or that the individual should be empowered to reject it. Consequently, our language does not allow the individual to fire the corporation, when clearly, hundreds of American corporations should be fired, as our newspapers reveal ad nauseam. When Sherron Watkins blew the whistle on Enron, she most definitely fired her company for cause—moral bankruptcy.

When you consider the power of the Bubble to alter the signposts we need to find the truth, it becomes clear how what is perhaps the most important word in the dictionary—*moral*—has come to be so maligned in modern times. *Moral*, in its original definition, is the adjective form of the Good. It is our ability to discern this Good, in all its forms, that separates us from animals and makes us human. By obscuring the definition of *moral*, and worse, making it a pejorative in some camps, the Market has been able to lead some to deny that the Good even exists. In this way, the two sides of human life, morality and productivity, have grown unbalanced in favor of productivity. You have to give the Market credit—it is one hell of a liar.

## Your Alternate Reality

As the Bubble has saturated our environment, as its appeals have grown more sophisticated, as the line between advertising and programming has blurred, as the sources of truth have been muzzled, and as our very language has been altered, we have slowly slipped our moorings and distanced ourselves from reality. In effect, the Market has crafted an alternate reality for us, which now surrounds us 24/7. Whenever we stop being conscious of the agenda behind all forms of commercial media and start thinking of it as reality, we have entered the Bubble.

We can describe the Bubble two ways, the first being what it stands for. The Bubble is a world of entertainment, pleasure, and fun, where happiness is derived from material things and sensual experience, where there are no limits on personal freedom, and where there are no consequences for our actions. Alternatively, we can define the Bubble by what it opposes: the Bubble exists to deny reality to us, to keep us from the truth, be it moral, or cultural, or spiritual, or aesthetic. Truth is like a pin, poised to pop the Bubble at all times.

So what is that missing truth? The last thing the Market wants you to do is see beyond its limited horizons to the ultimate questions of who and what we are, where we came from, and where we are headed. All such matters are either overlooked or made fun of. Nothing in the Bubble is to be taken seriously. Life is all a big joke. The reason is that "the big questions" engender a perspective that undermines market philosophy. They cause people to lead a simple life, a life centered on reflection, on contemplation, on learning, and on family and friends, rather than on consumption. You won't find many commercials broadcasting that message. The very last thing the Market wants us to know is the most obvious: We are mortal. We arise from we know not what, return to the same, and spend only the shortest time in between. Who will work an eighty-hour week for that Euro sedan once he realizes that? To the market, *carpe diem* only means "buy now!"

The Bubble thus represents the great narrowing of human horizons away from ultimate questions of meaning and purpose, being and existence, soul and God, and toward the cash register. The dulling of the intellect, the decline of philosophy, of religion, of literature, and the humanities in general, all begin here. The Bubble has largely succeeded in stopping us from having any conception of who and what we are anymore. The most essential terms defining the human being—terms like *body, mind, spirit, self, soul*—lie in a heap on the floor, where they are kicked around without thought as to what they really mean, as if it didn't even matter. "Free yourself from them," the Market says. "Buy something, and stop taking life so seriously!"

In this unreal environment, where a human being does not even know what makes him human, or a being, it is impossible to find happiness. Disconnected from truth, we are plagued by anxiety, as the pharmaceutical companies are only too happy to confirm. The Market has no interest in making us happy, since satisfaction represents a limit to desire. Instead, it sees our pain as a market opportunity, and sells us a constant stream of antidotes. "[Celebrity] magazines are proliferating for the same reason prescriptions of antidepressants and other psychotropic drugs are proliferating," says one magazine columnist. "They dull our emotional pain."[30] We find the same escapism in the movies. In 2003, the blockbuster films—*Finding Nemo, Pirates of the Caribbean,* and *The Return of the King*—were all fantasies.[31] And if you want to escape the rat race for a while, the Market will be happy to provide you with a yoga class, a weekend at a spa, or a weeklong vacation at Hedonism II. But it will never give you the critical knowledge necessary to find lasting happiness on your own. That would shut down a lucrative earning stream. The only way to find the happiness—is to pop the Bubble.

# 4. Flatland

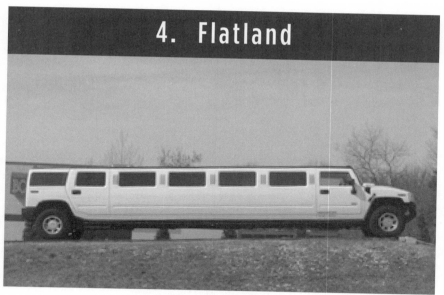

A Hummer Limousine: $1,000 per night.

In *The Republic*, Plato describes the nature of the ideal state. Its central organizing principle is what he identifies as "the Good." The best state, said the West's preeminent philosopher, should be a moral hierarchy, with the best people naturally at the top. This was the original meaning of *aristocracy*, rule by the best, although there is nothing to prevent this republic from being a meritocracy, too.

Plato's model creates a society shaped like a pyramid, with three tiers. On the bottom is the largest group, the Producers: the farmers, smiths, and builders of the city. Producers are ruled by their bodily appetites, and are not particularly bright, strong, brave, or well educated. The middle tier is the Auxiliaries. These are the people who defend the state, the soldiers and police. They are known for their courage and strength, and are somewhat educated. The top tier is the Guardians. These people manage the state. They are exceptionally intelligent, virtuous, and wise, highly educated, and focused on good itself.

Naturally, this moral hierarchy is the Market's worst nightmare, as it finds itself completely subservient to the Good. The Market has therefore countered with its own hierarchy, where the central organizing principle is money. The more money you have, the higher you are. It's that simple. This *market hierarchy* helps organize society along more productive lines. Democracy even supports this trend, for it empowers the great mass of producers, a point Alexis de Tocqueville made in *Democracy in America:*

> Democracy encourages a taste for physical gratification; this taste, if it becomes excessive, soon disposes men to believe that all is matter only; and materialism, in its turn, hurries them on with mad impatience to these same delights; such is the fatal circle within which democratic nations are driven round.[1]

Today as we look around the American republic, we find Plato's nightmare and de Tocqueville's I-told-you-so. The hierarchy of the Good has collapsed, and the Market rules. Plato's republic has been turned on its head: The producers are on top and the philosophers are at the bottom. Success in America is neither moral nor spiritual nor intellectual nor artistic these days, but financial. We like to call this system a "meritocracy," but we neglect to add that we are talking about market merit alone. One does not get to the top of the American ladder by being a great philosopher like Plato. One gets there by becoming rich, and it doesn't matter how.

To put it mildly, this is not actually the way our economy is supposed to relate to our society. At the time economic theory was founded, people like Adam Smith always assumed that the economy would operate on top of a moral foundation. It would be restrained, in other words, by higher values. They never anticipated that the Market would grow so powerful that it would erode that foundation itself—or that this was its hidden agenda. But since then the Market has succeeded in freeing itself from higher authority. In Darwinian fashion, it has used its power of selection to triumph in the marketplace of ideas. As billionaire philanthropist George Soros has noted:

> There has been an ongoing conflict between market values and other, more traditional value systems, which has aroused strong passions and antagonisms. As the Market mechanism has extended its sway, the fiction that people act on the basis of a given set of nonmarket values has

become progressively more difficult to maintain. Advertising, marketing, even packaging, aim at shaping people's preferences rather than, as laissez-faire theory holds, merely responding to them. Unsure of what they stand for, people increasingly rely on money as the criterion of value. What is more expensive is considered better. The value of a work of art can be judged by the price it fetches. People deserve respect and admiration because they are rich. What used to be a medium of exchange has usurped the place of fundamental values, reversing the relationship postulated by economic theory. What used to be professions have turned into businesses. The cult of success has replaced a belief in principles. Society has lost its anchor.[2]

The tremendous irony of this passage is the use of the term *nonmarket values* to refer to all moral, spiritual, and cultural values. We have now reached the point where the very nature of what makes us human is defined relative to the Market.

The collapse of the Good, and the concurrent rise of the Productive, is known as "externalization." It is a negative form of "inversion" (which can also occur in the other direction) and the natural result of a hypermarket. When this phenomenon strikes a society, all elements within it are affected. Individuals, organizations, professions, and democracy itself are all pulled inside out, so that they serve the Market. Society is pressed flat. In metaphysical terms, externalization is a shift from the interior to the exterior, from the deep to the superficial, from the spiritual to the material. It is the collapse of the moral hierarchy to a single point, the market price.

## The Pro-Con

Let us consider for a moment how the Market thinks about us. Each of us is part of the economy. We produce and we consume. Since the Market's raison d'être is increasing the productivity of the economy, it is intent on maximizing both of these functions. Every individual is clay to be molded into a highly efficient two-stroke engine, a *pro-con*.

Obviously, we all need *some* pro-con in us, but there is a lot more to us as well. Our original, innate identity, the very nature of who we are, is not a product of the market economy. It may contain elements that the Market finds productive, but it is also connected to principles that go well beyond market principles, and in a completely different, interior direction. This creates the Market's challenge. At some point, the human interior always stands in the way of increasing productivity. Our own unique identity, and our moral and spiritual nature, become limiting factors. They put the brakes on materialism, on greed, on conformity. In order to maximize the productivity of its resources, the Market must therefore cut us off from our authentic selves and redefine us on its own template. It must *externalize the individual.* It must draw us out of ourselves, separate us from all higher ground, and focus us on the external, material world, thereby reconstituting our character. It must pull its veil over the window of our mind so that all reality beyond the economic is hidden. It must separate us from our spiritual ground, from moral and aesthetic principles, from authentic meaning, and from any higher purpose than itself, from our community to our culture to our God. In the most ancient terms, it must steal our soul.

All arms of the market octopus are brought to bear on this task, including the Bubble. "There is a latent formation system in a culture economically based upon the continual expansion of products, consumer goods and productivity. This formation system, whether deliberately constructed or not, has a tendency to educate human persons into a mode of thinking, believing and acting that serves the imperatives of the economic system itself."[3]

The natural first step in externalizing the individual is to cast the human interior in a negative light. Instead of being yourself, and connected to a larger world of meaning and purpose—the route to true freedom—the Market broadcasts the opposite: The human interior is full of chains. One should not embrace moral or spiritual truth, but seek to free oneself from it. There are no higher standards. In their place, one should adopt the cornerstone of market philosophy: "Anything goes." This is supported by a doctrine of tolerance, which is stretched so far that—you guessed it—anything goes. Meanwhile, to defend itself from criticism, the Market clamps down on the free exercise of moral judgment. The result is curbs on speech that challenge the Market's hegemony, a phenomenon known as political correctness, but which is more accurately termed *market correctness.* In this way the Market aims to build an entire "post-moral age" (to quote the *Washington Post*) in which there is no distinction to be made between right and wrong, in which there are no higher principles, no absolutes, no truth, and all things are relative. We have all seen this insidious ideology unfold in recent years, so it needs no further explanation. What we have not recognized is why: it is the handmaiden of the hypermarket.

The economic benefits of this ideology are clear: Once you adopt it, all sales channels are open. Once "anything goes," we are free to turn *The Texas Chainsaw Massacre* into a cult film, free to celebrate the mob in *The Sopranos,* free to turn the Simpson murder trial into a media event, free to capitalize on the latest pedophilia charges against Michael Jackson, and free to watch *Growing Up Gotti,* A&E's reality show on a mobster's family, as if the Mafia were just another lifestyle choice. The Market can now package and sell the most glaring immorality without the slightest irony, such as the *Rolling Stone* magazine cover on a rap star that announced THE ART OF VIOLENCE. As long as it makes money, it's all right.

The success of this ideology can be seen in how many people are actually afraid to stick their necks out and make a simple moral judgment these days, a real fear of the Market's wrath. When Kathleen Toomey, director of the Georgia Division of Public Health, was asked to explain why teens in Rockdale County, Georgia, were having orgies after school, she responded: "The teens had formed their own social network, their own group, and they got approval from that group. And sadly the approval required them to perform in more and more bizarre ways—*at least what we would consider to be bizarre ways*—and carry out higher and higher risk activities."[4] Translation: "I am afraid to unequivocally state that teens having orgies after school is bad." No threat to the porn industry there.

Today such market philosophy is so firmly entrenched that it has disabled our common sense. Consider the following opening to a news story: "A rap performer affiliated with the Murder Inc. music label was shot dead on a street in South Jamaica, Queens, late Thursday, the authorities said yesterday."[5] The stunning irony in this line would be funny, if there were not someone lying dead in the street. Here's another one: "In the calculating eyes of music industry executives, the rap artist Jamaal Barrow possesses the sort of street credibility that instantly draws fans and sells records—a prison sentence."[6] Amazing. Yet we do not feel free enough to state the obvious: this is the purest sign of a precipitous social decline. That would be economically incorrect.

When moral judgment collapses like this, true individual freedom dies with it. The individual is no longer free to decide what is good or bad. Instead, the Market decides. If it sells, it is good, which means if it is popular, it is good. We find ourselves not looking within, to make our own determination, but looking out, to see what we should think, and how we should act, leaving us at the mercy of you-know-what. The result, not surprisingly, is that the market price defines the value of everything.

In one recent example of this phenomenon, I was sitting in a theater, watching a series of "movie facts" appear on the screen prior to the lights going down, when up came: "What was the first $100 million movie?" What an amazing question. It wasn't the quality of the movie itself that was important (*Jaws*), but how much it made at the box office. As if this had any relevance to me whatsoever. Why should I care about the corporate earnings of a movie studio? Why should anyone, except a stockholder? The message was that the audience should simply be excited by the idea of *all that money being made,* by someone, regardless of whom. Just the thought of it! The next thing you know, every Coke will come with an annual report.

Once the philosophy of "anything goes" empowers the Market, the transformation of the individual begins in earnest. In addition to looking to the Market to decide what is good or bad, the newly minted pro-con begins looking to the Market to define his own identity. As he is pulled into the external world, the Market becomes the ultimate role model, a Big Brother:

> Consumerism was the triumphant winner of the ideological wars of the 20th century, beating out both religion and politics as the path millions of Americans follow to find purpose, meaning, order, and transcendent exaltation in their lives. Liberty in this market democracy has, for many, come to mean freedom to buy as much as you can of whatever you wish, endlessly reinventing and telegraphing your sense of self with each new purchase.[7]

Naturally, the self-seeking consumer finds innumerable people in the marketplace willing to define who he is, for a price. And many new ways in which he learns that he is inherently deficient, from the hairstyle on his head to the shoes on his feet, and every failure in between: too fat, too thin, too tall, too short, bad skin, bad breath, small breasts, big breasts, wrinkles, crooked teeth, stained teeth. Then, of course, there is everything he does not *own*. This may seem like a small matter with regard to any single market message, but if you consider that by the time an individual graduates from high school he has seen well over half a million television commercials, that means he has been told, via this form of media alone, that he is deficient half a million times.

In America, one result of this feeling of self-deficiency has been a boom in plastic surgery, especially among women. In 2003 alone, there were 8.7 million cosmetic plastic surgeries, an increase of about a third over the previous year. The most common forms were eyebrow lifts, face-lifts, and breast implants. Nonsurgical alternatives, such as Botox shots, went up 41 percent. Some women are even having their pinkie toes removed now, the better to fit into pointy shoes. According to one clinical psychologist, "One woman gets Botox and then her neighbor and relatives look at her and feel relatively unattractive and feel they need to do something, too."[8] The booming market for a new body is so good now that dermatologists, gastroenterologists, and gynecologists are all rushing to get into the act. In California, a new bill in the state legislature would even allow dentists to perform cosmetic surgeries.[9] Not to be left out of the action, major networks have launched their own cosmetic-surgery reality shows, such as *The Swan* on Fox and *Extreme Makeover* on ABC, which take an imperfect human off the street and attempt to correct all their cosmetic deficiencies with modern surgery and other methods. "When it is all so overtly about appearance, personal identity becomes almost trivial," says Dr. Nancy Etcoff, author of *Survival of the Prettiest: The Science of Beauty*. "It's as if people would rather choose a mask, than look like themselves."[10]

On the male side, one sees a similar trend in the expansion of male cosmetics. One can only imagine how the cosmetics industry must lick its lips at the prospect of doubling the size of its market. The genesis of this movement naturally occurred in urban areas, where market pressures created a new form of life in the early nineties, a male noted for his vanity, and by extension, his desire for products that would make him beautiful, trendy, sexy: the "metrosexual":

> When Mark Simpson invented the term "metrosexual" in 1994, he
> described a dandyish narcissist in love not only with himself, but also

with his urban lifestyle; a straight man in touch with his feminine side. But mainly, he was addressing a man with a high consumption rate! This certainly contributed much to the success of the concept in the fashion and cosmetics industries. . . . At the end of the 1990s, artists, fashion creators and opinion leaders, highly sensitive to those evolutions and emerging trends, were eventually followed by industrialists eager to boost men's consumption. Fashion and cosmetic brands have capitalized on metrosexuality to develop men's markets.[11]

So the metrosexual would be more accurately termed a *market*sexual, someone who is a psychological captive of the cosmetics industry, and in a larger sense, the Market itself, which has managed, through its constant appeals to the self, to inflate his vanity. That old interior value, humility, simply makes no money. Here we see the power of the Market in spades, because it has managed to overcome even sexual identity. Indeed, it appears to be actively scrambling it, using the most clever of means. As it pushes the male toward traditionally feminine products, the Market has been very careful not to overly feminize its approach. Blush, for instance, may be applied with an instrument that looks like a shaving brush. Product lines are given appropriately masculine titles, such as Jean Paul Gaultier's obvious solution, Le Male. For fifty-eight dollars, you can get the eau de toilette spray, which comes in a bottle shaped like Arnold Schwarzenegger's torso, with a hand-grenade pin at the top, and the deodorant stick, which looks like the clip for an M-16. If you still don't get it, Gaultier's name is spelled with military lettering on the carton, the kind you see spray-painted on an ammo case. Overall, such gung ho approaches have apparently worked: the male cosmetics market grew 3.5 percent in 2003. And naturally, male spas and beauty salons have followed. Perhaps the male brassiere will be next.

The ultimate expression of the Market's power in this regard has been its ability to define beauty itself. In an interview with Linda Wells, editor in chief of *Allure* magazine ("the beauty expert"), National Public Radio's Susan Stamberg put her finger right on this point:

*Stamberg:* So is the answer to the question "Who says what's beautiful" . . . money?

*Wells:* A lot of it is money. A lot of it is commerce. It's a commercial country that we live in, and it would be nice to uphold a noble image of beauty, but I don't think that nobility is the most powerful force right now in our culture. I think it is commerce.[12]

What we see here is the evidence of a major transition. Nobility has been undermined. "The most powerful force" in our culture is the Market. The entire country is defined by it. The very idea of beauty is in its hands, and thus, we can infer, truth and goodness as well. The externalization of society is complete. This is the legacy of the hypermarket.

In sum, as the Market bears down upon the individual, a process of externalization unfolds. The human interior, with all its authentic values, is slowly eradicated, and the hierarchy of the Good collapses, like the center pole jerked from a tent. The individual then reconstructs his identity in the marketplace, transfers all meaning to external products and services, and focuses himself on productivity. The authentic individual is pulled inside out, becoming an efficient element in the economic engine: a pro-con. This same process operates at all levels of society as well, from companies, where it creates "the soulless corporation," to the corruption of the profession, including the law ("it's all about billable hours") and medicine ("my practice is primarily a business"). Everywhere today we see the transformation of the Good to the Productive, putting us all at increased risk.

Here we see the great lie of "anything goes" come to the surface. Having sold his soul to a Siren, the pro-con is anything but free. He lives in an amoral world, a slave to popular opinion and to the market price. He is not even free to turn off his television anymore, as it is the primary means by which the Market communicates with him, and thus, the primary source of his meaning and identity, his connection to what he thinks reality is: the Bubble. While preaching individual freedom, the Market is all the while controlling and homogenizing us, often in clever ways. Take the people who opt for cosmetic surgery: on the surface, creating one's own face would appear to be the ultimate means of self-expression. However, since there are a limited number of cosmetic surgeries that can be performed, and since they tend to seek a similar ideal of beauty, these surgeries are actually producing a mass-market face, an assembly-line look. Listen to the Market, and you quickly find yourself part of the herd.

## The Vortex

Once the individual externalizes himself, the Market has him. Not only does the Market define his identity, but it defines his value as well, via the usual means, the market price. To the Market, the value of a pro-con is reduced to a number, what the pro-con calls his net worth or, in annual terms, his compensation. With that number in hand, the Market can now pull on the pro-con's deepest lever: his self-esteem. And using this power, the Market will put the pro-con on a treadmill for the rest of his life. The pro-con will constantly search to improve his standing in the Market's eyes, first by making more money and then by spending it, thereby exercising the two sides of his personality. There is no end to this cycle. No matter how much money a person earns, the Market will always provide more ways to spend it. For every rung the pro-con climbs, there will always be another just beyond reach. In such a situation, the pro-con can never feel deeply satisfied with himself, which is just what the Market wants. Instead of relaxing and enjoying life, improving his mind, appreciating nature, spending time with family and friends, the pro-con will continue to work his fingers to the bone, until the day arrives when he cannot imagine doing anything else.

The pro-con typically assesses his place in the market hierarchy by evaluating his own financial success relative to those around him. Since he cannot peer into their bank accounts, he does this by looking at what they own, and they, him. This creates a certain pressure on the pro-con to show what he has, either by buying a larger house, or a more expensive car, thereby telegraphing his status. Otherwise, his local society may put downward pressure on him. The Market is also quite clear about which things elevate one's status, as certain brands are considered a step up from others, as their price tag indicates. Entire neighborhoods are the same way. In this way the market indicates the clothes, cars, and houses the pro-con should buy next—as well as the professions to pursue, the schools to attend, and the organizations to join.

The externalization of the individual thus creates an outward pressure that spreads throughout society, triggering a *market vortex,* an upward spiral of production and consumption in which everyone is trapped, at all levels. Today consumption pressure is so intense in America that it has caused a boom in self-storage rentals. As soon as people fill up their home, they place a few things in storage and go shopping. This includes even the largest purchases. For the first time ever, there are now more cars than drivers, according to the Transportation Department. Where do you park them, when your garage is full?

The market vortex is also the driving force behind displays of excess. As social competition has intensified, children's birthday parties have become increasingly expensive, involving professional performers, caterers, party planners, and numerous off-site entertainment options. The day of a simple cake and candles is gone. Then there are the toys: the cigarette boat with three enormous outboard motors strapped to the back. The $2 million RV that can drive into water. The street-legal 252 mph car. And finally, the suburban McMansion, the training ground for that ten-thousand-square-foot mega-house.

The psychological power of the market vortex should not be underestimated. It is immense. In fact, socioeconomic status is one of the two principal determinants of health, a statistic that points to the depth of the Market's connection with us. Even people who recognize that they are trapped within the vortex feel helpless to eject themselves, fearing the impact on their self-esteem. Professor Andrew Oswald of Warwick University has conducted several experiments that show that some two-thirds of people would be willing to reduce what they had if it meant that others would lose out and be worse off. Such studies reveal that it is not just a matter of what we have, and how it compares with others, but how we feel about ourselves that is our primary motivator. We commonly think of self-interest as being the driver of the market economy, but to be precise, it is self-*esteem*-interest that is driving us now, particularly as we long ago satisfied our purely material needs.

This is a critical point, for it is here that the Market has separated itself from Nature, spawning the hypermarket. In the past, we looked to Nature to satisfy our material well-being, just as the Market does today. But material well-being has innate limits. Once you have food on the table, a roof over your head, and clothes on your back, your material needs are essentially satisfied. You are free to pursue the other joys in life. This natural balance makes a society self-sustaining, because it takes only what it needs. It also makes it antithetical to the Market, since it imposes a ceiling on productivity. When one reaches a point where one simply has enough, it is the death knell of economic growth. By seizing hold of the lever of self-esteem, however, the

Market has made the urge to consume essentially unlimited. This has created a highly unnatural society, a society that is inherently unbalanced. A society run on self-esteem inevitably becomes self-destructive, simply because the resulting vortex eventually becomes unsustainable. When divorced from the human interior, the natural source of balance, the Market becomes a monster.

## The New American Hero

As the hierarchy of the Good has collapsed, the nature of our role models has changed along with it. In a Platonic republic, role models would be people who had achieved the highest Good in society: a great artistic work, a medical breakthrough, an act of heroism, a useful invention, a diplomatic advance, a distinguished record of public service. This is the natural, pre-Bubble state, one we actually used to enjoy in America prior to the advent of advanced media. We admired people worth admiring, authentic heroes. Today we have celebrities.

There have always been famous people, but celebrities are an invention of the Bubble. Unlike a hero, they do not need to have achieved anything of merit, or to have any talent at all. The noble life is not their priority, to put it mildly. They are a media image sold to the public, a human brand. Even their name is typically manufactured. We do not even consider them to be one of us, as we do the hero, but to exist in a world of their own. They usually come from the entertainment industry, which profits from their popularity in the marketplace, however that is achieved. And like all competitors in the marketplace, they ultimately serve themselves.

Naturally, the cult of celebrity is supported by the entire Bubble, as seen by the profusion of celebrity media: magazines like *Us, People,* and *In Touch,* television shows like *Entertainment Tonight,* and the entire E! network. Here the celebrity brand is used to sell the media itself. Celebrities also act as style symbols and may frequently hawk products directly. There has been tremendous coverage in the U.S. media regarding the fact that one character in the TV show *Sex and the City* happens to wear shoes by Manolo Blahnik, a previously obscure footwear designer. People then buy such shoes in order to fantasize that they are living in a TV show, not reality; that they are, in fact, the very celebrity brand themselves. Jamie Gavigan, a colorist at a Georgetown hair salon, doesn't own her own home, but owns twenty thousand dollars' worth of Blahniks. Two or three times a year she makes special shopping trips to Blahnik's New York boutique, where she is known by name, to refill the closet.[13]

The tremendous success of the media in creating this cult of celebrity has even created a new psychopathology, celebrity worship syndrome. As described by a team of researchers in the U.S and Britain led by James Houran, a psychologist with the Southern Illinois University School of Medicine, CWS is an unhealthy interest in the lives of the rich and famous—and almost a third of us have it. After surveying more than six hundred people, Houran's team devised a celebrity worship scale to measure the level of dysfunction, which is as follows:

*Level I: Entertainment social.* This is casual stargazing. The level of celebrity worship here is really quite mild: "My friends and I like to discuss how Ben could have moved from Gwyneth to J. Lo."

*Level II: Intense personal.* The person seems to feel a connection with the star: "I consider Halle Berry to be my soul mate."

*Level III: Borderline pathological.* Here, admiration has gone stalkeresque: "When he reads my love letters, Brad Pitt will leave Jennifer Aniston and live happily ever after with me."[14]

Dr. John Maltby, a lecturer in psychology at the University of Leicester, has put his own numbers on these levels. His survey of three thousand people showed that around 1 percent were level III, 10 percent were level II, and 14 percent were level I, adding up to a quarter of the population with a celebrity problem.[15] The media, of course, is pushing the extreme: MTV has created an entire reality show, *I Want a Famous Face,* in which people are surgically altered to look like their favorite movie stars. The cult of celebrity has thus joined forces with the plastic-surgery industry.

The result of this externalization from the Good to the Profitable is that, instead of elevating authentic heroes, we elevate people like Pamela Anderson, one of the most successful names in Hollywood, to the very summit of our culture, a person whose sole assets are made of silicone. Even her best-selling novel was written by someone else. We make Monica Lewinsky the star of her own cable TV show by virtue of the fact that she fellated the president. We have forgotten Olympic medalist Nancy Kerrigan, but we follow the fortunes of Tanya Harding, the fellow skater who attempted to maim her: first the inevitable sex video, then her new boxing career. What such people are actually like, we have no idea, nor do we care. If they titillate us, we make them rich; if they fail us, we are happy to tear them to pieces. When Courtney Love stands in court because of a cocaine problem, we don't care why, or what role we may have played in sending this sad case to rehab. The story ends up in the style section, where the focus is on her sweater: "The sad little cardigan, with its horizontal stripes, vaguely recalled a letterman sweater—but one plucked from a Goodwill store. It had the poor look of something unexpectedly found rather than sought out, and it subtly suggested that perhaps Love's lawyer was working pro bono." [16] Funny. This same image engine has manufactured an entirely new class of celebrity, the "supermodel." Here the Market has crafted the perfect flat person, a product so shallow and superficial that it becomes famous by walking without talking. Even Pamela Anderson spoke her lines.

While the Market has drowned the hero as a social ideal, it is certainly not above making money from the concept. The rise of the celebrity culture has actually created a market opportunity in this regard, as people search for what has been subtracted from their lives. So instead of real heroes, we have Bubble heroes, which we swallow like Prozac. Why give heroes away for free, when you can sell them?

Exhibit A is the most famous soldier of the second war in Iraq, army private Jessica Lynch. Lynch was straight out of modern central casting, the woman warrior from West Virginia who took on the evil Iraqis single-handed after her jeep crashed in an ambush. News reports initially claimed that Lynch fought fiercely, emptied her M-16 into numerous Iraqi soldiers, killing several of them, and was shot and stabbed several times herself. Hollywood promised to make a movie out of it. Later on it was revealed that Lynch's gun had jammed, that all her injuries were sustained in the crash, and that she was actually unconscious throughout most of her ordeal. NBC made a TV movie anyway. Since Ms. Rambo was out, *Saving Jessica Lynch* put a new spin on the tale: her "dramatic rescue." Here the Bubble was popped by none other than the U.S. military:

A few hours after the last members of Task Force 20 [the special operations team that rescued Lynch] flew away in helicopters, a contingent of U.S. tanks and trucks rolled up to the hospital's front door without firing a shot.

Central Command's public affairs office in Qatar geared up to make the most of the rescue.

"We wanted to make sure we got whatever visuals were available," said one public relations officer involved. . . . "We knew it would be the hottest thing of the day." . . .

"It took on a life of its own," said one colonel who tried to answer the barrage of media queries. "Reporters seemed to be reporting on each other's information. The rescue turned into a Hollywood concept." [17]

Ironically, it was all the people who tried to use Jessica Lynch's broken body for their own purposes who made her a real hero, when she made the facts public.

Like all market philosophy, the Market has crafted a phalanx of defenses to protect the cult of celebrity. If you were to criticize the popularity of Pamela Anderson today, you would inevitably hear "Hey, she's a smart businesswoman!" because she has parlayed her implants into millions of dollars. The implication is that this financial success is all that matters. Certainly, it is more important than the collapse of our culture. If you were to point this collapse out, you would hear "Well, that's what sells!" as if the Market should be the arbiter of all value. Finally, and most revealing of all, if you were to commit the ultimate faux pas and state that good culture should triumph over bad, you would inevitably encounter the Market's last gasp: "Oh my God, you're an elitist!" That's right: the entire United States may be organized in a market hierarchy, in which the rich are considered better than everyone else, but for some reason "elitism" only applies to those who dare to use their own aesthetic judgment. The message is clear: The Market knows best.

## The Closing of the American Mind

Once you become savvy to the Market's ways, it allows you to untangle even the most complex of situations. One of these is *The Closing of the*

*American Mind,* the title of a bestseller by Allan Bloom, and one of the most intelligent books on American decline ever written. As we have seen, there is nothing that closes the mind faster than the Market's veil. As society externalizes, all things noneconomic pass out of view. As the university increasingly comes under the Market's sway, this means that all aspects of intellectual life that are not directly relevant to increasing productivity will inevitably be devalued. This is precisely what has happened to the humanities. In an age when a third of undergraduates declare economics as their major, the humanities are like a deep-sea diver who has run out of air.

The Market's attack on the humanities has proceeded on multiple fronts, as it often does. As the material assembly line has consolidated its grip on our society, the university has responded. The science budget has dwarfed the humanities budget and skewed resources and talent in its direction with gravitational force. Instead of teaching people how to think and widening their intellectual horizons, the university has evolved toward a vocational model, with the degree valued primarily as a résumé enhancer. Philosophy, the Market's number one enemy, has plunged in value. Many graduate with minds that think only in terms of technical systems, without an understanding of where their culture came from, the ideas behind it, or the ability to criticize it, particularly in writing. As the standards of truth have been cut, and political correctness taken over, an attack on Western civilization, led by the Academy itself, has resulted in the burning of our great books, at least in effigy. Ironically, as the market price has become the standard of value, careers in education have been devalued across the board, including the once-esteemed professor. In California, prison guards make fifty-one thousand dollars a year, ten thousand dollars more than a first-year professor in a state university.[18] The two notable exceptions are the football coach and the head of the endowment, who frequently outearn the university president. The head of the endowment at Harvard was paid $6.9 million last year.[19]

With its responsibility for educating the public, the university participates in a feedback loop with society. University graduates shape society, while at the same time society shapes the university agenda. It is therefore not surprising that as the humanities have declined, reading has declined, although assessing primary responsibility is a chicken–egg debate. The U.S. Census Bureau's surveys of public participation in the arts over the past twenty years show an accelerating decline in American readers across all demographic groups. Between 1982 and 1992, the percentage of people who read literature fell 5 percent. Between 1992 and 2002 another 14 percent were lost. The National Endowment for the Arts has issued a clarion call, "Reading at Risk," which draws on the census data. "What this study does is give us accurate numbers that support our worst fears about American reading," says Dana Gioia, the chairman of the endowment. "It quantifies what people have been observing anecdotally, but the news is that it has been happening more rapidly and more pervasively than anyone thought possible. Reading is in decline among all groups, in every region, at every educational level and within every ethnic group." [20] Further evidence suggests this trend will continue. While the average American child now spends close to five hours a day in front of a television, he only spends an hour with books, newspapers, or magazines. [21]

Other reasons for the decline of literature have to do with the nature of reading itself. While the Market is an externalizing force, drawing us out of ourselves, literature is a purely internal experience. It is about reflection, contemplation, meaning, about exploring new ideas and wakening the life of the mind, for its own sake. This puts the Market at odds with the very idea of literature, since it has no practical benefit. To the Market, a great work of literature is a waste of time. The Market is not about the life of the mind, the unfolding of who you are, and what you can be—it is about putting the individual to productive work, a job that always exists outside himself. In this conflict, the Market has the upper hand, for as time goes on, and the economy increases in efficiency, the individual not only stops wanting to read literature, he no longer has the time, and in many cases, the interior silence. The stress of the hypermarket is a literature killer, just as it is a soul killer. When parents arrive home from the office exhausted at 7 p.m. and then face domestic tasks until bedtime, who can afford a great book?

Since literature mainly targets the intellectual and aesthetic sensibilities, it can't compete with sensory media, either. To a mind barraged by sexual and violent stimuli on a daily basis, literature is a weak voice shouting in a storm. People conditioned to seek ever-higher doses of shock value become numb to the subtleties of literary art. Instead of engaging a great work, with all its levels of ideas and understanding, its insight into the human condition, and meeting the voice behind it, we expect to pay for a measured dose of entertainment that requires nothing from us. In other words, we turn on the television.

As the demand for literature has shrunk, the publishing industry has responded accordingly. Today there is pressure to find authors (of all people) who are "media-genic" rather than merely great writers. Here the author's photo is key, a fact that would have taken Virginia Woolf out of the running for a bent nose. Publishers have also lowered the bar on what constitutes literature, a preeminent example being a new genre called "street lit." This "literature" is characterized by its subject matter (guns, drugs, sex, violence), its bad spelling, and its frequent use of expletives. According to a senior editor acquiring the books, "We noticed that it is very lucrative, very popular, you know, so the bookstores, the chain bookstores, wanted to have access to the product, just like the independent stores, so it behooved us to get on board and acquire these people."[22]

In a well-publicized article in *The Los Angeles Times* entitled "Dumbing Down American Readers," Harold Bloom, one of our foremost literary critics, underlined the state of American literature today with simple poignancy:

> Our society and our literature and our culture are being dumbed down, and the causes are very complex. I'm 73 years old. In a lifetime of teaching English, I've seen the study of literature debased. There's very little authentic study of the humanities remaining.[23]

Bloom is right, but the cause is only complex when you look at it from a bottom-up perspective. When you look at the fate of literature through the Market's eyes, it all makes perfect sense.

# 5. Jolts Per Minute

LEFT: *The Creature from the Black Lagoon,* 1954; RIGHT: *Friday the 13th,* 1980.

As we move from the level of the individual to that of society, the interior manifests itself as culture. Culture is the authentic identity of a society, and expresses the Good in various forms. As the poet Shelley put it, "Those who imagine and express this indestructible order, are not only the authors of language and of music, of the dance, and architecture, and statuary, and painting; they are the institutors of laws and the founders of civil society, and the inventors of the arts of life, and the teachers, who draw into a certain propinquity with the beautiful and the true that partial apprehension of the agencies of the invisible world which is called religion." [1]

Like the human interior, however, culture inevitably becomes a limiting factor to the Market. At some point, cultural values will inevitably come into conflict with market values. While the Frenchman enjoys a two-hour lunch, and while such civility may well be a moderating force in his life, the Market wants him gulping fast food at his desk. As the Market intensifies, it will therefore erode all forms of authentic culture, just as it does the human interior. In their place it breeds *market culture,* a culture where all ways of living serve a productive end, and where all standards are set by the market price. The Market is not just amoral, it is *acultural.*

Today this process is well advanced in the established market economies, what we revealingly call the "industrialized countries," with America leading the pack. We commonly refer to this market culture by a different name, "consumer culture," but this is another example of the Market's linguistic sleight of hand. Clearly, you cannot have a consumer culture without a producer culture, too. We only use the former term because it implies individual choice, as if the Market were serving us. In reality, any culture that places production and consumption, the twin pistons of the economy, at its summit, is serving the Market at the expense of the individual. We also refer to the market culture as popular culture, as if by making the Market sound democratic we can overlook its excesses. The truth is, popular culture originally meant the common traditions of a culture, which were rooted in the seasons and the cycle of annual festivals. This had nothing to do with shopping.

The collapse of authentic culture, and the rise of market culture, is by no means over, so it is instructive to take a look at how the process works, what it is doing to America today, and where it is taking us.

## The Jolt Machine

The creation of a market culture is driven partly by the economics of the media, the very walls of the Bubble. If society is a bell curve, where the mass of consumers is in the middle, then the Market will ensure that most products, most advertising, and most media is pitched to this bulge bracket, since that is where the money is. This creates a general cultural mediocrity, as the middle of the bell curve is the very definition of what is average. This trend is well known in market economies and has been remarked on for decades. But it is only part of the story. In market economies, the bell curve is paired with another powerful mechanism, the jolt machine. It is this mechanism that drives the mass market to the bottom.

Since the material world is the world of sense, the Market's primary appeal is sensual rather than intellectual. You see this in advertisements: all furniture is plush, hotels offer to pamper you, amusement parks offer a thrill, even Julie, the automated Amtrak voice, can hardly restrain her excitement at the thought of your next trip. From the very beginning, the life of the mind is deprioritized, and through it, your intellectual well-being, as suggested by the very word *sensation-alism*. The Market simply gains little from improving your mind.

This distinction splits the most powerful form of media, television, into two camps. The smaller camp, public television, is focused on elevating the mind. The Market's dominant voice, commercial television, is focused on keeping the viewer riveted to a particular channel in order to compete commercially. It does this by constantly producing sensory stimuli, a process known as "jolts per minute."[2] These sensory jolts take many forms: car chases, fistfights, jokes, sex scenes, murders, explosions, arguments. They are moments designed to excite the senses. Entire categories of content, such as sports and police shows (typical male jolts) and game shows and soap operas (female jolts) have arisen accordingly. Even volume levels and film cuts are part of the jolts-per-minute calculus. Haven't you ever been drawn out of a conversation by a television flickering in the room? In the end, if the jolts per minute are delivered well, ratings will rise, and advertisers will spend. If viewers get bored, they hit the channel button, and advertising revenues go with them. For this reason, the delivery of jolts per minute has been called the First Law of Commercial Television.[3] It also explains why you don't see many car chases on PBS.

These sensory appeals are fundamentally different than intellectual appeals. They actually skirt the intellect to reach deep into our most basic instincts, the area of autonomic reaction. They are jolts of fear, of sexual arousal, of sadness. In extreme cases, the pace and intensity of video images can even cause adverse physical reactions, a phenomenon found in video games. In 1997, seven hundred Japanese children were rushed to the hospital when the bright flashing lights of a televised Pokémon video game caused optically stimulated epileptic seizures.[4] Video games now warn of these effects in their instruction booklets, and certain forms of video are also banned in American schools.

This type of raw stimulation further can be very addictive, as seen in a classic experiment with rats:

Wires are inserted directly into excitement centers in the rat's brain, then attached to a depressible pedal in its cage. After discovering the connection between the pedal and the pleasure it brings, the rat depresses the pedal with growing frequency. Gradually the animal neglects other activities. In time it even forgets to eat—and starves to death.[5]

But that's rats and wires, you say. Can one really become addicted to tele-jolts? A recent article in *Scientific American* suggests you can:

> Psychologists and psychiatrists formally define substance dependence as a disorder characterized by criteria that include spending a great deal of time using the substance; using it more often than one intends; thinking about reducing use or making repeated unsuccessful efforts to reduce use; giving up important social, family or occupational activities to use it; and reporting withdrawal symptoms when one stops using it. All these criteria can apply to people who watch a lot of television.[6]

Such findings are supported by scientific studies of populations that have suddenly been denied television. In such cases, people go through the symptoms of withdrawal: "The family walked around like a chicken without a head," as one participant put it. A similar phenomenon is found on the Internet. In Finland, for example, a number of military draftees have been discharged early because of addiction to the Internet. Doctors found they missed their computers too much, since their online gaming had come to replace other hobbies and friends.

In America, the most compelling evidence for the success of the jolt machine is the stunning statistics we have already seen on American television viewing. Is it just a coincidence that America is also the global leader in the field of commercial television? In addition, many Americans freely admit to having a TV problem. Gallup polls in the nineties indicated that two out of five adults said they spent too much time watching television. Other polls consistently show that around 10 percent of Americans consider themselves TV addicts.[7] That still seems awfully low, when the average American is spending twelve years of her life in the jolt zone.

This addiction is very valuable to the Market, as it turns the "plug-in drug" into an instrument of control. Each program may be at the mercy of the remote, but the television as a whole is not. The addict needs his programming, and the Market controls the supply. Since sensual pleasures are transitory, the

TV addict develops a constant search for new stimuli, a manic channel surfing the Market is only too happy to encourage, via several hundred cable channels.

The nature of the medium further ensures the Market a receptive audience. The jolt machine is a one-way flow from programmers to viewers. It conditions the audience to be passive receptors of sensory stimuli rather than active thinkers. This manifests itself, as you would expect, in less mental activity and lowered alertness. The result is the couch potato, a person sitting four or more hours a day receiving commercial messages from a box in his living room. Surprisingly, this effect even manages to survive the on-off switch: "The sense of relaxation ends when the set is turned off, but the feelings of passivity and lowered alertness continue. Survey participants commonly reflect that television has somehow absorbed or sucked out their energy, leaving them depleted."[8] The result is a population conditioned to receive the market message without thinking about it.

In addition to attracting eyeballs and converting minds, the reduction of programming to jolts per minute is a classic example of unbridled market principles at work. The Market cannot control the creative process, or what emerges from it. It cannot put a number on something new and different. It can only price a known commodity. By reducing art to jolts per minute, however, programming becomes a formula—and there is nothing the Market likes more than that. A formula is the equivalent of an assembly line. Since you understand demand for the product, returns can be projected with greater accuracy, soothing management. Consequently, programming in a hypermarket becomes increasingly subordinate to the formula, until it is merely the envelope in which the jolts are delivered. "This trend towards explicit sexuality exists because there's a creative void," says entertainment magnate Robert Halmi. "It reflects the taste of the executives, but it's also pressure from the corporate heads who want networks to perform like stock portfolios, with a 26 percent growth rate."[9]

Another way to put this is that the Market strips the meaning from whatever it touches. The Market will take the most appalling aspects of life, and the very best aspects of life, and reduce them all to mere entertainment, another joke, a passing interest, packaged for immediate sale. All that matters is the numbers. So it is that we speak of "slasher films" now as a socially acceptable genre because their predominant meaning is box-office receipts. Behind this lies the simple fact that all market prices are nothing but quantity. So as the commodification of Nature continues, it blankets the globe in amoral digits, a process of *quantification* supported by the entire material assembly line: science, technology, industry, business. "As we rely throughout the culture on this imperium of numbers," writes TV producer Norman Lear, "we too easily forget that no numerical scale can truly represent the values that are most important: The spirit that makes a worker want to give his or her best. The persistence that helps a less-endowed competitor prevail. The altruism that yearns to be used. The artistic impulse that creates a film or novel or TV show that becomes a cherished cultural symbol."[10]

## Lowering the Bar

Over time, our mental jolt zone operates much like the body's response to a drug. It becomes conditioned to the dosage. As the jolts continue, the mind becomes desensitized to them, to the point where they no longer do the trick. Consumers can even become so immune to the same old jolts that they bore them. This causes a perpetual crisis for programmers and advertisers, who are always at risk of losing their audience. They are the perpetual victims of their own success. At this point the programmers have two choices. One is to increase the number of jolts per minute. This approach quickly reaches a natural limit, however, as there are only so many screen cuts that can be made before the screen becomes a blur, only so many jokes that can be told before the laugh track never stops. The other approach is to increase the intensity of each jolt. This is done by making the language cruder, the jokes more vulgar, the sex more bizarre, the violence more bloody, the explosions larger, the plots more outlandish.

In 2000 the Parents Television Council published a report, *What a Difference a Decade Makes*, that put some hard numbers on the Market's ability to lower the cultural bar in this way. They measured the levels of offensive language, sexual content, and violent content broadcast in prime time on every commercial television network in the first four weeks of the 1989–1990 season and compared it with the same period in 1999–2000. They found that the use of vulgar language had risen 565 percent, while the level of sexual content had more than tripled. "In the last decade, writers, producers, directors, and network programmers have continually pushed the envelope," said entertainer Steve Allen. "The advertising community must also shoulder some of the reponsibility for the rise in vulgarity. After all, without the support of corporate America, nothing would ever make it on television."[11] The PTC has since followed up with separate studies on foul language, violence, and sexuality. Overall, violence and foul language increased in every time slot between 1998 and 2002.[12] Sexual content decreased some during the family hour, but became more graphic. "In 1998, non-marital sex, references to prostitution, transvestitism, adultery, nudity and pornography accounted for less than 3% of all sexual content. In 2002, such material accounted for 26% of all sexual content. In addition, references to masturbation, strippers and oral sex accounted for an additional 8%."[13] On cable TV the plunge has been even swifter. The number of "raunchy" sexual references on cable TV shows more than doubled between 2000 and 2002, growing to more than twice that of network TV.

Our culture has responded to this barrage, as seen in a new word, *smashmouth,* which began in the world of football to describe an aggressive attitude and spread out into American society in general, where it now describes everything from politics to business, and appropriately names a rock band. "Clearly the word has captured something essential in a world of violent lyrics and movies, political attack ads, and dog-eat-dog reality-TV shows," says *The Wall Street Journal.*[14]

Extend this same phenomenon across all media and the result is a precipitous decline in cultural standards across the board, a reduction to the animal—or should we say, the octopus—that has been ongoing for decades. So it is that the hip-grinding of Elvis has become the tattooed rapper Eminem flipping you off today. Even our best work now fixates on the lowest aspects of humanity, as two of the 2003 Academy Award winners reveal: *Mystic River,* in which child molestation leads to murderous revenge, and *Monster,* about a serial-killer prostitute (and a lesbian, too!). Demand is so great for violence that a Los Angeles company, Suspect Entertainment, does nothing but provide real Latino gang members for Hollywood movies: "They will also provide consultation for appropriate gang dialogue and character motivation; they'll bring lowrider cars and tricked-out bicycles, scout locations, spray graffiti and bring all the extras any filmmaker could want: worried moms, young wannabes, old gangsters, junkies, thieves, victims, predators."[15]

Should we be surprised, then, when American soldiers fed on this diet since birth begin to torture Arab prisoners in Saddam Hussein's prison? Consider how one American soldier describes his experience in Iraq: "I was just thinking one thing when we drove into that ambush. 'Grand Theft Auto: Vice City,' " he says, referring to a video game. "I felt like I was living it." [16]

This plunge has not taken place overnight, but step-by-step. People have their limits, so the media can push them only so far. Over time, this creates a continuous cycle: the media pushes a little, and the general public accommodates itself to the new low, to include whatever value shifts are necessary. "The world adapts—by desensitizing in the same way that certain bacteria develop a tolerance to the sulfuric acids in stinking geothermal pools." [17] One can see this trend in the lowering standards of movie ratings. In another decade-spanning study, the Harvard School of Public Health found clear evidence of "ratings creep" in films, a consistent lowering of standards that turned the R movies of 1992 into the PG-13 movies of 2003, and the PG-13s into Gs. "A movie rated PG or PG-13 today has more sexual or violent content than a similarly rated movie in the past." An example is Disney's film *The Santa Clause,* which was rated PG in 1994, while its comparable sequel, *The Santa Clause 2,* was rated G in 2002.[18]

Senator Daniel Patrick Moynihan once famously referred to this cultural phenomenon as "defining deviancy down." As he explained it:

> I proffer the thesis that, over the past generation . . . the amount of deviant behavior in American society has increased beyond the levels the community can "afford to recognize" and that, accordingly, we have been re-defining deviancy so as to exempt much conduct previously stigmatized, and also quietly raising the "normal" level in categories where behavior is now abnormal by any earlier standard.[19]

Moynihan was speaking broadly of social decline, in terms of crime, the family, mental health, etc. But the key idea here is not what sector of society has dropped its standards, but why they fall to begin with.

Here the Bubble has much to teach us. The Bubble is the ultimate jolt machine. It is a veritable engine of desensitization. It has bombarded us with messages bent on lowering the cultural bar, year in and year out, for decades. In such an environment, how could we *not* define deviancy down? How could we *not* accept higher and higher and higher levels of graphic sexual and violent content? How could we *not* lower our moral, aesthetic, and spiritual standards across our entire culture? How could we not pitch our culture into decline?

The psychological power of deviancy is now so great in our society that we promote it even when it makes no economic sense. We simply assume that it must. In the movie business, R-rated films are less than half as likely as PG releases to gross $25 million. Yet Hollywood produces many more R-rated films.[20] The same discrepancy is even more true of G-rated movies. In a study of ten years of rated films (1988–1997), the average G-rated film produced a rate of return 78 percent greater than the average R-rated film. Yet in that same period, 17.4 times more R-rated films were produced.[21] The reason is that the idea of "pushing the limits" has become synonymous with Hollywood culture, and thereby central to career advancement—as if pushing limits alone were synonymous with artistic achievement. In our jolt machine, Monet is forbidden from painting his garden, for fear of boring the consumer.

One finds this same distortion in the print media, where the assumption that "sex sells" triumphs over the facts. One study of the media's focus on *Sex and the City* counted 2,000 articles on its star, Sarah Jessica Parker. Meanwhile, Ray Romano, the star of *Everybody Loves Raymond,* received only 805 articles, even though his audience is approximately four times the size of Parker's. Likewise, the star of *Law & Order,* Jerry Orbach, received only 193 articles, even though his show has 1 million more viewers than Parker's. Similarly, advertisers continue to line up to support violent programming, even when evidence suggests that violent programming impairs the viewer's ability to remember advertising. At some point, our market-driven emphasis on social deviance has simply taken on a life of its own.[22]

The power of the Market is such that we have been unable to reverse this trend even when we know that it is damaging our own children. For instance, since the 1960s, the public health community has issued repeated warnings about the impact of violence on television:[23]

- National Commission on the Causes and Prevention of Violence (1969): "Violence on television encourages violent forms of behavior."
- National Institute of Mental Health (1982): "The consensus among

most of the research community is that violence on television does lead to aggressive behavior by children."

- American Psychological Association (1993): "There is absolutely no doubt that higher levels of viewing violence on television are correlated with increased acceptance of aggressive attitudes and increased aggressive behavior."
- Joint Statement of the Public Health Community (2000): "At this time, well over 1,000 studies point overwhelmingly to a casual connection between media violence and aggressive behavior in some children."

The result of these warnings? The National Television Violence Study (1994–1997), the largest study to date, found that children's programming is actually *more* violent than other types of programming today, with more than twice as many violent incidents per hour. If a child watches two hours of cartoons a day, he will see ten thousand violent incidents in a year.

## Main-Street Porn

Nowhere is the success of the Market in lowering standards and changing values more apparent than in the mainstreaming of pornography in American life. Here the Market's unrelenting pressure has managed to create an unprecedented barrage of sexual content encouraging virtually all forms of deviant behavior that is available in one's home at all times. This transition has occurred in a relatively short period of time, beginning, as is often the case, with relatively innocent moves, gaining momentum, and finally entering free fall, the stage we are in today.

So why should we care? One of the reasons for the Market's success has been our general failure to answer that question. We hear moral indignation, but no moral explanation. Here one of the comments from observers of the Rockdale County case, where the after-school orgies of kids were linked back to their parents' materialism, provides a starting point: "Is it any surprise that children raised in such an atmosphere would value 'things' above relationships and perhaps even come to regard their bodies as a thing?" That is the essence of pornography: the body as a thing, a thing that provides sensual pleasure, like all market products, and is valued accordingly. It is not that this is wrong, in and of itself, as obviously the body *is* a thing, and pleasure is certainly part of it, and of being human, too. The problem is that this philosophy is pursued to the exclusion of all else, thereby eradicating all the other values that surround human sexuality and the meaning they provide human life. Pornography strips love from sex, emotion from sex, commitment from sex, caring from sex. It takes sex out of a person's innermost identity, his private self. It is purely meaningless, flat sex. In this way, pornography parallels so much of the Market, which seeks to strip all meaning from anything, leaving only productive behavior behind. Indeed, one could argue that pornography defines the Market, since it reduces all aspects of human life to the price of sensation. There really is no difference between an individual flaunting her body and one flaunting her BMW. From flat people to flat culture, the Market extols the pornographic life.

A few statistics reveal the extent of the Market's success, the degree to which pornography has penetrated American life. While Hollywood produces four hundred feature films a year, the $10 billion porn industry churns out eleven thousand. Nearly one out of every five movies rented by an American is a porn movie, a total of 800 million porn films a year. As of July 2003, there were 260 million pages of pornography online, eighteen times more than in 1998. Most visibly, porn has, like the naming of baseball stadiums, reached into cultural space that was previously off-limits. In one episode of *Friends,* then TV's number one rated show, the cast becomes obsessed with watching a porn channel. Private sex videos, from Pamela Anderson to Paris Hilton, are placed online and capture the attention of the nation. Pay-per-view offers a reality show, *Can You Be a Porn Star?* ABC broadcasts *Victoria's Secret Fashion Show,* in which parts of the models' bodies have to be blurred out. HBO offers a documentary series, *Pornucopia: Going Down in the Valley.* Playboy playmates enter the world of reality shows, competing on NBC's *Fear Factor.* The Abercrombie & Fitch catalog is so graphic today that you need to show an adult ID to get one. Porn star Jenna Jameson is on a Times Square billboard advertising her XXX Web site. "A wave of confessionals and self-help guides written by current or former stars of pornographic films is flooding bookstores this year, accompanied by erotic novels, racy sexual-instruction guides, histories of sexual particulars and photographic treatments of the world of pornography."[24]

As part of this trend, the "stripper aesthetic" is taking off. The spiked heels and overknee boots of the average lap dancer now populate the fashion runways. Encouraged by the pole-dancing of (who else) Madonna and Pamela Anderson, brass stripper poles, striptease-for-exercise DVDs, and pole-dancing classes are all the rage. Anderson has even been transformed into the comic-book hero Stripperella, with a weekly show on the Spike Channel, adding a layer of celluloid to her silicone. As *The Washington Post* concludes, "There is something unique about an era in which the average woman thinks nothing of doing a lap dance in gym class."[25] As part of its larger marketing strategy, the Market is increasingly pushing this porn chic at an ever-younger audience. *Hustler* magazine has even come out with a new teen gift line, such as makeup bags with the Hustler logo embroidered on it.[26]

Since art pursues the chic, it is not surprising that we have seen art embrace porn, too. In *Untitled,* a videotape shown at the Friedrich Petzel Gallery in Manhattan in June 2004, "the artist is seen having sex in what some have characterized coyly as 'every imaginable position' with an unidentified American collector who paid her close to $20,000 to participate in this curious 60-minute work of art."[27] The dictionary defines this as prostitution. The porn industry currently has its own version of the Academy Awards to recognize such "art," but not for long. This year, for the first time, Hollywood is not trimming its content to avoid the once dreaded NC-17 rating, but embracing it, a step toward the day when Best Actor will go to a porn star.

In the music industry, rap and porn have quickly grown close together since 2001, when Hustler Video distributed *Snoop Dogg's Doggystyle.* It was the top-selling adult tape of that year, according to *Adult Video News.* It was also the first hard-core video ever put on the *Billboard* top music-video list. Since then, the rapper 50 Cent has produced an interactive sex CD called *Groupie Luv,* in which the viewer can choose the partners, sexual positions, and camera angles of the performers; several rap stars have launched a series on Playboy TV; a new magazine, *Fish'n'Grits,* has been formed to exploit the rap–porn connection; and Snoop Dogg has followed up with *Hustlaz: Diary of a Pimp,* the top-selling video of 2003.[28]

In order to sell such material more effectively, Tower Records has hosted porn stars from Vivid Video, one of the leading porn brands, while Virgin Megastore has opened an adult-entertainment zone in its San Francisco store as a test market for the entire country. Naturally, one of the features is a stripper pole, in order to entertain customers.[29]

Ultimately, the conflation of movies, music, and porn has made porn stars celebrities in the larger culture, thereby completing the cycle: As more people ape porn celebrities, demand rises for porn music, porn accessories, porn cable, and all the products advertised on it. Many of these emulators, of course, are teenagers. "What's most striking today is the headlong convergence of youth culture and porn culture," concludes *Time* magazine.[30] While this convergence is new, it has already deeply penetrated our top universities. Smith, Vassar, M.I.T., Swarthmore, and Yale have all launched their own student-run porn magazines, as has Harvard, a school founded to graduate ministers, where the *H Bomb* porn mag was approved without objection by the faculty-run Committee on Student Life.[31] One Yale senior has already taken the next step and organized a campus "sex week," which took place in early 2004. The slate of topflight speakers included a porn star, the creator of the *Girls Gone Wild* spring-break videos, and a masturbation expert.[32]

The staff of *H Bomb*, Harvard's first student-run porn magazine, pose for the centerfold of their debut issue.

As with so many elements of market life, when you dig down into the spread of porn, what you find is a great deal of lying. In order to lower the bar more easily, the purveyors of porn, and all those who jolt for dollars, have sought to disguise their motives behind various facades, either to make themselves feel good or to con others. Telling people you are trying to manipulate their animal instincts for profit is simply nowhere near as effective as claiming, for instance, that stripping is "the final frontier of the neo-feminist movement," as one pole-dancing instructor put it.[33] The art-porn purveyors, of course, have the very highest aesthetic principles to point to. "All of my work is about what we want from art, what collectors want, what artists want from collectors, what museum audiences want," explains the "artist" who videotaped herself having sex with a "collector." "By that I mean, what we want not only economically, but in more personal, psychological and affective terms."[34] Meanwhile, the faculty adviser to Harvard's for-profit student porn magazine, *H Bomb,* was only doing it for the students: "There is a need for students of this age to have a voice, a medium of expression, and a magazine is a terrific place for this. It makes no sense to censor such expressions because doing so does not change the current climate. It is a time of change, and as adults, I would rather know about how students of this age feel about sex and sexuality than to be caught off guard."[35] Only the Market is bold enough to use moral arguments to sell pornography.

This explosion of American porn has been greatly facilitated by changes in American law, particularly when the Community Decency Act of 1996 was deemed unconstitutional. Since then the number of state and federal prosecutions under obscenity laws have dwindled, and major corporations have stepped in to profit from the creation and distribution of porn, encouraged by its rising social acceptability. Porn companies list their shares on NASDAQ. Holiday Inn offers their products. Visa and MasterCard process their charges. As the Market has changed our values, the law has bowed to its wishes, regardless of the social cost. Consequently, our society is being bombarded with a consistent message: Human sexuality has no meaning. The self is nothing but the senses, and other human beings are material objects to be used for pleasure. There are no limits to indulging yourself, and there are no consequences to your physical or mental health if you do. More market lies. Sex has been decoupled from emotion, from identity, from self-respect, from soul. As that message spreads from home to home, from teen to teen, it is unclear what the impact will be. But an FBI profile of serial murderers and sex offenders over the past twenty years suggests it won't be positive. Nearly all of them were addicted to adult and child pornography.[36]

## Entertain Me

If one wants hard evidence for the limits of market culture, one needs to look no further than the Super Bowl. The Super Bowl is the most popular event in American culture. In 2004, 89 million Americans tuned in, plus an untold number of international viewers. So like the Olympics, the Super Bowl provides America with an unequaled opportunity to showcase its culture, both domestically and to the world. And certainly, with the cost of a thirty-second commercial going for $3 million, the NFL and its commercial supporters were blessed with the financial resources necessary to achieve the highest goals.

So what was the result in 2004? First came the commercials, featuring a crotch-biting dog, a flatulent horse, insinuations of bestiality, graphic brutality, a child who spoke like a sailor, and a spate of drugs for erectile dysfunction. Then came a crotch-grabbing rapper who convinced an assemblage of cheerleaders to rip their skirts off. Finally came "the incident," when singer Justin Timberlake pulled the front of fellow singer Janet Jackson's top off, revealing her right breast, synchronized with the subtle lyrics: "I'm gonna have you naked by the end of this song." Thus did the clouds disperse, revealing not only the nature of American culture today, but market culture in general, for all the world to see. With all the money and attention generated by the event, this was the very best the Market could do.

In the ensuing days, the market culture continued to expose itself further. Media giants Viacom, CBS, and MTV were all publicly vilified for their lack of discretion, but the next day Viacom stock went up. Apparently the potential for a $5 million fine didn't faze investors, not when Viacom enjoyed $26.6 billion in earnings in 2003. Rather, investors recognized that the event was an advertising dream, even better than Madonna kissing Britney Spears. Indeed, the search engine Lycos enjoyed the greatest number of Internet searches since 9/11, as millions ran for a rerun of Jackson's jolt. Not to be outdone, the other networks clambered to take advantage of the situation:

> Citing the Jackson flap, [NBC] decreed that two split-second shots of an 80-year-old woman's breast in an emergency room sequence in "E.R." be excised. But the "E.R." star Noah Wylie [sic] then went on NBC's "Today" show the morning of the broadcast to joke about the decision, and the network-owned NBC affiliate in New York used the banned breast as a promo for its post-"E.R." news broadcast: "What you won't see on tonight's episode of 'E.R.'—at 11!" Thus did NBC successfully transform its decision not to bare geriatric flesh into a sexual tease to hype ratings. This is true marketing genius, American-style.[37]

The greatest beneficiary, of course, was Janet Jackson, whose professional stock rose faster than Viacom's. Shortly after the Super Bowl, she began hosting a ten-part series on BET, a network owned by Viacom, which noted in its press release that Jackson would be dressed in classic black—just as she was at the Super Bowl.[38]

So what was the cost? What the 2004 Super Bowl reveals is the Market's ability to strip the meaning from whatever it touches. The Super Bowl may appear to be the last place in the world you would look for meaning, but that is the point: There is a framework of meaning that surrounds all elements of culture, a framework we often take for granted until it is lost. Just think about what was stripped away from the Super Bowl in addition to Jackson's top. First of all, all those directly involved in the affair had to believe that Jackson's actions had no meaning, or at least, the profit that they would enjoy from her actions took priority over any other concerns. So either profit was king, or life was a meaningless game, or more likely both. This meaninglessness enabled the participants to prioritize themselves over everyone else—what else stood in the way? There could be nothing more important than them. This further implies a lack of respect for the audience, which included many kids. To Jackson & Co., the boobs were in the living rooms and sports bars of America as well as on the screen. So there was no meaningful connection in that direction, either. This lack of respect included, at the largest level, the entire United States, since this was a national event. In order to drop her top to the crowd,

Jackson had to care very little, if at all, about the dignity of the American enterprise, and how it looks to the rest of the world. To pull off her stunt, Jackson also had to ditch her own self-respect, the idea that her own body was worth more than national publicity. She sacrificed that for a higher value in the market. Finally, for the entire stunt to pay off, the Market had to like it, to appreciate it, to want more. There had to be millions who, like Jackson, could no longer demand anything better than another jolt. After decades in the Market Bubble, there were:

> Addiction in individuals occurs when a person stops seeing a reason to risk the vulnerability required for real fulfillment. A drug may be so powerful that it simply replaces the struggle to build a satisfying life. Or sometimes a person's life circumstances make fulfillment of normal dreams and desires unlikely. But usually there is something more fundamental, more at the level of meaning. The person's life story has become inadequate to inspire him or her to live life fully.[39]

Of course, Jackson & Co. were banking on this. They understood the market culture. They knew that shock had long since triumphed over substance. The unknown Brandi Chastain had stripped off her soccer jersey and become a household name. The cult of celebrity is pure market value, a momentary number placed on a celebrity's head, however it gets there. There is no meaning to it at all. Indeed, in a world governed by the Market, all attempts to inject meaning are met with resistance, as the Super Bowl itself revealed. When MTV suggested to the NFL that Bono, a star to eclipse Jackson, perform the song "An American Prayer" at halftime in order to increase awareness of the AIDS epidemic in Africa, which has already killed almost 20 million people, the NFL turned the request down. Instead, we got an aging tit on the tube.

And what of the football game itself? Meaning is an elusive idea, regardless of how essential it is, but when one reaches the pinnacle of sport, it can be an experience like *The Old Man and the Sea,* in which all the powers of nature are on display. That is the meaning in it, and what die-hard sports fans live for: the great match. It achieves what art achieves, in a very different fashion. What Jackson did was strip that meaning from the game, and from all those who played it and watched it. The game became subordinate to the halftime show, and to Jackson herself. What will the world remember of the 2004 Super Bowl, after all? It is difficult to muster much sympathy for people as grossly overpaid as professional athletes, but when the halftime show garners more publicity than the game, it is another sign that the Market has succeeded in inverting the natural order. You might as well build the stadium within the concession stand.

# 6. Borrowed Time

Tract homes, Delaware.

Like the meltdown of the nuclear family, the decline of our natural environment is another area of long-standing concern that appears to be the product of innumerable complex causes but that can be vastly simplified by looking at it from the Market's point of view. To the Market, which puts a price on everything, the natural environment is primarily real estate, and secondarily the value of all the natural resources that exist therein: timber, minerals, oil, etc. The latter form the raw materials from which a third category, technology, is created, from a simple hand tool to a computer chip. The Market's challenge, on the largest scale, is thus to transform the natural environment, which has no market value unto itself, into a commodity, be it a quarter-acre lot, the lumber cleared from it, or the tract home built upon it. In this way the Market fuels the growth of the economy.

The Market has met this challenge by building a vast material assembly line, a flat factory consisting of four stages. The first is scientific research. This provides the Market with new ideas, prototypes, and know-how. The second is technology development. Here the basic science is translated into a viable new prototype. The third stage is manufacturing, in which the technology is mass-produced. The fourth and final stage is distribution, in which all products are sold through various marketplaces, powering the entire economic engine. It is here that the Market has its say, through the market price. From here its power extends all the way back to the beginning of the assembly line, shaping the entire process. This influence becomes greater as the market economy becomes more efficient, such that the Market drives even the most basic science.

The material assembly line reveals an important point about the nature of the times we live in, the so-called modern age. There have been those who define modernity in terms of science, technology, industry, and business. But now we can see that all of these are part of a much larger scheme, an assembly line controlled by the Market. Science is not the active principle in the modern world; it is not an active principle at all. Science must operate within the market economy, like every other sector of society. Science provides a tremendous amount of know-how, but it does not, in the end, decide whether the product will live or die, the building will be built or not, the industry will survive or not. That is the role of the Market. And without its support, science would be just another struggling nonprofit.

While the material assembly line ends with the distribution of commodities, the Market is only halfway done with its work. Production is naturally followed by consumption. Here the economy reveals another chapter taken from nature. Unlike a common factory, the economy is self-evolving. It is like a brick factory that uses its product to expand its own walls. When the material assembly line produces a faster form of transportation, for instance, it can use it to become more efficient. In this way the productive infrastructure is continually being upgraded, from individual transistors to global networks. As old elements become obsolete, wear out, or fulfill their purpose, they are discarded, ending a cycle that began with Nature in the raw. Natural resources have been turned into products that have been turned into trash.

The Market is thus not only the mind of the economy, it is the brain that runs an entire alimentary canal. The market economy is a system for ingesting natural resources, digesting them, distributing the resulting value, and expelling the waste, mountains of it. It is one enormous organism.

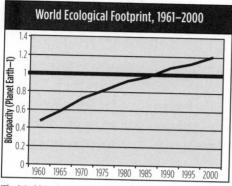

The World Ecological Footprint measures the total human consumption of renewable natural resources, using Earth as the unit of measure (1 planet = the total biological productive capacity of the Earth/year). Since 1987, the human race has been spending its natural capital faster than it can be replaced—a trend that cannot continue indefinitely.

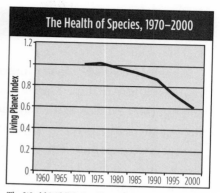

The World Wildlife Fund's Living Planet Index measures the average trends in the populations of species worldwide. From 1970 to 2000 it declined about 40 percent.

## The Obvious

Like all organisms, the market economy has a metabolism, but unlike other organisms, that metabolism has no ceiling to it. As we have seen, the market economy is quite capable of running past red line, and if left to its own devices always will. The entire Bubble exists to make this happen, to drive production through consumer demand. By basing demand on the psychological principle of self-esteem, the Market has liberated itself from all natural limits. This has created an unbalanced relationship between the market economy and Nature. A systemic form of incest has occurred, whereby the market economy, one of Nature's own offspring, now ravages Mother Nature herself.

The results of this modern development are well known, but bear repeating, at least in summary. In fact, they are one of the few things that cannot be repeated enough, particularly when linked to their primary cause. Let's begin with a report from the UN and the World Bank, among others:

There are times when the most difficult decision of all is to acknowledge the obvious. It is obvious that the world's national economies are based on the goods and services derived from ecosystems; it is also obvious that human life itself depends on the continuing capacity of ecosystems to provide their multitude of benefits. Yet for too long in both rich and poor nations, development priorities have focused on how much humanity can take from our ecosystems, with little attention to the impact of our actions.[1]

The impact of this uncontrolled development has been stark: "The current rate of decline in the long-term productive capacity of ecosystems could have devastating implications for human development and the welfare of all species."[2]

One way this decline is measured is through the World Wildlife Fund's Living Planet Index, which charts trends in populations of hundreds of species of birds, mammals, reptiles, amphibians, and fish. Between 1970 and 2000, these populations declined by approximately 35 percent, "a quantitative confirmation that the world is currently undergoing a very rapid loss of biodiversity comparable with the great mass extinction events that have previously occurred only five or six times in the Earth's history."[3] There are two main factors driving this global environmental disaster. One is how many people inhabit the earth and the other is how much we consume. Here the Market works both sides of the fence. On the one hand, we have seen that the evolution of market economies tends to stabilize population growth. On the other hand, it also spikes consumption, which tracks rising income levels. The net result has been that globally, consumption pressure has been rising around 5 percent per year. At that rate, it doubles every fifteen years.

This consumption pressure is measured using another index, known as the global ecological footprint. An ecological footprint is a quantitative assessment of the biologically productive area (i.e. the amount of nature) required to produce the resources (food, energy, and materials) and to absorb the wastes of an individual, city, region, or country. It is measured in hectares of land. To get a feeling of how the entire planet is doing, mankind's total footprint is compared with the total biological capacity of the earth (1.9 hectares per person). According to this measure, humanity breached the level of environmental sustainability in 1976 and has been taking more than nature can restore ever since. This is not a situation that can go on forever, any more than you can spend more than you earn forever. It means that we are rapidly depleting our savings, which is living on borrowed time. Some of us, furthermore, have been spending our natural capital a lot faster than others. While the ecological footprint of the average Asian consumer is 1.4 hectares, and the EF of the average Western European is 5 hectares, the average American eats up a whopping 9.6 hectares, the largest individual footprint on Earth. By 2050, mankind's footprint is likely to grow from between 180 percent to 220 percent of the earth's biological capacity, a spending spree whose ultimate repercussions are unknown.[4]

As grim as it is, the ecological footprint does not capture the full story. It is only a measure of consumption, not of its impact, such as pollution, species degradation, and extinction. But it does give us a way to measure the rpms of the market engine, and how much fuel we have left. When you combine this knowledge with what drives consumption, we are left facing an unsettling truth. It's not that we are expanding our footprint to provide for a growing population. We are raping the earth to boost our self-esteem.

## Global Warming

One of the most serious repercussions of the market economy's voracious appetite has been global warming. While there has been a great deal of debate about the science behind this phenomenon, the results are in. From the National Academy of Sciences to the U.S. Environmental Protection Agency to the American Geophysical Union to the United Nations, there is no longer any doubt that global warming has occurred, and is continuing. The big question now is what the repercussions are going to be.

Global warming is caused mainly by the burning of fossil fuels like gasoline and coal. This produces gases that trap heat in the atmosphere, creating the so-called greenhouse effect. Since the beginning of the Industrial Revolution, the concentration of greenhouse gases in Earth's atmosphere has been rising. Carbon dioxide has increased nearly 30 percent, methane has more than doubled, and nitrous oxide has risen by about 15 percent. Consequently, there has been a rise in global temperature. In the twentieth century, the temperature on Earth rose about 1 degree Fahrenheit, a trend that is accelerating. The last century's ten warmest years all occurred after 1985, with 1998 being the warmest ever recorded. Scientists now predict that in the next century we could experience as much as a 10-degree rise, with almost half of that in the next fifty years.[5]

Such swings in temperature have much greater repercussions in a global ecosystem than they do in everyday life. The snow cover in the Northern Hemisphere, the size of mountain glaciers, and the floating ice in the Arctic Ocean have already decreased substantially. The Arctic ice pack has lost about 40 percent of its thickness over the past four decades. Meanwhile, the global

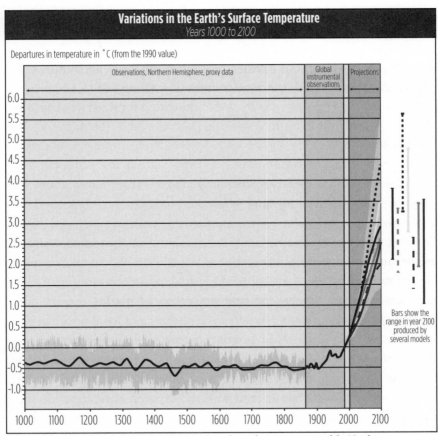

**Variations in the Earth's Surface Temperature**
*Years 1000 to 2100*

Departures in temperature in °C (from the 1990 value)

Observations, Northern Hemisphere, proxy data | Global instrumental observations | Projections

Bars show the range in year 2100 produced by several models

From years 1000 to 1860 the chart shows variations in the surface temperature of the Northern Hemisphere, as reconstructed from proxy data (tree rings, corals, ice cubes, and historical records). The line shows the 50-year-average, the gray region the 95% confidence limit in the annual data. From years 1860–2000 variations are global and derived from instumentation. The line shows the decadal average. From years 2000 to 2100 the line is based on projections of globally averaged surface temperatures drawn from several different scenerios and models.

sea level has risen four to eight inches in the past century, a rate three times faster than the previous three thousand years. Worldwide precipitation over land has also increased by about 1 percent, with extreme rainfall events increasing in frequency throughout much of the United States.[6] So far these changes have all been more or less manageable. What concerns scientists, and increasingly the general public, is what will happen as the temperature continues to rise. Since the climate system is complex, and our planetary experiment unprecedented, no one is sure of the answer, but some macro trends are clear. As the climate warms, evaporation will increase, thereby increasing average global precipitation. Soil moisture will likely decline, while intense rainstorms will become more frequent. Along most of the U.S. coast, the area level is likely to rise two feet. As noted by the UN, climatic change can trigger diverse repercussions in many areas: health (weather-related mortality, infectious diseases, respiratory illnesses), agriculture (crop yields, irrigation demands), forests (composition, range, health, and productivity), water (water supply, quality, and competition for water), coastal areas (erosion, inundation, and the cost of protection from the same), species and natural areas (loss of habitat and species).[7] The great fear is that the change in temperature will be strong enough to generate a sudden climatic crisis. Scientists liken global warming to rocking a canoe: You can push only so far before you reach the tipping point.

The Market is quite adept at creating solutions to the problems it creates. One might even say it lives off them. We have seen this phenomenon already: as the human system becomes obese, for instance, the result is aerobics classes, stomach stapling, and the South Beach Diet. In this way the problems the Market creates become the next generation of market opportunities. To prevent global warming, Columbia University oceanographer Wallace Broecker has proposed a logical solution: the creation of giant machines that would extract carbon dioxide from the atmosphere. Here we see global warming becoming the beginning of a highly profitable enterprise, a new form of environmental utility company, one that will ensure that the air is the right temperature, and free of pollutants, too. So it is that one day we will all be paying our local climate utility a monthly fee for the air we breathe and a stable height to the ocean.

Here we see the Market's deeper strategy of commodification emerge. In addition to creating market opportunities by creating problems, the Market seizes control of the most basic aspects of life, areas that were once considered to be in the realm of Nature, and hence, free of charge. Today in America, for instance, two of the most basic aspects of life, exercise and drinking water, have already been thoroughly commodified. Exercise is frequently performed in gyms, for a monthly fee. Drinking water was originally part of your water bill, but in one of its more hysterical successes, the Market has now successfully convinced much of the American population to pay for bottled water, water that is frequently no better than that which emerges from your kitchen tap. In fact, municipal water is used as a source for approximately 25 percent of the bottled water sold in the United States, including Coke's Dasani and Pepsi's Aquafina—the pictures of mountains and snow on the label notwithstanding.[8] The implication is that the Market can do it better than your local town, a statement that becomes self-fulfilling as people shift their allegiance to the packaged solution. The public water thus becomes like the public schools, an unpalatable option you are forced to take when you can't afford the private alternative. Given these successes, it is therefore not surprising that the Market would start to wrap its fingers around the global climate, one way or another, particularly when you consider the size of the market opportunity. Once every region has its own Enviro-Clean 3000 Atmospheric Sanitizer, we will all be able to sit back and watch while Houston traders rig the climate market to increase demand for bottled water.

The reason this cycle continues is that the alternative, regulating the Market, is met with fierce resistance, even when the planet is at stake. How will anyone profit from regulations that reduce emissions? This resistance is particularly strong in America, which uses more energy than any nation on Earth, and also emits about 20 percent of the world's greenhouse gases:

To most scientists, global warming is a truly successful hypothesis. The evidence overwhelmingly shows, as predicted, that human behavior is altering the climate, with potentially catastrophic results. And yet it seems strangely difficult to scare or reason or argue Americans, the critical audience to reach, into recognizing the truth and acting on it. The world's population is trapped in a malign paradox. Instead of taking the lead, the United States—the country with the highest emissions and the most excessive consumption, as well as enormous potential to produce innovative energy technologies—knows and seems to care the least about global warming. Short-term self-interest is a powerful buffer against reality.[9]

In effect, what the global warming problem represents is the ultimate ceiling on the Market. It is a global concern that is greater than productivity. Barring a suitable economic solution, the Market's strategy has thus been to go on the offensive and deny that global warming even exists. For decades, the science of climate change, a phenomenon first described in 1896, has been vilified by all sorts of industry groups. An example is the Greening Earth Society, which was founded on Earth Day 1998 to promote the idea that increasing levels of atmospheric $CO_2$ is actually good for mankind. The Greening Earth Society is funded by the Western Fuels Association, a cooperative of coal-dependent utilities in the western states. In that same year, the hottest ever recorded, "coral reefs around the world suffered the most extensive and severe bleaching and subsequent mortality in modern record."[10] To the Western Fuels Association, however, this was merely a stellar opportunity for coral reefs to excel:

Coral bleaching, long considered an indicator of reef demise, creates an opportunity for corals to adapt by creating a new symbiotic relationship with different, better-adapted algae. Bleaching may be an excellent strategy employed by corals to sacrifice short-term benefits for longer-term gains.[11]

Opportunity, strategy, sacrificing short-term benefits for long-term gains—are we reading their annual report?

Such resistance from industry, while expected, has been complemented by those who view global warming as an affront to the "free market" itself. Groups like globalwarming.org ("an on-going coalition of market-oriented national and state-level policy and activist groups") have joined industry in attacking climate science, as if the scientific community were conspiring to undermine their ideology rather than pointing out an issue that is simply *more important than the Market*—because they do not recognize that anything is. The line between "free market" ideology and religious dogma has evaporated. Here the standard argument is that attempts to control global warming will cost us too much money—as if our environment had little value. One imagines these groups still broadcasting from a mountaintop as the water level rises.

At the political level, where these issues are ultimately resolved, the key to containing global warming has been the Kyoto Protocol, a global agreement for limiting greenhouse-gas emissions. In order to be ratified, the Protocol requires enough signatures from industrialized countries to account for at least 55 percent of their $CO_2$ emissions, using 1990 as a baseline. As of April 15, 2004, 122 countries had ratified or acceded to the Kyoto Protocol, but the key player, the U.S., withdrew from the process in 2001. As a result, the industrial countries have met only 44.2 percent of their target, and the Protocol remains unratified. The reason for the U.S. withdrawal? The Bush administration cast doubt about the science involved and said the Protocol would put a strain on the U.S. economy.

Meanwhile, even industrial leaders are defecting. Recently the CEO of British Petroleum broke with his industry to step forward and recognize both the science behind global warming and the threat it poses to the planet. In an article in *Foreign Affairs*, John Browne clearly expressed why global warming is a critical issue for us all:

> The most dramatic scenarios, although unlikely, would have grave consequences for humanity and ecosystems. Rapid changes in climate could upset the circulation of the North Atlantic, for example—which, ironically, would cause much colder regional temperatures in northern Europe by weakening the heat-rich Gulf Stream. The Amazon rain forest could deplete dramatically due to drying in the atmosphere, in turn releasing huge volumes of carbon that is stored in trees. And an accelerated rise in sea level from melting ice in Antarctica could occur. These uncertain consequences do not lead to crisp timetables for policy. But they mean that precaution and improvements in measurement and learning will be crucial . . . we still have time to take measured steps. But if we are to avoid having to make dramatic and economically destructive decisions in the future, we must act soon.[12]

When the heads of oil companies start making statements like this, it is time to sit up and listen. Nevertheless, some of the "free market" crowd will still try to pull themselves off the mat and say, "See, the Market is working! It is self-correcting!" Inherent in this last gasp is the idea that the Market is somehow moral, a pure contradiction in terms, as revealed by the statement above. Browne is not making a productive argument—i.e. an argument whose end is to increase economic productivity—he is making a moral argument, whatever its financial impact may be. By definition, the Market is incapable of such thinking, otherwise we would not be in this predicament. Instead, its unending emphasis on economic self-interest as an end in itself continues to stand in the way of the very measures needed to avert planetary catastrophe. Or as the UN tactfully put it, "Significant environmental problems remain deeply embedded in the socio-economic fabric of all societies in all regions. Progress towards a global sustainable future is just too slow."[13] A recent review of several books on global warming contains a similar message:

> The true puzzle of global warming isn't the mechanics of man-made climate change—the feedback loops, the damage to the ozone layer, the shift in oceanic oscillations, the melting of the icecaps, the desertification of formerly productive agricultural lands. These can be studied and understood. The true puzzle is human nature. In every one of these accounts of climate change and environmental degradation, the authors note the inertia of the global system.[14]

That "human nature" is the self-interest leveraged by the unbridled Market, a power that has become so great that even a threat to the planet cannot overcome it.

## A Diabolical Force

Of all the empirical evidence for the danger of the unbridled Market, none is more obvious, more omnipresent, and more poignant than the fate that has befallen the American landscape. From sea to shining sea, our once beautiful country is now drowning in sprawl. As we circumnavigate virtually any major American city, we find ourselves in an identical world of strip malls, chain stores, fast-food restaurants, tract homes, and cookie-cutter communities with artificial names, all connected by miles of blacktop and utility cables, and in half of all cases, submerged in bad air. As James Howard Kunstler has evocatively put it:

> We drive up and down the gruesome, tragic suburban boulevards of commerce, and we're overwhelmed at the fantastic, awesome, stupefying ugliness of absolutely everything in sight—the fry pits, the big-box stores, the office units, the lube joints, the carpet warehouses, the parking lagoons, the plastic townhouse clusters, the uproar of signs, the highway itself clogged with cars—as though the whole thing had been designed by some diabolical force bent on making human beings miserable.[15]

Ah yes, and what could that "diabolical force" be? We profess not to know. "Most recognize the undesirable symptoms of the disease and many have already come up with cures for it; unfortunately, most lack a complete understanding of the underlying causes of it."[16] Like family breakdown, sprawl is another great mystery of our time, one that remains so until you look at it through the Market's eyes.

The term *sprawl* was first used by Earle Draper, a Tennessee Valley Authority official, who told a national conference of planners in 1937: "In bursting its bounds, the city actually sprawled and made the countryside ugly, uneconomic [in terms] of services and doubtful social value." In 1958, urbanist William Whyte, author of *The Organization Man,* popularized the idea in a *Fortune* article called "Urban Sprawl," in which he wrote:

> In the next three or four years Americans will have a chance to decide how decent a place this country will be to live in, and for generations to come. Already huge patches of once green countryside have been turned into vast, smog-filled deserts that are neither city, suburb, nor country, and each day—at a rate of some 3,000 acres a day—more countryside is being bulldozed under. You can't stop progress, they say, yet much more of this kind of progress and we shall have the paradox of prosperity lowering our standard of living. . . . It is not merely that the country-

side is receding; in the great expansion of the metropolitan areas, the subdivisions of one city are beginning to meet up with the subdivisions of another.

In the almost half century since then, Whyte's worst nightmare has come true. Between 1970 and 1990 alone, more than 19 million acres of rural land were developed. Today two acres of farmland are lost every minute, the fastest such decline in American history, only to be replaced by suburban blight. The American Farmland Trust reports that an astonishing 70 percent of remaining prime or unique farmland is in the path of development, creating the potential for coast-to-coast sprawl.[17]

As we have lost our countryside to sprawl, the nature of sprawl itself has been the subject of debate. Like family breakdown, sprawl has been attributed to many causes: cheaper land, population increases, growing affluence, the automobile, differentials in government services (especially schools), racial attitudes, ease of development, federal tax policy, and land-use regulations. Others see the suburban flight that powers sprawl as an attempt to escape the urban market environment. This is like the horror movie where the woman flees the house and jumps into the car, only to find the murderer in the backseat. While all of these factors have certainly contributed to suburban development, none of them is the primary cause of sprawl, simply because sprawl is not synonymous with development, no matter how many farms give up the ghost. Development merely creates the environment we live in, an environment that can be uplifting or depressing, depending on the principles underlying it. Building a paradise on earth would take development. So what sprawl represents is *bad development,* a negative, virulent form of physical growth.

So why are we locked in this spiral of development hell? Why can't the United States, with all its vast financial and technological resources, make a decent main street anymore? The answer goes to the heart of what sprawl is—and indeed, what the Market is. Sprawl is what happens when human beings relinquish control of their environment to the Market. We call this "uncontrolled growth," but such growth is really controlled by market forces, as opposed to city planners and regulators, who constrain and harness them. In this way, sprawl is akin to commercial television, or market culture

**Top 20 U.S. Cities Threatened by Sprawl**

Seattle 7

Minneapolis-St. Paul 8

Kansas City 5

Chicago 2

Akron 5

Washington 3

Cincinnati 4

10

Las Vegas 3

Los Angeles

Denver 6

St. Louis 5

Raleigh 2

San Diego

Phoenix

Little Rock

Atlanta 1

Austin 2

McAllen 1

Pensacola

Orlando 1

Daytona Beach 4

West Palm Beach 4

Ft. Lauderdale 9

**Population**

◆ 1 million +    ☐ 200k - 500k

⬤ 500k - 1 million    ✪ dishonorable mention

in general: it is what you get when you strip away any higher principles from the enterprise. The entire built environment loses its meaning as a public space serving the community, the city, the country. Performance triumphs over art, creating the architectural equivalent of pornography.

## Marketecture

In designing an environment for living, the critical issue is the balance between the natural and the artificial. As Frank Lloyd Wright famously noted, a good building, one that is organically integrated into its site, actually *improves* on Nature, a principle we can extend to development at all scales. If one travels the Irish countryside, for instance, one typically leaves a village and enters miles of beautiful countryside before entering another village. The result is that one always has the feeling of living within Nature. Or take a city like San Francisco, with its dramatic rolling perch overlooking its namesake bay. Certainly the footprint of San Francisco has obliterated much of the natural environment it occupies. And yet the result is one of the most strikingly beautiful cities on Earth. So development, in and of itself, need not necessarily mar the landscape, as long as it serves a higher set of principles: aesthetic, moral, spiritual, cultural. If not, it upsets the natural balance, with tragic effect on the individuals who live within it. As Wright also noted, the environment we live in reinforces certain values in us. It shapes our character, our well-being, our outlook on life, an influence that exists at all scales, from the individual home to the largest public spaces.

Sprawl arises when the Market erodes the higher principles of design and seizes control of the suburban development process, such that the key players involved simply do whatever maximizes their profit, regardless of the consequences. In other words, it is another case of inversion, the collapse of the human in the face of the productive. The result is a chamber of architectural horrors, in which all the common pathologies of the unbalanced Market are made highly visible. In fact, we live in them.

Take tract homes, for instance. In suburban home construction, the tract home is the equivalent of the fast-food hamburger: cheap, mass-produced, and lacking nutritional value. In order to save money on design costs and streamline production, every example looks like the next one. Since pennies add up on the assembly line, great effort is applied to reduce costs everywhere, creating minimal framing, paper-thin walls, and other materials chosen to survive a week longer than the new home warranty. Cheap labor rounds out the picture, yielding substandard construction—although you may not notice right away. Nothing is built to last. This same market philosophy extends out to encompass the entire building site. Instead of saving trees, which are difficult to work around, the entire future neighborhood is bulldozed on day one. The site is then divided into (what else) identical lot sizes. A few saplings are then planted, creating a market for tree growers and commoditizing yet another element of nature.

A similar process manages the development of Kunstler's "gruesome, tragic suburban boulevards of commerce." Here the term *sprawl* becomes inadequate, since these hellish highways are found well beyond the edges of our cities. A better term would be *marketecture,* although the result is the same. Individual buildings are designed without any attempt to fit them into their surroundings. Just the opposite: diverse surroundings are forced to accept the same building. Here the archetype is McDonald's, the first company to apply the assembly line to restaurant construction. The efficiencies involved allow McDonald's to open a new building every two hours. These and other chain stores, of all kinds, are then placed side by side in so-called commercial zones, without any pretext of aesthetics at all—as if, by virtue of the fact that we are eating, or shopping, or getting our oil changed, we no longer need beauty in our lives. The very expansion of these businesses is done by demographic analysis, so that as soon as population and earnings levels dictate, the cinder block is laid. When you add this commercial marketecture to the residential variety, what you get is the classic "cookie-cutter" suburb, another term right off the assembly line. This process erases local distinctions, further homogenizing entire regions, even nations.

The true nature of sprawl is revealed by a telling fact: in the past fifty years, as the sprawl phenomenon has unfolded, it has redefined the center of a town, its civic space. Instead of the town square, we have the mall, a far more productive commercial experience. Like sprawl itself, malls are the product of real estate developers and are designed down to the last nail to maximize their profit. As consumer researcher Paco Underhill notes in *The Call of the Mall*, the food courts exist to prolong a shopper's stay, the restrooms are placed down a long dingy corridor so they don't eat up more valuable retail space, the floor plan funnels browsers to the most profitable locations. Every store is governed by its "conversion rate," the measure of its ability to convert browsers into spenders, and beholden to the real estate company for more than rent, as the landlord gets a percentage of sales. Since women's apparel is the number one category, malls are primarily designed for female shoppers. So it is that pictures of supermodels loom over the cosmetic counters like cult rulers. As a building, the mall is typically the ugliest of all marketecture, a huge windowless box that makes Wal-Mart look welcoming. "A big wall with a little mouse hole," as a top mall designer describes the typical entrance. The entire edifice focuses within, trapping everyone in an intensely commercial space, where you cannot even see outside. But why would you? The link to the community is that of a prison:

> Next time you're at a mall, instead of going directly inside, stroll around the perimeter of the place. It will be one of the more joyless promenades you'll ever make. You'll be very alone out there, on a narrow strip of sidewalk, assuming it has a sidewalk—many malls don't—with maybe a se-

curity guard or two to keep you company. . . . There will almost certainly be shrubbery, neatly clipped, but it's greenery of the most generic kind. Nobody thought you'd ever look too closely at it. Its only job is to be green.[18]

Nevertheless, consumers endure these tortures, and keep coming. The Mall of America, a name to make a novelist blush, is not only the largest mall in the country, it has more visitors than Disney World, Graceland, and the Grand Canyon combined. It is also an ironic choice for a name because you give up your right to free speech the moment you walk in the door. The mall may be the public square of today, but it is privately owned, so you have no right to voice your opinion to your fellow citizens there, no matter how many of them there may be. The Market does not appreciate demonstrators. Instead, you can go back to the old town square, where no one is.

In addition to commodifying trees, homogenizing buildings, and imprisoning shoppers, the Market also incorporates other aspects of its philosophy into the environment, creating a self-reinforcing trend. As competition increases and community sentiment breaks down, people retreat into suburban existences where life revolves around the automobile. The idea of the bedroom community arises, a place to sleep between commutes, rather than a place to live. People grow isolated from one another, until they are "bowling alone," as Robert Putnam famously put it, a breakdown in community association that mirrors the broken bonds of loyalty in corporations. Marketectures sets these social trends in stone—and asphalt, which now covers 2 percent of the entire country, as well as 50 percent of many metropolitan areas.[19] Gated communities flourish as a bulwark against the world, associating wealth with social isolation, and reinforcing indifference to the rest of society. Demarcated developments of all kinds are marketed as local brands, with faux names carrying varying degrees of status. Since size is everything, the Market pushes bloated homes as the ultimate form of conspicuous consumption, and quite successfully. Over the past thirty years, home sizes have doubled as families have shrunk, fueling the rise of the McMansion, another homogenous franchise. Like the American population as a whole, we are experiencing the obesity of architecture. Instead of living a simple life in a modest home that serves our authentic needs, as part of a larger community, one that is part of an even larger natural environment, many of us spend two hours in our car every day just so we can make the mortgage payment on a house twice as large as we need. We do this because, since the house is larger than average, we can hold our head up in American society and feel good about ourselves. Meanwhile, each McMansion symbolizes the very overconsumption that is overwhelming the earth. They are architectural signs of an unbalanced life.

This march of marketecture represents a significant departure from the past. Prior to the market efficiencies of modern real estate development, individuals had a much greater say in the construction of their own surroundings. Since the distance between the consumer and the developer was often zero, towns were the collective result of individual action. The result was, not surprisingly, well-built homes and villages that people actually wanted to live in, and communities with a sense of place, a human scale. There were common architectural styles, like the Cape Cod, which drew communities together, but also a great deal of individual variation on a theme. Today the evidence for the attractiveness of this approach is the tourism that many of the old towns of America generate, from the former colonial ports on the East Coast (Newport, Annapolis, Charleston, Savannah) to Mendocino and Carmel on the West—all charming environments that have remained so by heavily regulating their central historic districts. As the Market has grown in efficiency, however, individuals have relinquished their own control over their surroundings to the Market's middleman, the developer, and hence, to the Market itself. From the mobile home to the tract home to the suburban development with four different styles of colonial to choose from, the home has become another external product, the result of choices made outside us, choices that do not respond to our needs or serve to uplift us as much as they fit us into a predefined, homogenized environment designed to extract as much money from us as possible. This not only subtracts from the aesthetics of our surroundings, it increasingly subtracts from their quality as well:

A gathering rumble can be heard across the [architectural] profession about the way America builds. The country has garnered a reputation for overlooking gaping joints, sloppy measurements and obvious blemishes, and refusing to deviate from even the most outmoded standardized practices. Having exported its expertise, in the 80's and early 90's, to destinations from Singapore to Dubai, it is now facing stiff competition from Europe and Asia, where the building traditions favor singularity, craftsmanship and durability over speed and cost.[20]

There are many exceptions to this trend, of course, including various attempts to try to re-create the village feel of the past and the resurgence of craftsmen. But by definition, sprawl is marketecture, and there is more sprawl in America than anything else—or anywhere else. The reason the word *development* has become a pejorative to so many people is that it is now synonymous with *market* development, in the same way that *progress* has come to mean material progress.

The marketscape that has emerged from this evolution is one of the great differences between America and Europe. The vast majority of European towns were laid out and constructed prior to the twentieth century. In contrast, over 80 percent of everything ever built in America has been constructed in the past fifty years. One reason Europe remains such a popular destination for American tourists is that by going there one can escape our suffocating sprawl and enjoy a more ancient, human environment, where all the roads and buildings haven't been built in a hypermarket. "There is one difference between America and the other First World nations, and that's sprawl," says travel writer Douglas Morris. "They have the violent video games, the television, the movies, the cell phones. They have all the material opulence that we do, but their physical landscape is still connected."[21]

Like stress, the human impact of sprawl is difficult to quantify. It is the root cause, or a contributing factor, in many adverse social effects. In human health, it has been linked to everything from obesity (all driving, no walking) to pollution (more auto emissions) to violence (social isolation). In the environmental movement, it is viewed as the terminal stage in ecosystem destruction. All of this would be mitigated, if not halted, by viewing development in the context of higher values. But that is precisely the balanced perspective that the Market fights at all times.

In its war against Nature, the Market uses the incremental strategy, just as it does with the spread of porn. As sprawl oozes across the countryside, people adapt, bit by bit, until one day the two-lane roads are all four, five, or six lanes, the scenery is all gone, and Main Street is one large franchise operation, serving a traffic jam. Along the way some people notice and put up a fight, and occasionally they even win, preventing Wal-Mart from dropping its mall-in-a-box in their backyard. But the reason sprawl continues to spread is that the power of the unbridled Market has so far overpowered most resistance. The source of the systemic inertia that prevents progress on global warming is the same one actively promoting the spread of sprawl. It is the gears of unbridled economic self-interest. If you put up legal roadblocks, it is amazing how many ways the sprawl lobby will discover to circumvent them. Those who wield the economic ax, it seems, are more powerful than those who would seek to deflect its blows. The individual is often thrust in the position of reacting too late, if he even has the time and money to get involved; meanwhile, out of sight, another incursion is under way. Vested interests are strong, well organized, and well rewarded; organized resistance is usually a nonprofit.

New Jersey, a state whose name has become synonymous with sprawl, is a prime example of the power of the sprawl lobby. Controlling sprawl is a universally popular idea in New Jersey, the most crowded state in the union. In his State of the State Address in January 2003, first-term governor James McGreevey promised to take on "those who profit from the strip malls and McMansions" and adopt the toughest antisprawl legislation in the nation. Within nine months, however, McGreevey was forced to abandon his Blueprint for Intelligent Growth in favor of "less controversial legislative and regulatory changes" after strong resistance from special interests, led by the New Jersey Builders Association, divided the legislature.[22] Meanwhile, the rest of the country continues to think of the "Garden State" as the exits off I-95.

The objective of this war, from the Market's standpoint, is to create a productive environment, a physical Bubble. By isolating people, sprawl atomizes society, turning people into discrete productive elements in a commercial landscape. To this end, sprawl is just a beginning, like the bulldozer leveling the forest for the tract homes. It is the preparatory stage to urbanization. As the bedroom communities extend farther out, business leaders decide to move their offices closer to home. Office buildings arise to meet demand, transforming the flat landscape of car dealers and doughnut shops into a rising skyline. The market temperature rises accordingly, changing the temper of society. The next thing you know, the local paper is talking about road rage and guns in school. The final stage of this evolution occurs when the stars go away, drowned in fluorescent light, signaling a narrowing of perspective. One can no longer see beyond the physical Bubble and ask the questions the stars require. The marketscape is a vast stadium that keeps your eyes focused on the game, 24/7.

But don't worry, if you want a star, you can always buy one. Really. If you go to www.yourstar.com, you can name your own star for $39.95. In return, you will get a certificate and a map showing its location in your chosen constellation. Even the heavens are now part of the sprawl.

## Annapolis: A Case Study

Annapolis, the capital of Maryland and the town in which I live, is a vivid example of the diverse issues surrounding sprawl. Annapolis has some great neighborhoods, one of the most successful being Epping Forest (www.eppingforest.org), which was established on a then-isolated peninsula on the Severn River, part of the Chesapeake Bay, in 1926. In those days, it was a long trip from Washington or Baltimore all the way out to the Atlantic Ocean, so Epping Forest, like several other nearby river communities, was a practical solution for a summer vacation. The community evolved as a family summer camp, with simple cottages connected by pathways, a beach, and a clubhouse, all located within a primary-growth forest of hundred-foot trees. Over the years the paths were paved, but their original twists and turns were retained, without sidewalks or curbs. The private clubhouse expanded, adding a marina (residents are offered a boat slip with their house), a bar and restaurant open throughout the summer, tennis courts, a summer camp for kids, a swim team, and a beach volleyball league. There is also a waterfront park and a picturesque, ecumenical chapel. Almost all the original summer cottages have now been winterized and expanded, but of some 250 homes, there is only one McMansion. After years of personal renovations, the houses have all taken on an individual flair, and no two look alike. Indeed, it is hard to find a plumb-and-square surface in some of them. There are relatively few community rules, but they include no fences without approval. Residents reflect a diverse socioeconomic mix, with some families staying through multiple generations.

Life in Epping is the original meaning of popular culture, a series of annual festivals, including the Christmas-tree lighting, the bull and oyster roasts, which take place on the beach, the Fourth of July golf-cart-and-wagon parade through the forest, the summer ice-cream cruise (a boat trip to down-town Annapolis), a full slate of Labor Day family events, and the winter home tour, affording residents the opportunity to check out their neighbor's cot-tage. All of this is on a take-it-or-leave-it basis (although the boat-club party is not to be missed). Most amazingly, the entire community is self-governed on a volunteer basis, creating lively community meetings that double as the-ater. Using a tax rebate from the county, Epping Forest Inc. operates its own water supply, plows its own roads, and even makes a small profit on the club-house, which serves to employ its teenagers. The community has benefited tremendously from the applied talents of its residents, including the many tradespeople who live there. Self-management has kept costs extraordinarily low. Annual dues, also known as the water bill, are under $500. A slip at the pier is only $400 a year—the monthly cost elsewhere—including the Hurri-cane Isabel damage premium. The summer camp is $75 per week. It is hard to imagine what one could reasonably expect to add to this picture, particularly when the community has fewer than one thousand people in it, except this: home prices have more than doubled in the past five years and now exist on a bell curve from $250,000 to almost $1 million (waterfront), excluding the McMansion. The average home is well under three thousand square feet.

So what is the underlying cause of this tremendous success? Why isn't Ep-ping Forest scarred with marketecture? Primarily because it is not the prod-uct of the Market. Epping Forest was not built by developers. It was built by its residents, people who valued the trees and the bay and focused on creating a great community for themselves, one step at a time. All in all, an extraordi-narily simple recipe, one that took a long time to mature, like a fine wine, but was worth the wait. Instead of sitting in their cookie-cutter suburban home dreaming of a McMansion and a Euro sedan, residents now get to spend an inordinate amount of time strolling through the forest, boating on the bay, and having dinner at the beach.

Two miles beyond the community entrance, however, a very different picture emerges. Between Epping Forest and downtown Annapolis lies an ar-chitectural horror. In a short ten years, the main roads have doubled in size, the fields and forests have been leveled, and marketecture has spread every-where. The monolithic Annapolis Mall has more than doubled in size, and three other large shopping areas have been built. The usual collection of chain stores, convenience stores, fast-food franchises, and service stations has arrived: Home Depot, Sam's Club, Staples, PetSmart, Best Buy, 7-Eleven, Office Depot, RadioShack, Safeway, Giant, Dunkin' Donuts, McDonald's (2), Burger King, Taco Bell, Red Lobster, Fuddruckers, Friday's, Pep Boys, Trak Auto, All Tune & Lube, Firestone, Exxon, Shell, Mobil, etc. etc. etc. ad nauseam. Two enormous townhouse developments, Harbor Gate and Sea Breeze, neither of which has either, now exist where a forest once stood. All told, several square miles have been transformed into one flat commercial-

TOP: Annapolis, MD: 18th and 19th century; BOTTOM: Annapolis, MD: 20th century.

ized space, paved with blacktop, lined with parking spaces, and punctuated by one colored flat-roofed box after another, all connected by overhead power lines and chain links of traffic, creating what my six-year-old son nicknamed a "trash road." Nor is the pace of change slowing. The largest project of them all, a 1.8-million-square-foot mall and apartment complex to be known as "Annapolis Towne Centre" is just taking off. Needless to say, it is a long way from the real town center, although with metaphorical flourish it will occupy the site of a former prison.

The great irony of this swath of aesthetic destruction is what lies at the other end: the historic district of Annapolis. Here one finds the largest collection of eighteenth-century buildings in America, and what is arguably the most charming Main Street as well, a brick thoroughfare, lined with wrought-iron lamps and hanging flower baskets, that begins with an Episcopal church straight out of the English countryside and slopes downhill through a row of shops to the Chesapeake Bay. When one digs into the historical causes of this pleasant facade, one finds that, while many buildings have been restored, almost all were built prior to the twentieth century. One also finds comprehensive planning. In 1694, Governor Francis Nicholson devised the city plan based on the Baroque capitals of Europe, with several sunburst patterns in the streets that serve to elevate the soul above the modern grid. So as one leaves this model of urban charm and enters the horror of the sprawl around it, it is not only a shift in location, but a change in eras, that one experiences. When one moves from the architecture of the eighteenth century to the twentieth, one can see, block by block, a regression into ugliness, the very ugliness that arises whenever the Market is put in charge of anything.

One local development that has been a great aesthetic success is Quiet Waters Park.[23] The public park was constructed on 340 acres of beautiful rolling land on the South River, another Chesapeake tributary. There is a six-mile bike trail that meanders through the woods, kayak rentals, an elegant Victorian visitor center with restaurant, a huge fountain that doubles as a skating rink, two children's playgrounds, a dog beach (for letting your dog swim, of course), scenic overlooks of the river, several pavilions for outdoor events, a formal garden with attractive sculpture, a wedding pavilion, and innumerable places for picnics, including a large gazebo sitting on an island in a pond. The entire ambience is one of refined elegance, a public estate. The only problem is, hardly anyone goes. On one absolutely beautiful day in June, I counted fewer than twenty cars at the park. On that same day, I lost count of cars at the Annapolis Mall. There were literally *hundreds* of cars at the mall, an enormous, air-conditioned white box with hardly a window.

But if you think about how the Bubble works, all this makes sense. No one serves to make money from an Epping Forest, which is run by volunteers, any more than they serve to make money from Quiet Waters Park, which is run by the county park service. So there is no advertising for either one. But if you add up the advertising for every store in the mall, from Nordstrom's to Hecht's to Banana Republic to GAP to every movie in the cineplex, the combined impact on the consumer is tremendous, certainly enough to generate social pressure. And if you pick up the real estate section in your local paper, you will not find ads for self-run communities. What you will find is page after page of townhouse communities, apartment communities, and suburban developments. These are environments that are ultimately constructed to maximize the profit of developers, rather than to maximize social happiness. And what they reveal is the deep nature of our market society, a society that is not set up to support an individual's life, but to prey upon him for financial gain—the essential difference between a civilization and an economy.

The sprawl that is afflicting Annapolis is endemic in the entire region, where Washington, D.C., Baltimore, and Annapolis are rapidly congealing into one continuous megalopolis. The Maryland Office of Planning estimates that in the period from 1995 to 2020, more land will be converted to housing in the region surrounding the Chesapeake Bay than in the past 350 years. According to the Chesapeake Bay Foundation, more than ninety thousand acres are consumed by sprawl each year in the bay states. With this sprawl has come declining air quality. The Baltimore–Washington area has been rated by the American Lung Association as the seventh worst metropolitan area in the United States. Maryland was once a national leader in anti-sprawl legislation, but like New Jersey, its ambitious Smart Growth program has been scaled back.

Our failure to stop sprawl has put tremendous pressure on the Chesapeake Bay, which receives agricultural runoff from deep into Pennsylvania, raising levels of nitrogen and phosphorus. In the past few years, we have experienced several Pfiesteria outbreaks, a fish disease that can be passed to humans, major fish kills, crabs coming to the surface for lack of oxygen, the appearance of an enormous dead zone in the center of the bay where no life can exist, the disappearance of 20 percent of the bay's grasses in a single year, and warnings not to eat certain species. In one double-edged announcement, the Department of the Environment opined that children and women of childbearing age could avoid significant health risks by limiting consumption of rockfish to one meal per month. Men could have two. Even the notorious Asian snakehead fish has now established itself in the Potomac. But people adjust. Most people don't know that the bay was crystal clear forty years ago, when enormous oyster beds were still alive to strain the water. They think it always looked like a can of turpentine, after you've cleaned the brush.

These changes were brought home to me one afternoon when my sons and I went fishing on a nearby pier. We noticed that some of the sunfish we were catching had funny red spots on their fins, but others didn't. My son had an aquarium, so he took a decent one home, where he put it in a tank by itself. A few days later we noticed a tendril hanging from one of its fins, but didn't think much of it. A few days after that, the fish was lying dead on the bottom. We scooped it up and placed it on a piece of newspaper. It appeared to be moving. This was because of the thousands of squirming parasites, small thin worms, that had eaten it inside and out.

## Theory Meets Reality

Academics and policy makers can argue about capitalism in the abstract all day long. Meanwhile there is undeniable, hard empirical evidence lying all around us that proves without a shadow of a doubt that something is decidedly wrong with free-market theory, particularly in lots where there are no trees. The reason is that sprawl, the product of the unbridled market, is an unmitigated disaster. With huge financial resources, a talent pool of over 200 million people, and a continent of breathtaking natural resources to work with, the best America has been able to do is strip malls, fast food, and bad air. "It could be much better," Paco Underhill writes of the mall, "more vivid, intelligent, adventurous, entertaining, imaginative, alive with the human quest for art and beauty and truth. But it's not. It's the mall." One could add, it's the suburb—and increasingly, the nation. The unbridled application of capitalism has created a world that is less and less livable with each passing day, a world created not for us, but for the economic system itself, at our expense. The "free market" sounds nice in theory, but it has failed the acid test: it doesn't work, at least not on its own.

As concrete evidence (no pun intended), sprawl debunks several myths of the Market, while illuminating the nature of the Market itself:

*The Market Is the Will of the People.* Clearly this is wrong, since sprawl is not what the people want. Who the heck wants to live in sprawl? Who likes ugliness, traffic, sameness? Yet sprawl is exactly what the Market has produced. The reason is that the Market is not the entire will of the people—it is only their *economic* will, a very different idea. It is the product of people thinking purely in terms of economic self-interest. Yet human beings are motivated by higher values, too. So the collective will of a society would have to take all such values into account. The Market cannot do that. As we have noted many times previously, and as many other observers have confirmed, the Market is purely amoral. Since human beings are not, the Market can never be a complete reflection of human desires. It is only half the picture: productivity without morality. By extension, the Market should never be considered "democratic," since democratic values are simply not its end.

*The Market Serves the Consumer.* Since no one wants to live in sprawl, the Market is not providing what the consumer wants. Instead, the Market is providing what the economy wants: a productive environment. As systems theory explains, the system has its own independent existence, and when it comes to the economic system, the Market is serving it, not us. When people go on vacation, they choose to go to national parks and historic districts for a reason: these are places that have been *protected* from the "free market," not enabled by it.

The idea that the Market responds to consumer choice is still true, but only partly so. Consumers also respond to the will of the Market, forming the other half of the feedback loop. The market-driven developer cannot create an environment so bad that you will not buy it. At the same time, he is not interested in providing you with the best possible environment to live in. He is trying to maximize his profit. So there is a balance of power between the consumer and the Market, between the individual and the assembly line, at all times. In these dynamics, profit does not equate with excellence. Like Wall Street banks, developers know that their misdeeds may cost them a few customers, and even a lawsuit or two, but the profit to be gained from cheaply made cookie-cutter homes is clearly worth it or it would not be happening. Aesthetic crime pays, just as financial crime pays. When it comes to malls, the hidden restrooms, the haphazard parking lots, the fortress exteriors, the bad lighting, the mediocre food, and the useless mall map are all good enough. Like the Bubble, they reflect a reduction to the mean, rather than an effort to lift a civilization to its highest potential. No one wins from this, since we all have to live in the result, including every shareholder in Taco Bell. Even real estate developers have to go to the mall sometimes.

This reality hit home personally when my wife and I were looking for our home in Annapolis. We were interested in a simple cottage on a wooded lot. We didn't see any of those in the paper. Instead, we were confronted with page after page of mass-produced center-hall colonials, the domestic equivalent of the office cubicle. Consumer choice, the vaunted benefit of the market economy, had been constrained by the development assembly line. Since then, I cannot count the number of people who have entered Epping Forest and said, "I never knew a place like this existed!" When one considers that the entire East Coast was once primary-growth forest, fully capable of supporting thousands of such affordable, human-centric communities, and the social problems they ameliorate, the opportunity cost is staggering.

The great irony of all marketecture is that there is no economic reason why it has to be so ugly. Certainly an oil company could afford to hire a great architect to design one attractive gas station before replicating it across the country. Similarly, there are boundless inexpensive yet attractive options to the tract home that could be built if their developers cared one iota about their impact on the individual and the community. Consider Rush Creek, a community of forty-nine houses in a wooded area near Columbus, Ohio. Built in Frank Lloyd Wright's organic style, which seeks to integrate a house into nature, the homes have attracted a religious following, yet the average size is only two thousand square feet. "Without getting grandiose about it, we look at our house as a work of art," one resident says. "We're here for life." Another adds, "This house is sculpture in another dimension." Recent prices ranged from about $250,000 to around $350,000, about a 25 percent premium over conventional local houses.[24] The model for Rush Creek is Wright's Usonian houses, which the great architect designed as an affordable alternative for the American middle class—over half a century ago. So I ask you, what would you prefer to live in, another center-hall colonial, or one of the many variations of the Usonian house, designed by America's greatest architect?

*The Individual Pursuit of Economic Self-Interest Leads to Collective Good.* Clearly this isn't true, either, because sprawl is the result of individuals pursuing their economic self-interest. On the other hand, this does not imply that individuals should always be held accountable for the negatives associated with sprawl. Many problems are the cumulative result of relatively innocent individual actions. The destruction of an ecosystem occurs one tree at a time—but is everyone who took down a tree responsible for the destruction of the ecosystem? Is the individual who buys a suburban home these days responsible for the growth of cookie-cutter suburbs? This kind of incrementalism reveals the independence of the system, where the sum is greater than the parts. The Market is quite capable of creating a collective nightmare for which few are to blame. Such adverse effects require that communities be particularly vigilant about what is being created around them. Yet this is precisely the approach that is undermined by excessive faith in economic self-interest.

When you cut through the ideology, economic self-interest is really an excuse for selfishness, for indifference to society, for rejecting higher values. It is the doctrinal rationale for "anything goes." The simple fact is that collective acts of selfishness do not magically produce good, particularly when you factor in the quality of the lives that are being lived on a daily basis in such a system, rather than merely looking at the impersonal economic results: the size of the malls built, the number of burgers sold, and our favorite metric, the GDP. You don't create a civilization worth calling one without citizens who see that as a common goal. The "free market" is simply incapable of providing what a combination of aesthetic education, sound planning, *and* the Market can achieve, when properly balanced.

The entire idea that unbridled self-interest creates "Good" is made patently false, and farcically so, when one considers the countless stories of what actually happens when greed is considered good. There is no corrupting force more powerful than the unbridled Market, as the Nature Conservancy can attest. If ever there was an organization established to resist the adverse effects of the Market, the world's largest and most well funded environmental organization should be it. And certainly the people at the top of that organization, its board of directors, would be the ones most likely to ensure that this was so. And yet in 2003, the Nature Conservancy was caught selling undeveloped land to its trustees for home sites and giving them interest-free loans to buy them. Now there is the Market at work.

*The Market Liberates the Individual.* This is the most insidious claim of the "free market" because it appears unassailable. But like many aspects of the Market, a close look reveals that the truth is not so black and white. The market*place* may be free, in the sense that you can enter and leave at will, buy what you want, and even create your own company, but the Market itself, the force that arises from all the economic self-interest displayed in the marketplace, could care less about your freedom, and will happily cage you in sprawl if it will make the economy more productive.

Those who see the Market as the source of their freedom commonly attack all other forms of authority, from other individuals to professions to governments, thereby putting their faith in a force that is purely amoral. Ironically, this is actually the death of the individual, not his salvation. The only free individual is one who is free to express a moral, aesthetic, or cultural opinion, and the only way to inject that judgment into the world is to give that individual the appropriate authority to do so. Like suburban development, authority should only be rejected in its bad form, otherwise all the benefits of wise authority are lost. The timeless challenge is thus to create institutions and professions that elevate the best among us so that we maximize the wisdom at the top. That takes hard work, but such institutional mechanisms are what elevate a civilization, rather than pound it into barbarism. The assumption that the Market should perform such a role is not only patently false, it reflects a lack of faith in the individual and the social institutions he commands. "Who are you to tell me what to do?" asks the libertarian, overlooking the fact that there will always be people more qualified to make certain judgments than others—if we can only identify and promote them. Meanwhile, the system in which he places his faith is only too happy to tell us all what to do, and how to live, to cast a Bubble around our minds that separates us from reality, and to build a physical environment that separates us from nature, while destroying it at the same time. Tyranny does not just flow from individuals, it arises just as easily from the Market.

# 7. The Ozone Hole

Car dealer, Maryland.

It was a war of each against all, and the devil take the hindmost. . . . You went about with your soul full of suspicion and hatred; you understood that you were environed by hostile powers that were trying to get your money, and who used all the virtues to bait their traps with. . . . The great corporation which employed you lied to you, and lied to the whole country—from top to bottom it was nothing but one gigantic lie.

—Upton Sinclair, *The Jungle*

If you want to understand the nature of the Market, the natural destination is Wall Street. There the power of the Market is as great as anyplace else on Earth. With millions of dollars at stake every day, the environment inside a securities firm, or on a trading floor, is like a crucible, burning away any other principles but market principles, any other forces but market forces, any other values but market values. It is an ongoing orgy of selection. Consequently, Wall Street represents the best laboratory imaginable for studying the impact of the unbridled Market on society, and may even be viewed as a predictor of where a society is headed, once it surrenders to it.

It may seem like ancient history today, but not long ago Wall Street traders were playing a gentleman's game. As late as the 1980s, there were still strong bonds between employees and their firms. This created distinct corporate

identities, some strengthened by ethnicity, which encouraged a sense of be-
longing. Even entire markets enjoyed a sense of community. Before the boom
years of the eighties, the U.S. Government Market, the largest bond market of
them all, comprised only a hundred and fifty traders, all of whom knew one
another, forming an extended family in which entrance was gained through
nepotism or friendship. Each year the entire market had a party for the holi-
days. Traders came in at nine thirty, got going around ten, started wrapping
up at three thirty, and left at four. If things got slow, they played cards. Within
the firm, everyone was on the same team. Competition existed mainly between firms. But even there limits prevailed. Other firms wouldn't dare poach
your employees, for example; it was considered out of character.

This was all incredibly inefficient, of course, from the Market's perspective. If traders were loyal to their firm, they couldn't be attracted to a new
firm where they might be needed. If firms were loyal to their employees, they
could not be so easily fired. At all levels, there were human bonds holding
society together, bonds that were fundamentally moral, not economic. So
the Market proceeded to cut them. Productivity was maximized when each
man had to look out for himself—when there was risk on his head and no
place to hide.

The catalyst for this transformation was the stock-market crash of 1987.
In its wake, Wall Street employees were fired by the thousands; by the end of
1990 the securities industry had cut 20 percent of its employees. People who
had come up through the ranks and served at a firm for twenty-five years
suddenly found themselves out in the street. High-salaried people in their
forties and fifties were thrown out in favor of cheaper bodies in their twenties. Meanwhile, senior executives continued to take home $3 million to $8
million pay packages. Company loyalty was never the same again. The team
players of yesterday gave way to free agents and mercenaries to whom firms
were nothing more than places to hang your hat, collections of electronics
whose history and culture were irrelevant. Instead of making an investment
in people and promoting from within, management became a matter of hir-
ing superstars from the free-agent pool and keeping them happy. Employees
became contractual commodities purchased or discarded as the Market de-
manded, and only as good as their last trade. Like professional athletes, the
life span of these traders depended on their continued ability to compete
against the rookies. The best were greatly rewarded for it; the rest weren't. Or-

ganizations were run by a few insiders taking home immense pay packages. Wealth was not something to be built through a joint effort, through team-work in the firm, and shared with others, but by seizing power with a small group of insiders and leveraging the rest. Business was nothing but oppor-tunism, in which you seized on short-term opportunities, maximized your profit from them, and moved on. Nothing was built to last. Executives did not lead, they exploited and preyed upon those below them: This was their right. Trading was a zero-sum game, in which profit always came at the expense of someone.

As this winner-take-all society broke out, the temperature of the trading floor began to rise. Pressure intensified, driving everyone into their corner, and civility evaporated. People starting moving faster, talking faster, and get-ting more emotional. They screamed at each other with more frequency. They swore at each other. They threatened each other. They threw things at each other. Occasionally they even hit each other. This state of nature quickly became the norm. New people forgot what it used to be like on the desk be-cause they had never seen otherwise. People came in during their twenties and were burned out by thirty-five. Health problems among traders rose dra-matically, though few discussed it publicly, for fear of giving someone else a competitive edge. Some turned to drink, others to drugs, others to antide-pressants. The trading floor became the embodiment of Darwinism. It was the closest thing on Earth to a pure market society, if *society* is even the right word for it.[1]

At the deepest level, what the Market had done was alter the way people relate to one another. The intensity of the market environment changed their values, in the same way military basic training breeds soldiers. One could even see this transformation take place in a microcosm, with certain new recruits. They would enter the trading floor with the traditional values of American society, the values of the middle-class home, and in a larger sense, of the Judeo-Christian tradition, and be transformed in short order into very different people, or be forced out. Do not bring your moral code in here, the Market said. We play by the Market Code.

This critical transformation began, as it does today, with the redefinition of good and evil. The Market does not respect the idea of good, which is in-nately moral, as there are many instances where what is good is downright unprofitable. Good is an ideal, and the Market is purely pragmatic: it only cares about what works. Good and evil thus morph into profit and loss. The distinction between truth and lie likewise disappears. The victors write history, in the Market's view. So one should say, or do, whatever is necessary in order to win, making truth a matter of effectiveness. Similarly, justice has no meaning to the Market, because might makes right. Justice is thus equivalent to power. The Market has no concept of beauty, either, apart from its economic value. Van Gogh never sold a painting—so he was worthless. The only thing that is aesthetically pleasing to the Market is an efficient business, a mechanism sculpted so perfectly that it consistently creates more economic value. Love and hate are also unknown to the Market. If the Market needs to bind two elements together, it uses a legal contract. This ensures performance. If there is a failure to perform, the Market simply advises breaking the contract. Underlying this idea is the principle of cynicism. To the Market, courage is the strength to be selfish no matter what. Finally, the Market redefines meaning as money. Since money is the only criterion of value, it has to define all meaning, and that is that.

The end result of this remarkable transformation is a set of principles that you will not find on any trading floor, just as you will not find it on any corporate wall, or in any Constitution. It is the unwritten Scripture of the market society:

> Good is Profit
>
> Truth is Effectiveness
>
> Beauty is Efficiency
>
> Love is Performance
>
> Courage is Selfishness
>
> Justice is Power
>
> Meaning is Money

As this Market Code takes over, one of the first symptoms, quite naturally, is a confusion in terms. For example, you begin to hear people talk about "success" without making any distinction between a moral success and a financial success. Instead, getting rich becomes success itself. Likewise, a lack of distinction arises between a financial decline and a moral decline, economic prosperity and human happiness, financial power and moral authority, material progress and spiritual progress, market value and moral value, market principles and moral principles, market failure and moral failure, net worth and moral worth, and economic poverty and spiritual poverty. Under extreme circumstances, the distinction between what is moral and productive is completely lost. So it is that greed becomes good.

## Playahs

In order to understand the power of the Market Code, one need only consider the impact of September 11 on some of our financial elite. If ever there was an event tailor-made to shock an individual out of the Market's spell, the destruction of the World Trade Center was it. And yet in several noteworthy cases, this is not what happened at all. Consider this article, which appeared in *The New York Times* on September 16, 2001:

As smoke filled the skies above Manhattan on Tuesday, with most of the nation still paralyzed by the horror of watching the World Trade Center's twin towers collapse, almost seven miles north in a Midtown office building, Alan S. Weil was calling his landlord.

Like millions of other people, Mr. Weil had been stunned by the images on television—more than most, however, since along with the Midtown offices, his law firm occupied five floors of 1 World Trade Center. As many as 600 of his friends and colleagues at the law firm, Sidley Austin Brown & Wood, might have been lost in the catastrophe.

Once Mr. Weil received word that most of the staff had gotten out safely, his relief was tainted by a chilling thought: if his 135-year-old firm was going to recover, he would have to act quickly.

Within three hours of the twin towers' collapse, that call to the landlord had secured leases on four additional floors in the Midtown building for his dispossessed lawyers and staff. By the end of that day, others within the firm had arranged for the immediate delivery of 800 desks, 300 computers and cell phones by the hundreds; contractors were hired to string cables to expand the firm's computer network.

"It's just amazing what you can get in New York overnight," said Thomas R. Smith Jr., vice chairman of the firm's management committee and head of what was its World Trade Center offices.[2]

Now let's put this in perspective. It is but an hour or so after the twin towers have fallen. America is paralyzed. Graphic images of over twenty-seven hundred people being crushed to death are on every TV channel. One of our great national landmarks had just been destroyed. There has been a simultaneous attack on the Pentagon. Fighter jets are patrolling overhead. No one knows if another strike is imminent. In such a situation, one might expect a normal human reaction to be tracking down all your fellow partners and employees, the people you pass in the hall every day, and to worry about the city you call home, a city now covered in ash, its shoeless residents streaming across the Brooklyn Bridge. Instead, Alan Weil is focused on getting new office space.

As the rest of the article relates, shortly after the attack Weil received a call from John Connolly, his director of administration, who had fled the World Trade Center just in time to avoid his death. It must have been a dramatic conversation ("I am seeing burn victims whose skin is hanging off," Connelly told the *Times*, fighting back sobs. "I'm seeing women whose hair is singed and burned off their heads"). He tells Weil that their employees "seemed to have left the building safely"—and given the chaos in the hours after the collapse, in which phone lines were overwhelmed, one can certainly understand his uncertainty about the whereabouts of six hundred people. But with "most" of his employees safe, Weil decides he has more pressing matters to attend to, like getting an edge in an already shrinking real estate market. Three hours later, he has got the jump on everyone and secured four new furnished floors, a superhuman feat. And what were his motives? "Trying to keep the firm alive," as the *Times* kindly put it. However, given the fact that 135-year-old Sidley Austin Brown & Wood was at that time the fourth largest law firm in America, with thirty-three hundred people worldwide, and that it was heavily insured, including an art collection valued at $1.5 million, one suspects that this noble crowd of seven-figure salaries could easily have taken a day off to reflect on the worst national disaster since Pearl Harbor, particularly when their office was destroyed by it.

September 11 doesn't seem to have changed the modus operandi of Howard Lutnick, either. As you may remember, Lutnick was (and is) the CEO of Cantor Fitzgerald, which occupied some of the top floors of One World Trade Center. When that building collapsed, Lutnick lost 658 of his employees, more than any other company, and barely escaped with his own life. Late for work that day, he watched the tower fall, killing scores of people he knew, including his own brother.

A few days later, in a tear-filled interview with Connie Chung, Lutnick promised to take care of the families of all his employees. This sounded like a truly noble commitment, and a real turnaround for Lutnik, who had a reputation on Wall Street for brutal business dealings. As *The New York Times* put it in 1996, Cantor had "an office culture that makes Oliver Stone's vision of Wall Street look beatific by comparison." Then, two days after the interview, Lutnick, whose net worth was estimated at over half a billion dollars, cut off all payments to the families of the dead. A media firestorm struck him, led by both Chung and Bill O'Reilly, who claimed that Lutnick's tears had been nothing but a public-relations stunt. By early October Lutnick had reversed his position and created a new and generous financial plan for families, some of whom had gone to the media with stories of how untrustworthy Lutnick was. Lutnick later explained that he had cut off the payments "Because I needed my bankers to know that I was in control. That I wasn't sentimental and that I was no less motivated or driven to make my business survive."[3] Further fighting broke out between the firm and the families over issues like reimbursement for lost vacation time and bonuses. Cantor then took the remarkable step of suing the 9/11 Victim Compensation Fund, set up to help the families of the dead. Among Cantor's many claims: the family of a young trader should receive $5 million for lost income, not $3 million, while the grant of an additional $250,000 for pain and suffering was "woefully inadequate." Compare this with the benefits the U.S. government pays out for casualties of war: about $225,000, mostly in life insurance, plus a $10,000 annual pension for widows.

In the midst of these battles, Lutnick set out to write a book on his post-9/11 experiences with his college buddy, writer Tom Barbash, to help clear his damaged reputation. Though Barbash clearly set out to craft a sympathetic portrait, a *New York Times* reviewer found that "Throughout the book, Lutnick's unwavering focus is almost unnerving, particularly since it seems nearly identical to the way he operated before Sept. 11. He does not seem racked with survivor's guilt, or to have experienced any second thoughts about a life spent in relentless pursuit of money. To the contrary, the profit motive has been transformed, for Lutnick, into a source of redemption."[4]

In the two years since 9/11, this peculiar "source of redemption" has spawned a rather long legal record. In November 2001, Cantor was sued by Dow Jones, owners of *The Wall Street Journal*, for breach of contract, and to end their business relationship. In the spring of 2002, experts in the advertising industry accused the firm of exploiting the tragedy of 9/11 in a series of television commercials, in which Cantor employees were filmed talking about their experiences.[5] In the summer of 2002 a British High Court judge issued a split ruling in an ugly suit brought by Cantor against rival firm Icap, claiming that Icap had poached three of its employees in a deliberate attempt to weaken Cantor in the wake of 9/11. Two Cantor brokers charged they had been bullied into leaving the firm; one testified that a senior Cantor manager had wiped spit on his face (ironically, the case mirrored one brought against Cantor in 1999, when Cantor was found guilty of poaching twenty brokers from Icap's predecessor[6]). In October 2002, Municipal Partners, a former unit of Cantor, filed an arbitration complaint with the National Association of Securities Dealers against Cantor and Lutnick, accusing them of anticompetitive business practices and for failing to honor the terms of a contract between them. In the suit, Municipal (which lost twenty-six of its thirty employees on 9/11) charged that Cantor "continues to wrongfully retain fees and revenues that . . . do not belong to Cantor."[7] In May of 2003, Cantor Fitzgerald was sued by the property owner of the World Trade Center, Larry Silverstein, for failing to pay its last month's rent prior to 9/11, even though all other major tenants of the towers had done so. The outstanding bill was over $1 million. In August 2003, a British judge awarded $1.5 million to former Cantor derivatives trader Stephen Horkulak, who accused the firm of psychological abuse, forcing his premature resignation. The judge found that Horkulak's boss, Brooklyn native Lee Amaitis, constantly shouted and swore at him. Horkulak even claimed that Amaitis called him at home during his daughter's birthday party and threatened to "break him in two." Cantor stood by Amaitis, claiming he was "a proven leader with tremendous energy and fortitude" whose style was appropriate to the trading floor.[8] In the fall of 2003, Cantor began negotiating to buy a new building one block from Wall Street, signaling its return to the downtown area. Cantor had already successfully lobbied a sympathetic U.S. Congress for a special appropriation for companies that had suffered heavy loss of life on 9/11: $24 million of that $33 million appropriation went to Cantor, which had further been earmarked for an additional $6 million from the federal fund to rebuild lower Manhattan. But the total $30 million award was not enough for Lutnick, who began demanding an ever-larger array of subsidies from New York City as well. As one former city administrator put it, "With all due respect for the enormous loss of life at Cantor, the company shouldn't trade on the horrors of 9/11 to get an unconscionable windfall for a single company." [9]

United We Stand.

Finally, how can we forget Dick Grasso, the former president of the New York Stock Exchange? Five days after the 9/11 attacks, the entire world watched as Grasso reopened the shell-shocked exchange for business, a richly symbolic act. The New York Stock Exchange is the nerve center of American capitalism, presiding over 90 percent of the stock trades in the country. With the World Trade Center gone, it had become the preeminent symbol of American capitalism as well, its front entrance draped in an enormous American flag. Around the world, TVs zoomed in on a familiar scene, the famous trading floor we frequently see on the nightly news. Only this time, the specialists in their multicolored coats were not screaming prices at one another, they were focused on Grasso, who stood near the opening bell. At nine thirty, Grasso bowed his head for two minutes of silence. When that was through, he sang "God Bless America" with the rest of the traders. At that moment, Dick Grasso became a new global symbol of America. He was even dubbed "the President of Capitalism."

Within two years, however, the NYSE was mired in scandal. Supposedly self-regulating, it was revealed in 2003 to be an insider operation set up to benefit its directors and the firms they represented. Investigators discovered blatant security violations had been ignored, and that investors had been pickpocketed on over 2 billion trades in the previous three years. The entire exchange had become a casino rigged for the profits of the house. This came as no surprise: since the entire function of the NYSE could be better performed by a computer, what else was its purpose but to enrich those who ran it? The icing on this corrupt cake was Grasso himself, whose combined compensation package was publicly revealed to be $187.5 million, forcing his resignation. Indeed, it turned out that his board of directors had awarded him a special $5 million bonus for his post-9/11 efforts to get the exchange back up on its feet. Not a bad windfall for a terrorist attack.

Grasso was subsequently deposed, but he made an enlightening appearance in January 2004 when Kappa Delta Phi, a secret Wall Street society of some 250 current and former senior executives, held its annual black-tie dinner at the St. Regis Hotel in Manhattan. In attendance were New York mayor Michael Bloomberg, founder of the Bloomberg financial information service, whose name is on every trading desk in the world, and Bloomberg's companion, Diana Taylor, who was being inducted into the group. As part of the induction process, Taylor and several others donned mock prison garb and began lampooning their audience with various skits and songs focused on the past year of Wall Street scandals. Some of the biggest laughs were had at the expense of Grasso, who sat laughing in the audience along with several of his former board members.[10] In a Hollywood ending, Taylor was subsequently made the superintendent of banks for the State of New York.

Today when I think of the great *playahs* of Gotham, and how blind they are to the rest of human society, what comes to mind is a New York City firefighter. He is some middle-class kid from the Bronx, climbing the infinite stairs of the World Trade Center, sweating profusely, lugging some heavy rescue equipment over his shoulder. It is an image etched in all of our minds. Yet for our society to work, this image must make sense to all of us—and today it does not. To the financial elite in their tall towers, that kid was like the doorman or the security guard, another business expense. Worse, he just didn't get *the way things are* in the market society. He was foolishly serving others when he should have been serving himself. He had failed to adopt the Market Code. And in their minds, that made him fair game.

## The Criminal Element

Now that we have seen the nature of the Market Code, and its tenacious grip on the human mind, it should not be surprising that the chief association one makes with the term *Wall Street* today, and American finance in general, is crime. One needs to look no further than the tapes

## Major Wall Street Fines in the Two Years Following 9–11 Attack

2003
**Sept. 4 | Goldman Sachs | $9.3 million**
Improper trading in U.S. Treasury securities and futures.
**Aug. 14 | SG Cowen, Lehman Brothers | $7.5 million**
Failure to supervise a rogue stock broker.
**July 28 | Citigroup, J.P. Morgan Chase | $305 million**
Financial misconduct pertaining to financial structures created for Enron.
**April 30 | Visa USA and MasterCard International | $3 billion**
Forcing retailers to accept higher fees.
**March 20 | Merrill Lynch | $6 million**
Involvement in collapse of Askin Capital Management.
**Feb. 20 | J.P. Morgan Chase | $6 million**
Profit sharing and tie-in trades related to initial public offerings.
**Feb. 20 | Merrill Lynch | $80 million**
Financial misconduct pertaining to financial structures created for Enron.
**Jan. 9 | FleetBoston Financial | $33 million**
Improper profit sharing related to initial public offerings during 1999 and 2000.
2002
**Dec. 31 | Bank One | $1.3 million**
Improper telemarketing practices in 28 states.
**Dec. 30 | U.S. Bancorp | $32.5 million**
Fraudulent stock research during technology boom.
**Dec. 20 | Bear Stearns, Credit Suisse Group, Deutsche Bank, Goldman Sachs, J.P. Morgan Chase, Lehman Brothers, Merrill Lynch, Morgan Stanley, Citigroup, UBS | $1.335 billion**
Fraudulent stock research during technology boom.
**Dec. 3 | Goldman Sachs, Morgan Stanley, Citigroup, Deutsche Bank, U.S. Bancorp | $8.25 million**
Violating e-mail record-keeping requirements.
**Oct. 11 | Household International | $484 million**
Largest predatory lending settlement in history.

**Oct. 2 | Bank of America | $490 million**
Misrepresented financial statements in NationsBank merger.
**Sept. 23 | Citigroup | $5 million**
Publishing misleading research.
**Sept. 19 | Citigroup | $215 million**
Predatory lending.
**Sept. 5 | Deutsche Bank | $58 million**
Manipulating market during acquisition of Bankers Trust.
**July 26 | FINOVA Group | $47.5 million**
Misleading financial statements.
**June 17 | American Express | $31 million**
Gender discrimination.
**May 30 | The Metris Companies | $5.6 million**
Unauthorized fees and charges.
**May 21 | Merrill Lynch | $100 million**
Publishing misleading research.
**March 27 | Providian Financial | $38 million**
False and misleading statements by executives.
**Jan. 17 | Credit Suisse Group | $100 million**
Charging extraordinary commissions on trades linked to IPOs.
**Jan. 7 | Knight Trading Group | $1.5 million**
Trading violations.
2001
**Dec 7 | American Express | $15 million**
Misclassifying full-time employees for tax benefits.
**Nov. 7 | Providian Financial | $105 million**
Unauthorized fees and charges,
**Oct. 12 | Bank of Bermuda | $65 million**
Raising money under false pretenses.

Total: $6,586,850,000

from the Enron trading floor to understand the culture the unbridled Market has created:

> One energy trader gloats about cheating "poor grandmothers." Another suggests shutting down a power plant in order to drive up electricity prices. A third, hearing of a fire under a transmission line that caused a power failure, shouts "burn baby, burn." . . . An exhaustive study released by the Federal Energy Regulatory Commission in March 2003 confirmed what everyone had long suspected—that Enron and other major energy companies manipulated California's energy markets in 2000 and 2001 in ways that cost the state billions. Now comes the most graphic evidence yet of the cynicism and ruthlessness with which Enron's floor traders, presumably with the endorsement of their superiors, rigged the market. The evidence is in taped conversations among Enron traders, obtained from the Justice Department by a public utility district near Seattle that wants to recover what it says are $2 billion in unjust profits. The tapes, which CBS broadcast last week, are remarkable not only for their cynicism but also their raw profanity—the average energy trader appears to have a vocabulary consisting of a half-dozen obscenities as well as "cool," "wow" and "awesome." [11]

Certainly financial crime is nothing new, as the old saying "Wall Street bilks Main Street" reveals. But what *is* new today is the nature, scope, and efficiency of that crime, the wholesale adoption of it as a common business practice, the types of people involved in it, and the sheer audacious scale of it. Since the early nineties, we have seen Salomon Brothers defraud the United States Treasury, Merrill Lynch bankrupt the largest county in America (Orange County, California), and virtually all the major Wall Street banks—including Bear Stearns, Credit Suisse, Deutsche Bank, Goldman Sachs, J.P. Morgan Chase, Lehman Brothers, Merrill Lynch, Morgan Stanley, Citigroup, and UBS Warburg—plead guilty to providing phony stock research to the entire American public, a massive fraud that fueled the technology boom and helped drive the entire U.S. economy uncomfortably close to deflation. We have even had a *global* investment boom fueled by more Wall Street "research." This was the emerging-markets boom in the mid-nineties, which involved the entire world's developing countries and culminated in the collapse of the Mexican peso, not to mention a $20 billion bailout of U.S. taxpayer money. More recently on the home front we had another boom, the explosion of Enron, a most elaborate fraud that was partly engineered by Merrill Lynch, Citigroup, and J.P. Morgan Chase; while the horizon of criminal finance has extended to encompass the entire mutual-fund industry, where large clients have been timing the market at the expense of small investors. And given this den of thieves, it was only a matter of time before the mob entered the cave. As *BusinessWeek* reporter Gary Weiss revealed in *Born to Steal: When the Mafia Hit Wall Street:*

> Although organized crime had participated in a smattering of stock scams years before, never had "wise guys" actually established and run brokerage firms. In the 1990s, firmly encamped in lower Manhattan, the six New York area crime families took a hefty chunk of the $10 billion-a-year trade in grossly overpriced microcap stocks. By the end of the millennium, Wall Street had become a leading Mafia cash cow.[12]

One of the reasons for the persistent crime wave on Wall Street is that rogue banks continue to operate unchecked year after year, my former employer Merrill Lynch being the best example. In 1995, Merrill Lynch was implicated in the collapse of Orange County, California, the largest municipal bankruptcy in American history. The people of Orange County, California, simply woke up one morning to discover that their entire county, including all public school systems, public works, trash collection, and the rest of the machinery that keeps the largest county in America going, was bankrupt, and that this bankruptcy occurred almost completely at the hands of Merrill Lynch, including several of its trading desks, its investment banking arm, senior management, and a salesman, Michael Stamenson, who had already been directly involved in a similar scandal in San Jose. Merrill Lynch ended up paying a $400 million fine to settle the charges against it, which has had no apparent impact on its modus operandi. In the past few years, Merrill has been instrumental in many other highly public scandals. It played a central role in the Enron fiasco, costing it another $80 million in fines. It was one of the chief targets of the federal investigation into Wall Street business practices, pled guilty to providing phony stock research to the public, and paid a $200 million fine. It was sued by over twenty-eight hundred of its female employees over sexual discrimination, settled with them, and then was sued again for not living up to the terms of the settlement. Henry Blodget, the champion of the $400 Internet stock, worked at Merrill, as did Peter Bacanovic, Martha Stewart's broker.

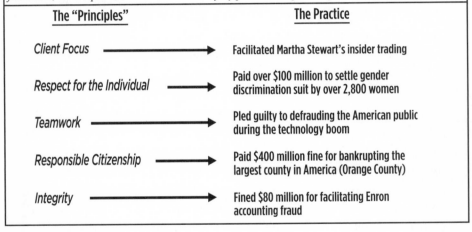

### More Bull: "The Merrill Lynch Principles"

*From the Merrill Lynch Web site: "The Merrill Lynch Principles are the foundation for our actions as leaders, colleagues, employees and citizens. Our commitment to guide our individual and organizational conduct by the Principles helps us in achieving status as one world-class company. As Merrill Lynch grows evermore diverse and global, the Principles will help us to define further who we are, what we believe and what we aspire to be for ourselves, our clients and stakeholders. As with any framework, the Principles—while rooted in history and tradition—are evolving with our business. As a community we share the belief that the Principles are a sound framework, but the question remains, "How do we fully put the Principles into practice?..."*

| The "Principles" | The Practice |
| --- | --- |
| Client Focus | Facilitated Martha Stewart's insider trading |
| Respect for the Individual | Paid over $100 million to settle gender discrimination suit by over 2,800 women |
| Teamwork | Pled guilty to defrauding the American public during the technology boom |
| Responsible Citizenship | Paid $400 million fine for bankrupting the largest county in America (Orange County) |
| Integrity | Fined $80 million for facilitating Enron accounting fraud |

The reason for this decade-long rap sheet is that our banks are more powerful than our government. Banks like Merrill keep committing their crimes and paying their fines, year after year, because they know our government won't stop them. The inevitable fines the regulators mete out, while seemingly large to the man on the street, are a mere pittance to these institutions. Merrill's $200 million settlement over phony research, for instance, represents less than *two days* of Merrill's revenue in 2000, when the technology boom was in full swing. Likewise, the "unprecedented" $1.4 billion settlement over corrupt business practices by all the major Wall Street firms, which was broadcast as a major triumph, represents only 2.4 percent of the $58 billion in pretax income these banks earned in 2000. Not much of a deterrent there. On Wall Street, crime has become just another form of risk to be evaluated, a matter of potential gain versus the costs of lawyers and fines. And when you compare Merrill's legal record with its corporate profits, you will certainly reach the inescapable conclusion that crime pays.

Compare this with Japan. When Japanese regulators discovered that Citigroup's Private Bank Group had violated the law, they simply shut them down. "A number of acts injurious to public interests, serious violations of laws and regulations, and extremely inappropriate transactions were uncovered at the Private Bank Group, which led us to conclude that continued future operations are inappropriate," wrote the Japanese Financial Services Agency in its order.[13]

Can we invite them here?

## The Wall Street Nation

The corruption of our economy is not limited to Wall Street, of course. As the temperature of the hypermarket has risen, it has spread out from its financial epicenter like a virus, encompassing not only New York, but America as well. In an extraordinary article in the *New York Times* called "City of Schemes" (for which that paper deserves great credit), Kurt Andersen eloquently exposed this connection, which has otherwise remained one of the great overlooked facts of our time:

> If you have to choose the primary breeding ground for the various business misdeeds now consuming national attention, New York, I'm afraid, is the place. . . . No matter where they are, lines of blame for the companies' current circumstances lead straight back to our city. And it's disingenuous to pretend otherwise . . . if infectious greed is the virus, New York is the center of the outbreak. . . . It was New York investment bankers who drove the mergers-and-acquisitions deal culture of the eighties and nineties and who most aggressively oversold the myth of synergy that justified it. It was New York investment bankers and their Wall Street brothers who trained a generation of obedient American CEOs (by means of stock-option-based compensation) to worry more about jacking up their share prices in the short term than about running their companies well for the long haul. It was they who permitted the

digital technology giddiness of the late nineties to spread beyond Silicon Valley; Palo Alto venture capitalists may have doled out most of the initial .com money, but it was New York investment bankers who took all those companies public for billions of dollars, thus enabling the national festival of greed. It was they who created an inherently corrupt equities research establishment. It was they—with their lawyers at the big New York firms—who invented the novel financial architectures of Enron and WorldCom, just as it was the New York consulting firm McKinsey & Co. that provided Enron with its egregiously go-go, ultra-fast-company ideology.

Moreover, it was the example of New York investment bankers, earning gigantic salaries for doing essentially nothing—knowing the right people, talking smoothly, showing up at closings—that encouraged business people out in the rest of America to feel entitled to smoke-and-mirrors cash bonanzas of their own.

New Yorkers didn't create the digital technology mania of the nineties. But while nearly all of the real achievements of the Wired Decade . . . were accomplished by people elsewhere, it was New Yorkers who made the scramble for instant wealth the endeavors' overriding purpose.[14]

It is hard to comprehend the full implications of this passage. Essentially what Andersen is saying is that the market elite in New York, led by the Wall Street investment banks, and supported by armies of corrupt lawyers and accountants, advertising and PR firms, have been preying upon the rest of the country. This is a description of a city without a soul, a prerequisite for the Market's capital. And who could be a more perfect symbol for such a place than its billionaire mayor, Mike Bloomberg, who not only made his fortune in the world of trading, but who invented the very financial information service that now sits atop the desk of every trader in the world? Not even Tom Wolfe would have been bold enough to invent a character like that.

Our new Wall Street Nation clearly had a long gestation, but its birth date was late 2001, when the Enron bubble finally burst. Since then we have seen an unequaled parade of corporate scandals on a scale never before seen in the United States, a crime wave involving some of our largest corporations that has yet to end. Consider the major corporate scandals that erupted in just the eighteen-month period following January 2002:

## Major U.S. Corporate Scandals, January 2002–June 2003[15]

| Company | Scandal |
| --- | --- |
| Abbott Laboratories | $622 million settlement for sales practices encouraging fraud of Medicare and Medicaid. |
| Adelphia Communications | Racketeering by Rigas family, including fraud, conspiracy, misuse of funds. |
| AES | Inflating revenues to bolster stock price. |
| Ahold/Tops Markets | Accounting irregularities, including $900 million in overstatements. |
| AOL/Time Warner | Inflating ad revenues to keep stock price inflated. |
| Arthur Andersen | Obstruction of justice. |
| Astra Zeneca | $355 million fine for sales practices encouraging fraud of federal health programs. |
| CMS Energy | Overstating revenue through fraudulent trading activities. |
| Bayer/GlaxoSmithKline | Agreed to jointly pay $345 million to settle allegations of defrauding Medicaid. |
| Bristol Myers Squibb | Inflating revenue by $1.5 billion. |
| Cendant | Inflating income by $500 million. |
| CMS Energy | Overstating revenue through fraudulent trading activities. |
| Computer Associates | Violating premerger rules. |
| Cornell Companies | Misleading statements. |
| Dollar General | Accounting fraud. |
| Duke Energy | Overstating revenue through fraudulent trading activities. |
| Dynegy | Overstating revenue through fraudulent trading activities. |
| El Paso | Overstating revenue through fraudulent trading activities. |
| Enron | Massive accounting fraud involving numerous senior executives. Charges include obstructing justice, wire fraud, money laundering, conspiracy, false statements. |
| Freddie Mac | Understating earnings by $4.5 billion. |
| Gateway | Accounting fraud. |
| GE | Excessive retirement benefits granted to former CEO Jack Welch. |
| Global Crossing | Fraudulent trading to inflate revenues. |
| Halliburton | Booking cost overruns as revenue; questionable trading activities. |
| HealthSouth | $2.7 billion accounting fraud involving numerous executives. |
| Homestore.com | Conspiracy to commit securities fraud, insider trading, accounting fraud. |
| HPL Technologies, Inc. | Accounting fraud. |
| IBM | Improper booking of sales revenue |
| ImClone | Insider trading, perjury, bank fraud and obstruction of justice, tax evasion. |

*(continued)*

## Major U.S. Corporate Scandals, January 2002–June 2003 *(continued)*

| Company | Scandal |
|---|---|
| Johnson & Johnson | False record keeping. |
| Kmart | Securities fraud, accounting irregularities, misuse of company funds. |
| KPMG | Role in Rite Aid, Xerox accounting scandals. |
| Lucent | SEC investigation over $679 million earnings readjustment. |
| Martha Stewart Omnimedia | Insider trading of founder Stewart. |
| McLeod USA | Offering investment-banking business in exchange for access to IPOs. |
| Merck | Overstatement of revenues leading to excessive charges for drug orders. |
| Metromedia Fiber Networks | Offering investment-banking business in exchange for access to IPOs. |
| Microstrategy | Accounting fraud. |
| Mirant | Inflating revenue over $1 billion. |
| Network Associates | Overstatement of revenues. |
| Pediatrix Medical Group | Irregular billing of Medicaid. |
| Peregrine Systems | Overstating $100 million in revenue. |
| Phar-More | Overstatement of profits. |
| PNC Financial | Overstated $155 million in revenues. |
| PricewaterhouseCoopers | Involvement in numerous accounting scandals. |
| Qwest | Overstating $1.2 billion in revenue from improper trading activities; offering investment-banking business in exchange for access to IPOs. |
| Reliant Energy | Inflating revenue through fraudulent trading activity. |
| Rite Aid | Massive accounting fraud. |
| Schering Plough | Obstruction-of-justice charges relating to its marketing practices. |
| Sotheby's | Price fixing. |
| Sprint | Excessive executive compensation. |
| Sunbeam | Accounting fraud. |
| Tenet | Overcharging Medicare. |
| Tyco | Massive theft of over $600 million in company assets by insiders. Charges include tax evasion, grand larceny, enterprise corruption, falsifying business records, securities fraud, enterprise corruption, grand larceny. |
| U.S. Technologies | CEO charged with twenty-two counts of securities, mail, and wire fraud. |
| Vivendi Universal | Multibillion-dollar accounting irregularities. |
| Waste Management | Overstated income by more than $1 billion. |
| Williams Cos. | Questionable accounting and trading activities. |
| WorldCom | Massive accounting fraud involving several executives who hid more than $11 billion in expenses; offering investment-banking business in exchange for access to IPOs. |
| Xerox | Accounting fraud involving $1.4 billion overstatement of earnings. |

One cannot read through this list, which encompasses the very breadth of American corporate life, including some of our very largest companies, without reaching the inescapable conclusion: corporate America is simply saturated with corruption. From one end of the country to another, and in all kinds of businesses and professions, people are lying, stealing, defrauding, conspiring, and otherwise breaking the law, led by those at the very top, the people who make the most money to begin with, who are most likely to have attended our best schools and to otherwise have benefited from all that America has to offer. As *BusinessWeek* concluded in its "Number One Lesson for the Year 2002":

> The problems revealed by the scandals were systemic, not the result of a few bad apples. While only a few CEOs may go to jail for breaking the law, the breakdown was endemic to both the corporate and financial systems. Most CEOs, not just a few, were overcompensated for success and protected from failure. Many, not just a few, accountants, analysts, attorneys, regulators, and legislators failed, to one degree or another, in ensuring the accuracy of financial statements and the free flow of honest data in the markets.

The only problem with this passage is "the scandals *were*." No—the scandals *are*. For almost four years now, our corruption has been continuous and ongoing. It has touched all corners of our economy, far more than we have space to address.[16]

So far, the most common form of corporate crime has been accounting fraud. In this scam, the books are cooked to make it look like the company is worth more than it is, thereby increasing the value of the CEO's stock options. This scam requires that the corporation co-opt an accounting firm to verify the phony numbers. This is accomplished by giving the accounting firms lucrative consulting contracts, a kind of payoff. The investor, of course, is left holding the bag. From 1997 to 2000, *over seven hundred companies,* many of them blue-chip, were forced to restate misleading earnings from past financial statements, costing investors hundreds of billions of dollars in market value.[17] And behind every one was an accounting firm verifying the books. When the SEC investigated one of the majors, Pricewaterhouse-Coopers, in the late nineties, it discovered an incredible eight thousand violations. Over half the partners were holding forbidden stock—stock in the firms they audited—including the CEO, James Schiro.

## Doublespeak

This widespread fraud has been supported by the carefully crafted marketing statements that have issued forth from companies under investigation. Consider the full-page letter to the public published in the *Washington Post* by the new CEO of Freddie Mac after the previous executive team was dismissed. It begins:

> Every morning when Freddie Mac's doors open, 4,000 employees begin working with one goal in mind: to open the doors of more homes for more of America's families. That's a special mission; one we take seriously—and personally.[18]

Naturally, there was no mention in this letter of how, or why, Freddie Mac had failed to report $4.5 billion in earnings over three years, in order to present a false image of steady earnings growth to Wall Street. Clearly, not all four thousand people go to work there with the same goal in mind.

This omnipresent deception reveals the fundamental dynamic at work in American business

### The Cover Lie

"Most of us made it to the chief executive position because of a particularly high degree of responsibility. . . . We are offended most by the perception that we would waste the resources of a company that is a major part of our life and livelihood, and that we would be happy with directors who would permit that waste. . . . So as a CEO I want a strong, competent board."

—*Tyco CEO Dennis Kozlowski, later convicted of leading a $600 million theft from his company.*

"It's more than just money. You've got to give back to the community that supported you."

—*Adelphia Communications CEO John Rigas, later convicted of looting hundreds of millions of dollars from his company and falsifying its financial condition.*

"You'll see people who in the early days . . . took their life savings and trusted this company with their money. And I have an awesome responsibility to those people to make sure that they're done right."

—*WorldCom CEO Bernard Ebbers, later convicted of orchestrating a record $11 billion accounting fraud.*

today: the con. There is a built-in dichotomy between word and deed. On the surface, American business waves the flag, surrounded by cheerleaders: business magazines, business schools, management gurus, and everyone else who benefits from hiding the unpleasant truth. Meanwhile, beneath the public screen, the rip-off is under way. This corrosive duality has become so prevalent that many of us not only expect it, but also consider it to be a normal part of life. When the editors of the *New York Times* hold forth on the Fourth of July, they conclude "our actual history all too often looks like a sprawling, brawling free-for-all that uses the high language of our principles as a kind of camouflage for what the market will bear." [19] And yet while this problem is not categorically new, the difference today is how many people are involved in it, and how intense the hypermarket has made it. Millions of us now lead a schizophrenic existence, caught between the public, surface world of the American Dream—the realm of the family, of God, of country, and of moral principle—and the hidden, subterranean world of Market America, a dog-eat-dog world run by major corporations, where everyone does what they can get away with. It is the secret fact of American life, the one we are all not supposed to admit.

One encounters this dichotomy from the very moment one goes to found a new company. This act necessitates that one choose a state to incorporate in. Instead of one's home state, the majority opinion is the tiny state of Delaware, which has intentionally crafted an entire probusiness legal code to attract corporations. They'll be happy to set up a mailbox for you, even

---

### HEALTHSOUTH 2001 ANNUAL REPORT

At HealthSouth, we're excited about the future of healthcare—and the future of our company. 2001 proved to be a year that clearly defined HealthSouth as the Fortune 500 company that will lead the way into a new era of healthcare.

"In 2001, we set new records as we pushed our revenues well over $4.3 billion and celebrated another year of fulfilling Wall Street expectations, maintaining our record as the Fortune 500 company with the second-longest streak for meeting or exceeding analysts' expectations."

**RICHARD M. SCRUSHY**
Chairman of the Board & Chief Executive Officer

11/4/03: Indicted on 85 counts in $2.7 billion accounting fraud

though you may never even step foot in the place. Similarly, Florida has become the number one place for CEOs to buy real estate and establish residency because the state has sheltered personal property from bankruptcy, thereby attracting wealthy citizens. In short, the law is being used to make money. And our own legal system is so used to this that we think of it as perfectly normal.

Within this fraudulent world, it is those who not only recognize the two levels of reality, but also know how to exploit the difference, who get ahead. They have learned to speak the Market's doublespeak without flinching. The very personality of the richest man in America, Bill Gates, has been described as "affable cold-heartedness." Some see this as the key to his financial success. On the surface, he is doing an honest business deal with Apple, while below the surface, he is walking off with the idea for Windows. Many of our businesspeople privately admire such talents. At the same time, the subterranean reality it represents—known by its code name, "the way things are"— is never admitted in public. You won't find it taught in any business school, where it would threaten the image, and you won't hear any CEOs admit to it either, even though so many clearly live by it. If anyone ever questions their motives, the proper response is to react with moral outrage, vehemently deny all charges, and, naturally, seek the best legal counsel. Even the victims of the scam sometimes refuse to admit to it, since they would prefer a more comfortable reality to live in.

In the broadest social sense, this dynamic has created a dangerous separation in America between an upper, predatory class and their prey, the middle class, which is still clinging to a unified value system. The middle class is fed the lies, carefully prepared by corporate communications, while the upper class winks and nods at one another on the way to the country club: they know how things *really* work. To the slick American CEO, the man of principle is a sucker. As this gyre widens, our entire democratic tradition becomes the shield for a corrupt elite. To the corrupt insiders, America is nothing but *ideology,* as Marx originally defined it: "the false system of thought elaborated by the ruling class to justify its rule in the eyes of the world, while hiding its real selfish motives."[20]

So why don't more people catch on to this? The answer is deeply embedded in human nature. When *The New Republic* was devastated by a reporter who had fabricated numerous stories, one of its editors, Leon Wieseltier, commented: "The reason that con artists get away with elaborate deception is that most people refuse to live in a world in which cynicism is the rule." In other words, it is the very existence of good people that allows bad people to thrive. Or as the Chinese philosopher Chuang-tzu noted in 300 BC:

> When justice and benevolence are in the air, a few people are really concerned with the good of others, but the majority are aware that this is a good thing, ripe for exploitation. They take advantage of the situation. For them, benevolence and justice are traps to catch birds. Thus benevolence and justice rapidly come to be associated with fraud and hypocrisy. Then everybody doubts. And that is when trouble really begins.[21]

## The Rich Get Richer

The trouble has begun, and it is called the income gap. In the United States, the gap between rich and poor has been widening since 1967. Our level of inequality is now higher than in any other industrialized country. As with many hypermarket phenomena, no one has quite figured out why. But once we lift the Market's veil, a simple answer suggests itself. A winner-take-all society has broken out in America, and the people at the top are lining their pockets at everyone else's expense. If you add together the thefts at Tyco ($600 million) and Hollinger ($400 million) alone, that is $1 billion stolen from the thousands by the few. Once again, free-market theory has failed us. Rewards are not being apportioned based on merit, but on the ability to form a powerful cabal at the top of a corporation and drain it of every cent. The centralization of wealth in the hands of a few is just one more symptom of the hypermarket.

This problem is epitomized by CEO pay, which continues to resist all attempts at significant reform. By point of reference, a CEO in Japan is paid twenty times what an ordinary worker makes; in Britain, thirty-five times. In 2002, the average U.S. CEO earned nearly 300 times what an average worker did—seven times more than in 1982. The average compensation in the Fortune 100 was $12 million.[22] Indeed, according to Responsible Wealth, the CEOs at twenty-three companies under investigation for accounting fraud actually made 66 percent *more* than the CEOs at clean companies: $62.2 million per year during 1999–2001.

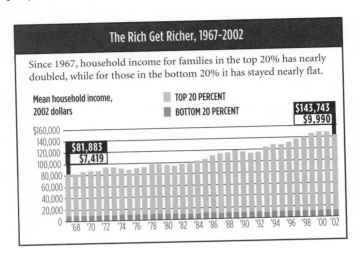

**The Rich Get Richer, 1967–2002**

Since 1967, household income for families in the top 20% has nearly doubled, while for those in the bottom 20% it has stayed nearly flat.

Mean household income, 2002 dollars

TOP 20 PERCENT
BOTTOM 20 PERCENT

$143,743
$9,990

$81,883
$7,419

To put it another way: If you were an average production worker in the United States, you made $25,467 in 2001. But if your pay had been increasing over the previous decade at the same rate as the average CEO's, your pay would have been $101,156. So where did all your money go? The money that did *not* go into your pocket went instead into *their* pockets, people who don't even need it, do not deserve it, and may well have broken the law to get it.

Here the perks tell the same tale. In American corporations, senior executives are routinely reimbursed for expenses small and large that ordinary employees are not. Martha Stewart, for instance, asked her company to reimburse her $17,000 a year for her weekend driver, for trips to her hairdresser, and even for coffee. Tyco was paying private-school tuition for some of its top execs, not to mention CEO Dennis Kozlowski's $6,000 shower curtain, $15,000 umbrella stand, and the $1 million birthday party in Sardinia for his wife. Former GE CEO Jack Welch got a Manhattan apartment and Knicks tickets—after he retired (he gave them up when this was made public in divorce proceedings. Even Oracle chairman Larry Ellison, one of the richest men in the world, billed his company $8,360 in 2000 for "personal fitness expenses." He was worth more than $50 billion at the time.[23]

If one now steps away from this picture and looks at the gap between rich and poor in the United States, one can see what is really driving it: a deep lack of integrity in how American business is conducted. The theory of free enterprise now has little bearing on our modern reality. It is, rather, just another element of the con. The truth is that massive rewards are going to some of the worst among us, and that the present system favors them. At the same time, that same system is necessarily selecting *out* the good people. Instead of the best rising to the top, the nature of American business makes it difficult to climb the economic ladder without becoming part of the problem, another slick and deceptive phony. To do what is right, and to expect the same from others, is to risk one's career and family.

The living proof of this reality is Sherron Watkins. Watkins was the courageous woman who stepped forward, when so many others did not, to expose the crimes at Enron. Since then, Watkins has had difficulty finding a job. "In terms of bigger corporations, I have had people talk to me about various things, and then the door gets slammed. When it comes down to the final decision, there's probably one or two people who say: 'Are y'all crazy? She's a whistleblower.' "[24]

The character of American business today is contained in this vignette. Hundreds of corporations should be beating down the door to hire someone of such integrity—if they had any themselves. What a positive statement that would make for any company that had nothing to hide. Instead, the silence of corporate America counsels the world that Watkins should have said nothing, no matter what crimes were being committed or how many people would be hurt by them. Moral courage not only has no value, says corporate America, it is a *vice*. In its place, cowardice reigns. After four years of corporate scandals, the American corporation remains a refuge for the gutless.

## Market Charity

Many people choose to look at the corruption in business as if it were unique to that world, a function of the profit motive. And yet the evidence clearly suggests this is not the case. The corrosive impact of the hypermarket has so changed our culture that even the nonprofit arena is awash in scandal. Here the most poignant example is human service organizations, which seek to address poverty, disease, and other social problems.

| | Major Scandals in Human Services Organizations, 1992–2002 | |
|---|---|---|
| Year | Organization | Scandal |
| 1992 | United Way of America | Misuse of funds, fraud, tax evasion, satellite business operations. |
| 1994 | National Association for the Advancement of Colored People (NAACP) | Misappropriation of funds. |
| | Jewish Community Center of Greater Washington | Embezzlement, misuse of funds, satellite business operations. |
| 1995 | New Era Foundation | Embezzlement. |
| 1996 | American Parkinson Disease Association | Embezzlement. |
| | Evangelical Lutheran Church | Embezzlement. |
| | Episcopal Church (national) | Misappropriation of funds. |
| | Roman Catholic Church (Brooklyn) | Misappropriation of funds. |
| | Hellenic American Neighborhood Action Committee (HANAC) | Unauthorized contracting by parallel entity. |
| | March of Dimes | Conflict of interest, misappropriation of funds. |
| 1997 | Three Rivers Regatta (PA) | Misappropriation of funds. |
| 1998 | Goodwill Industries (CA) | Systematic looting of funds over twenty-five years. |
| 1998–2000 | Bishop Estate (HI) | Mismanagement, conflict of interest. |
| 1999 | National Baptist Convention | Grand theft, racketeering. |
| | Head Start (NYC) | Embezzlement. |
| | Federation of Puerto Rican Organizations | Embezzlement, money laundering. |
| | Baptist Foundation of Arizona | Lost investment, fraud. |
| | Allegheny Health Education and Research Foundation (PA) | Theft, conspiracy. |
| 2000 | American Cancer Society | Theft, conspiracy. |
| | Freeport Daycare Center (NY) | Misappropriation of funds. |
| | Operation Smile | Misappropriation of funds, flawed accounting. |
| | Toys for Tots | Theft. |
| 2002 | United Way of National Capital Region | Financial mismanagement, misuse of funds. |
| | Capital Area United Way (East Lansing, MI) | Embezzlement. |

In the decade from 1992 to 2002, there was a steady flow of corruption from major human-services organizations, the most well-known example being the United Way. The United Way is currently composed of fourteen hundred local organizations that raise over $5 billion a year, making it on whole the second largest charity in America. In 1992, an investigation of the national chapter, the United Way of America, revealed that its CEO, William Aramony, a veteran of twenty-two years, had been using donations to fund an expensive condo, limousine service, and trips on the Concorde, at the same time as he was receiving a $463,000 salary. After being indicted by a federal grand jury, Aramony was convicted of twenty-five counts of fraud, amounting to a $1 million theft from donors, and sentenced to seven years in prison. This did not prevent him from suing his former employer over deferred compensation, however, and winning $4.2 million of it, as a result of the milewide holes in his employment contract. More donations in his pocket. One would think that the United Way would have learned an important lesson from this, particularly given how the negative publicity impacted its fund-raising, but it didn't. When the next CEO resigned four years later, individual board members pledged $292,500 to her as a parting gift, prompting a public outcry. Then, in 2002, a third wave struck, this time in the United Way of the National Capital Region, where another investigation revealed lax financial controls, including open executive expense accounts and charity-owned vehicles being sold at below-market rates to employees and their families. Management had deliberately hidden the critical reports of auditors from the board. The organization had also lied about its fund-raising levels, its overhead expenses, and paid $1 million into the CEO's pension plan. The CEO was fired, and the entire board resigned. Meanwhile, at the United Way in Lansing, Michigan, an investigation discovered that Jacquelyn Allen-MacGregor, the former vice president for finance and a twenty-year veteran, had embezzled $1.9 million, twice the Aramony amount and the largest embezzlement case in United Way history. She was later sentenced to four years in prison. Thankfully, she had no deferred-compensation plan.

Other major scandals in the human-services arena during this period included the American Parkinson Disease Association, whose CEO, Frank Williams, embezzled contributions in excess of $1 million over a seven-year period, and the NAACP, whose executive director, Benjamin Chavis, was fired for mismanaging funds, including settling a sex-discrimination suit against himself using NAACP money. But the clear winner of the Enron award goes to Goodwill Industries of Santa Clara, California, where seven employees, led by Linda Marcil, stole $15 million over twenty-five years by skimming money from cash registers and selling donated clothing, turning their city's charity into their own personal ATM. After one of them, Carol Marr, was discovered with $1 million in her bank accounts, she committed suicide.

Clearly, many nonprofits are suffering from the same kind of corruption as for-profits. And one reason is that the same people run them. Many nonprofit boards are influenced or controlled by corporate executives selected for their ability to give money as well as expertise, including those implicated in our many corporate scandals. An example is Paul Allaire, the former chairman and CEO of Xerox. After an SEC investigation alleged that Allaire and five others had inflated Xerox's profits by $1.4 billion, Allaire agreed to pay a $1 million penalty and give up $7.6 million in compensation. He was also barred from serving as a director of a public company for five years. This did not stop the board of trustees of the Ford Foundation—at $10 billion, one of the nation's largest private foundations—from keeping him as its chairman. Nor did it faze the boards of the New York City Ballet or Outward Bound, where he also serves as a board member. No matter how many waves of scandal batter our shores, the market elite takes care of its own.

## The Besieged Consumer

As the American economy has become increasingly corrupt and predatory, it has changed the relationship between business and the consumer. When dealing with American business today, at all levels, the consumer must be increasingly defensive about getting ripped off, particularly as the rip-offs are getting more and more sophisticated.

One of innumerable examples is deliberate overbilling. Here the consumer is charged for something he has not asked for or for a service that was never performed. And I use myself as the unfortunate example. Recently I bought a new tire at Firestone in Annapolis, Maryland. A week later I found the receipt and realized that I had been charged forty dollars for a "new tire warranty" that I had never been told about. I then had to place three calls before the "right person" was there to subtract this from my bill. I was also informed that it was "company policy" to add the new tire warranty to a bill unless someone decided against it—but how do you decide against something they don't tell you about? The same strategy has been applied to phone books in my area of Maryland. Three years ago I noticed that we had been charged fifty dollars for a Washington, D.C., phone book, which appeared unrequested on our doorstep. I called, the phone company promised to take us off their list, and the charge was removed from my bill. The same phone book showed up the next two years in a row, and each year I had to go through the same drill, until I finally took it to a supervisor. How many others never noticed?

Having experienced similar problems himself, *New York Times* reporter David Pogue reviewed his family records and found "at least seven cases where a service company (including at least three phone companies) overbilled us and didn't correct the mistake until we turned ourselves into human pit bulls." He then solicited readers to share similar stories, and was overwhelmed by twelve hundred responses in four days. Of the twelve hundred responses, only two people described being underbilled; the rest were overbilled. One respondee noted that "My experience with cell phone companies, airlines, and Internet providers has been so overwhelmingly dominated by 'mistakes' that I can't believe that it amounts to anything less than an insidious new business model developed to prey upon busy lives." Another opined: "They've cut to the bone to increase their bottom line. They train their front lines to blow people off, and give them no authority to make amends for problems. In previous eras, this was known as thievery. Now it's just the way things are done."[25]

In all these cases, the Market calculus is simple: in an age when people have so little time, many people will not notice an extra charge. If you make it difficult to subtract the charges, more people will forget or give up. At the end of the day, the amount you make by deceiving people will be greater than the expense of reimbursing them. Even if the law comes knocking, as it has for the cell-phone companies (Verizon, Sprint, Qwest, SBC, AT&T, and MCI have all settled class-action lawsuits related to fees and overbilling); there is money to be made. For instance, Verizon settled a class-action overbilling lawsuit for $20 million. But Verizon has 40 million subscribers. So all they need to do is overbill each customer fifty cents a year to break even. Verizon Wireless has even come up with a most ingenious strategy to make this happen. They don't provide an itemized list of calls with your statement unless you pay an additional monthly fee. So if you have been overbilled, you will never notice, while if you haven't, you have just paid for a clean statement. How many suits did it take to figure that one out?

The same market calculus now applies to the widespread use of rebates. If you go into the Best Buy retail chain, for instance, you will see price tags in big black numbers beneath all the electronics for sale. Normally, price tags tell you the price of a product, right? Not in the hypermarket. The fine print beneath these prices reveals that they are actually the "after rebate" price. The price at the *register* is much higher. To get the "after rebate" price, you will have to send in a completed form to the manufacturer with your receipt. This form will be printed out for you at the register.

Of course, all of this is an enormous scam at your expense. There is no legitimate purpose behind retail rebates. If its cash register can print out rebate slips, Best Buy can certainly pay the consumer the rebate on the spot and get reimbursed by the manufacturer. The only reason the consumer is being injected in the middle of this financial relationship between the manufacturer and the retailer is that the entire operation has been constructed to rip him off. First, Best Buy gets to advertise prices that appear to be lower than they really are, thereby deceiving its customers. "It's a wonderful trigger for purchasing, because it gives people the perception that they're saving money," says consumer psychologist Renee Fraser, president of Fraser Communications.[26] Second, manufacturers benefit from the fact that two out of five consumers never send in their rebate slips, either because they forget, or they throw them out by accident (the slip-in-the-bottom-of-the-bag syndrome), or because of the hassle factor: cutting the product code from the box, having the original store sales receipt, filling out the rebate form, writing down the product serial numbers, copying all the documents. If they do send them in, the rebates are frequently denied because they have not been filled out correctly (the slips have their own fine print). One of the common traps is the thirty-day deadline for submitting the paperwork, a fact you won't find on the Best Buy price tag. Of course, there are also many cases in which the rebate slips simply disappear into the void. You may not learn of this, however, until you call up to inquire why you never received your rebate—if you ever do. How many of us today have time to keep track of a thirty-five-dollar rebate over several months and then deal with the answering service of a "fulfillment company" on the other side of the United States? But of course the manufacturers know this, which is why the entire rebate system has been constructed this way. "The system is generally set up to make applying for the money as difficult as possible," finds *USA Today*. Apart from the obvious benefits, the system allows manufacturers a way of distancing themselves from consumer complaints, which fall on the fulfillment company. Such complaints are constant: next to tech-support woes, for instance, rebate complaints are the most common reason why *PC World* readers write seeking help from the magazine.[27] Since the rebate slips take an additional ninety days to process, manufacturers also benefit from sitting on their money that much longer. These well-known dynamics notwithstanding, the rebate scam is now such an integral part of the American retail sector that it is being taught in business school, as if it were a legitimate business practice. At least, that is what my local Best Buy salesman told me; he took the course.

Once one understands the sophistication of these relatively small scams, one can truly begin to appreciate the Market's major campaigns, such as the prescription-drug culture. In addition to harnessing the power of the Bubble, as seen earlier, the pharmaceutical industry has become its own market octopus, its many tentacles insinuated throughout the health-care system, and squeezing it for every cent. Marketing dollars are used to reduce human beings to an innumerable number of deficiencies, each one requiring its own cure. Clinical trials are structured to support these findings. Doctors benefiting from lucrative contracts with pharmaceutical companies are used to manage these trials. Negative evidence is suppressed. Detailing representatives offer significant incentives to physicians to prescribe a new product. Lobbyists influence lawmakers to allow direct-to-consumer marketing. Advertising raises patient awareness about a drug. Patients then put sales pressure on their doctor, who is, increasingly, running yet another business competing against other practices like his own. The cumulative effect is the creation of an entire prescription-drug culture, where you medicate issues once deemed spiritual or social or even natural. Here an enormous, well-funded industry has exploited the complexities of the modern economy to become a potent offensive weapon, one so powerful that it has managed, through constant pressure over many years, to undermine the medical profession, the most well defended of them all, with literally scores of standards organizations, in order to create an artificial demand, to the applause of investors and the detriment of public health.

And the response of free-market theory?

Caveat emptor!

That's right, let the buyer beware. This is the idea that, when you get ripped off, or sold a bill of goods, or prescribed a poison pill, it's your own fault, because you should have known better. How could we ever blame the system?

## The Ozone Hole

The evidence we have seen so far suggests that modern society is governed by an inexorable logic. At moderate temperatures, the Market is a beneficial force. But if the Market gets too hot, we lose our morality and adopt the Market Code. Corruption follows. This phenomenon is naturally more pronounced in large cities, where market forces are most intense, and less so in small towns, where the market temperature goes down and the human factor goes up. But over time it has been growing everywhere, to the point where we have now reached the boiling point. The amoral power of the Market has broken the bonds of our society and formed an entirely new state, like water turning into steam:

> The character of Americans has changed. Those values associated with the market hold sway in their most caricatured form: individualism and self-reliance have morphed into selfishness and self-absorption; competitiveness has become social Darwinism; desire for the good life has turned into materialism; aspiration has become envy. There is a growing gap between the life that many Americans want and the life they can afford—a problem that bedevils even those who would seem to have everything. Other values in our culture have been sidelined: belief in community, social responsibility, compassion for the less able or less fortunate . . . we're starting to feel like a corrupt banana republic—one of those places where a rapacious oligarchy sets the moral tone by ripping off the entire country and those below follow suit with corruption of every conceivable kind.[28]

To understand the scope of this tragedy, and its implications for the future, consider its impact on our youngest citizens. In 2002, a survey of twelve thousand high-school students found that 74 percent admitted to cheating on an exam at least once in the past year, 38 percent said they shoplifted, and 37 percent said they would lie to get a good job.[29] "They're basically decent kids whose values are being totally corrupted by a world which is sanctioning stuff that even they know is wrong," explained Michael Josephson, whose firm conducted the survey. Cheating is so widespread now that many teachers have given up trying to prevent it. Numerous Web sites (papers4less.com, schoolsucks.com, cheathouse.com) are devoted to selling papers to students. One, ivyessays.com, even specializes in applications to the Ivy League. When ABC's *Prime Time* investigated this cheating trend at one of the top public high schools in the nation, students explained their behavior thus:

> *Student #1:* Look at businesspeople. They cheat.
> *Student #2:* Yeah, all the big company scandals. Like Enron and all the others. Look at the court system. Whether you did it or not, if you can get the jury to say that you're not guilty, you're free.
> *Student #3:* Yeah, if you get a good lawyer, I mean, they can persuade anybody to say that, or to think that, you're not guilty.
> *Student #4:* Our own President a couple years ago. That statement he made to the court about the Monica Lewinsky issue. "I did not sleep with that woman." It was a complete lie.
> *Student #3:* What kind of example does that set for the students in this school? Why shouldn't we do it if he can do it?[30]

This cheating epidemic suggests that a generation of students has now absorbed the amorality of the hypermarket, ensuring widespread corruption for years to come. A moral ozone hole has opened up over America, and it is burning us all.

## The Light Goes On

So far we have focused entirely on the domestic operations of American business. But of course, we also live in a global economy, and the major American banks and corporations are almost all multinationals. So if they are lying, cheating, stealing, and manipulating markets here at home, one can only imagine what they are doing abroad, particularly in countries where laws are more lax and corruption is endemic, even accepted—places like Mexico, the focus of the emerging-markets investment boom, the one that preceded the technology boom and ended with the collapse of that country's currency; or Indonesia, the largest Muslim country in the world, which was devastated by the Asian financial crisis; places where, with the right incentives to the cabal at the top, an entire country can be turned into an Enron.

For example, the SEC is now investigating whether four major American oil companies—Exxon Mobil, Marathon, Amerada Hess, and Chevron Texaco—bribed the dictator of oil-rich Equatorial Guinea, Teodoro Nguema, a man widely accused of torture and other abuses. The allegations stem from the corruption discovered at Riggs Bank in Washington, where accounts revealed payments of $1 million or more by American oil companies to Equatorial Guinean officials and their relatives. A Senate investigation determined that "Riggs Bank serviced the E.G. accounts with little or no attention to the bank's anti-money-laundering obligations, turned a blind eye to evidence suggesting the bank was handling the proceeds of foreign corruption, and allowed numerous suspicious transactions to take place without notifying law enforcement."[31] One can only imagine the rage of a people oppressed by such corruption, particularly when they are subsisting on a few dollars a day.

This foreign corruption is very different from our domestic variety in one important sense: it is not one American ripping off another. Consequently, the victims of U.S. corporations, and the larger philosophy they represent, feel not only manipulated, and ripped off, and exploited, but oppressed by a foreign power: America. Once you make this connection, the light goes on. You can finally understand what corporate America is not telling you, the answer to the question that has haunted Americans since 9/11: "Why do they hate us?" You can understand why those most fervently opposed to living by the Market Code—religious fundamentalists—would attack us. And you can understand why they would target the global symbol of American capitalism, the World Trade Center—twice. The enemy is not just outside us, it is inside as well, whether we wish to admit it or not.

# 8. The Modern God

The statue of Darth Vader at the summit of the National Cathedral, Washington, D.C. This image is for sale in the National Cathedral gift shop.

Of all the institutional threats to the Market's hegemony, none is greater than religion. Every major religion proposes that mankind live by a belief system that is antithetical to the Market Code. This moral code, with its common set of principles—truth, justice, compassion, love, selflessness, etc.—governs the internal, spiritual, religious side of life rather than the external, material, economic side. The symmetry between these two sides is revealed simply by transposing the words *market* and *moral*. In this way, we can toggle between moral philosophy and market philosophy, moral principles and market principles, moral values and market values, moral behavior and market behavior, a moral society and a market society. In each case, *moral* or *market* refers to the different end being served, creating two very different sides to life, one Good and the other Productive.

In the West, our moral code arises from the Judeo-Christian tradition, where it stems, according to all believers, from a monotheistic God. It is an expression of the innate laws of the human interior, the logic that governs the soul. The Market Code, on the other hand, emerges from Nature, the laws of the physical universe. It is nothing but natural selection in economic guise. This established, early on, a central conflict in our civilization. As Jesus put it, "No man can serve two masters: for either he will hate the one, and love the other; or else he will hold to the one, and despise the other. Ye cannot serve God and mammon."[1]

This does not mean that God and the Market are mutually exclusive; it simply means that an individual cannot serve two completely different ends at the same time. God and the Market can coexist, but one must be subordinate to the other. So clearly, if you want the outcome to be Good, the moral code must take precedence. In this way the Market becomes not only the invaluable source of material well-being, but also the critical means of supporting the higher goals in life, providing it with the meaning and purpose the market economy can never fulfill.

This very same opposition is also commonly expressed in many other ways. In some cases it is referred to as "the spiritual vs. the material." In others it is "the sacred vs. the profane." In still others it is "the religious vs. the secular." A recent book comparing American and European philosophies of life puts it this insightful way: "It all gets back to a basic difference in the American and European Dreams. We strive for happiness by *doing*. Europeans strive for happiness by *being*."[2]

This last opposition, being vs. doing, finally takes us to the summit. God, of course, is an idea rooted in being, whether it is the Infinite Being of the Judeo-Christian tradition, the Pure Being of Buddhism, or any other of the Supreme Beings that populate man's religious life, while the Market is purely rooted in doing, the source of all productivity. One finds it hard to imagine converting Judeo-Christianity to a God of Infinite Doing, although the Bubble would certainly support this. Unfortunately the idea of God-as-being has been greatly obscured by those who confuse it with the institution of religion, with its specific doctrines, stories, and rituals, and further challenged by semantic disagreements (the Buddhists are neutral on whether Pure Being constitutes "God," for example). This creates some surprising results, once you cut through the fog. For instance, if, as suggested above, Europeans are rooted in Being, while Americans are rooted in Doing, this implies that

Europeans, who are statistically much less observant than Americans, are actually seeking God in a different fashion, while Americans, who claim much higher levels of religious observance, are actually living lives devoted to the Market. After all, what American would deny that his country worships the god of productivity?

In any case, regardless of your individual perspective—regardless of whether you choose to define the nature of reality as Good vs. Productive, spiritual vs. material, sacred vs. profane, religious vs. secular, or being vs. doing—what you are talking about, particularly in modern society, is the opposition between God and the Market. All the other manifestations of this opposition—the struggle between religion and science, say—are actually subsets of this larger duality, which pits the entire material assembly line against the human spirit—the human *being*—and its innate connection to all Being, the connection known as the soul. To deny this metaphysical reality is to collapse human beings to human doings, a suggestion that sounds patently ridiculous, but which is, in fact, the essence of the modern age.

It is this essential metaphysical divide that lies beneath American society today, creating two opposing codes of behavior. The Moral Code arises from Being, which is good, while the Market Code arises from Doing, which is productive. The result is a constant struggle in our minds, and in society itself.

As we have seen now many times, the Market hates being limited, and the ultimate limiting factor is morality. As Dostoyevsky argued: Without God, anything is permissible—the very "anything goes" attitude that defines market philosophy. To the unbridled Market, then, all paths to God lead in the wrong direction. The Market does not want the meek to inherit the earth, but the rich. The Golden Rule is another problem, if you think that a productive end should always justify the means. From here the list goes on and on, one commandment at a time, a conflict that has shaken the modern world, and challenged everyone in it:

The commandment against coveting warns against devoting energy to acquiring goods and possessions. Yet, the message to achieve wealth is the engine of a modern consumer society. The conflict between the commandment and the drive to consume is as much a conflict between the ethical demands of the ancient world and the practical reality of living in the modern one.[3]

It is this conflict that has created the core dynamic in our society today. As the Market heats up, it naturally begins to chafe against the moral harness, making God, even the idea of God, the Market's ultimate enemy. To put it another way: since the Market is purely amoral, it is naturally disposed to eradicate all moral restraints. So the more powerful the Market becomes, the more amoral, and aspiritual, society will become.

This is a mortal struggle with the highest possible stakes, one that has redefined the traditional axis of religious conflict. "I am beginning to think that for all the religions of the world, however they may differ from one another, the religion of the Market has become the most formidable rival, the more so because it is rarely recognized as a religion," writes theologian Harvey Cox. "The Market is becoming more like the Yahweh of the Old Testament—not just one superior deity contending with others but the Supreme Deity, the only true God, whose reign must now be universally accepted and who allows no rivals."[4]

| Religion | Wisdom |
|---|---|
| Native American | "Miserable as we seem in thy eyes, we consider ourselves . . . much happier than thou, in this that we are very content with the little that we have." (Micmac chief) |
| Buddhist | "Whoever in this world overcomes his selfish cravings, his sorrows fall away from him, like drops of water from a lotus flower" (Dhammapada, 336) |
| Christian | It is "easier for a camel to go through the eye of a needle than for a rich man to enter the kingdom of God." (Matthew 19:23-24) |
| Confucian | "Excess and deficiency are equally at fault." (Confucius, XI.15) |
| Ancient Greek | "Nothing in Excess." (Inscribed at Oracle of Delphi) |
| Hindu | "That person who lives completely free from desires, without longing . . . attains peace." (Bhagavad-Gita, 11.71) |
| Islamic | "Abundance diverts you, until you come to the graves." (Koran, 102:1-2) |
| Jewish | "Give me neither poverty nor riches." (Proverbs 30:8) |
| Taoist | "He who knows he has enough is rich." (Tao Te Ching) |

# The Secular Veil

Sometimes it is difficult to spot the trend in the short term, but if you widen your time horizon it becomes crystal clear. So it is with the impact of the Market upon religion. America was initially settled by people of various orthodox religions. As an exhibit at the Library of Congress described it:

> Many of the British North American colonies that eventually formed the United States of America were settled in the seventeenth century by men and women who, in the face of European persecution, refused to compromise passionately held religious convictions and fled Europe. The New England colonies, New Jersey, Pennsylvania, and Maryland were conceived and established "as plantations of religion." Some settlers who arrived in these areas came for secular motives—"to catch fish" as one New Englander put it—but the great majority left Europe to worship God in the way they believed to be correct. They enthusiastically supported the efforts of their leaders to create a "city on a hill" or a "holy experiment," whose success would prove that God's plan for his churches could be successfully realized in the American wilderness. Even colonies like Virginia, which were planned as commercial ventures, were led by entrepreneurs who considered themselves "militant Protestants" and who worked diligently to promote the prosperity of the church.[5]

American life as a whole has slowly moved from this extreme to another over its history, a process governed by one of the Market's great euphemisms, "secularism." Secularism is, ostensibly, the idea that the public square should have no religious element. In a democracy, the story goes, all faiths are welcome, so how can we favor one over another? Such arguments are extremely deceptive, however, because they fail to make the all-important distinction between religions, which are institutions unique to their followers, and the spiritual side of human life, which is essential to all of us. If multiple religions were really the problem, then the natural solution, if one were at all interested in recognizing the human interior, would be to eject religion while retaining that universal human attribute, the soul. This could be done in many ways. There is, for instance, the so-called perennial philosophy, which is the distilled wisdom of all the world's great faiths. There is also what you might call the Joseph Campbell approach, which is to treat all religion as mythology, while defining the myth as a story that points to universal truths. One does not even need to dip into religious texts to find spiritual wisdom ("Do not scorn me! I am not poor," says Leonardo da Vinci. "He is poor, rather, who desires many things"). But nowhere will you find the proponents of secularism advocating such ecumenical solutions, even though the vast majority of mankind (more than 90 percent) professes to believe in God and to follow one faith or another. The reason is that saving your soul is not the objective of secularism. Quite the opposite. The real purpose of secularism is to replace the moral code with the Market Code. It is another example of the Market's great sleight of hand, the spiritual version of ethnic cleansing. After all, when God is removed from the public square, what is the only power left behind?

Here we see another example of the insidious way the Market redefines our terms. Secularism is done in the name of "tolerance," when it is actually *intolerance*—the exact opposite. Secularism means that the spiritual side of life is not tolerated in public. In other words, instead of practicing spiritual tolerance, we practice secular tolerance. We tolerate all means of denying the soul and the existence of God.

In this way the Market undercuts the ultimate source of moral absolutes and leaves them in human hands, where it can better control them. Instead of statutory law, like the U.S. Constitution, embodying spiritual principles innate in man and universe, such as truth, justice, and freedom, statutory law is left wide open to commercial interests, their political pressures, and the Market's ever-present veil, "progress." The moral gives way to the "ethical," a stand-in for the utilitarian. The result is laws and social pressures that support the removal of religion from public life, and through it, the eradication of the American soul.

Since 2003 alone, we have seen a snowball of such secular attacks. The *Under God* phrase in the Pledge of Allegiance was struck down by a California court (the Supreme Court later overturned this on a procedural, rather than substantive, point), the Supreme Court ruled that a state could take away someone's college scholarship if they decided to study theology, and litigation arose aimed at banning Christmas Nativity scenes. At the same time, one is free to burn the American flag, use a federal scholarship to study popular culture, and to mainstream pornography. While Reuters initially denied the Methodist Church the right to advertise on its Times Square billboard, no one stopped porn queen Jenna Jameson from advertising her XXX Web site in the same location. These and many other acts of their kind communicate a consistent message: religion is a public menace. And since the word *religion* comes from the Latin, *religio,* meaning "to link back" (to God), by cutting that cord the Market has shut the blinds on any reality beyond itself. Today my right to believe in nothing trumps your right to believe in something. Nihilism rules, and nihilism is a primary symptom of the hypermarket.

In the annals of secularism, the Market's greatest victory was won in an Alabama courthouse, for reasons hidden beneath the usual veil. The West, like all the world's great civilizations, has a religious tradition at its core. Ours is clearly the Judeo-Christian tradition. The essential moral code of that tradition is the Ten Commandments of the Old Testament, or *Tanakh,* handed down from God to Moses on Mt. Sinai over three thousand years ago, as described in the Book of Exodus in the Bible. In Judaism these are known as the *Aseret ha-Dibrot,* the Ten Declarations, and treated as the categories of a further 613 commandments *(mitzvot).* But whether we call them categories or commandments, whether we change their order or tweak their translation, we are talking about the heart of Judeo-Christian morality, the binding agent of our civilization.

In the summer of 2003, a two-and-a-half-ton granite monument to the Commandments was ordered removed from the Alabama Judicial Building on the grounds that it was unconstitutional. Alabama Supreme Court justice Roy Moore refused, on the grounds that the Ten Commandments form the basis for U.S. laws, and was removed from office. While unfortunate, this action would have been understandable if the aim was the liberalization of religion. If Moore had been objecting to a more inclusive spirituality—say, by adding the rest of the *mitzvot,* or quoting from the Upanishads, or adding text from the Koran, or coming up with some universal spiritual symbol—he should have been removed. But that wasn't the point of the exercise, as no spiritual alternative was put in the monument's place. Instead, the rule of law, the bulwark of a civilization, was separated from God. The law, according to this judicial action, would now be guided by "secular" considerations alone, as if contracts, lawyers, litigation, and judges would be enough to hold us all together. The idea of a moral absolute was dead, and relativism ruled: Whatever human beings decided would be okay. This was a watershed event. The primary issue was not the separation of church and state, but the very character of our civilization, and of civilization itself. Every major civilization on Earth has a religion at its core.

The arguments mustered to undermine Roy Moore were Market classics. The media took pains to paint him as a religious extremist, a "Christian fundamentalist." They failed to note that the Ten Commandments are not extreme, but have been central to our civilization for several millennia; that they are not just Christian, but given to Moses. In reality, what the secularists were ultimately objecting to was not Christianity, nor a literal reading of the Bible, but spiritual absolutes, in and of themselves. They were objecting to a man who believed in something, instead of nothing. Roy Moore was not a nihilist.

What the Commandments controversy ultimately represented, then, was not the separation of church and state, but a battle between the spiritual and the material, a battle in which the material won, backed by U.S. federal law. The issue wasn't religion, it was the denial of any higher authority than man, or any moral code stemming from Him. This isn't secularism—it is a virulent atheism. The term *secularism* just makes the ugly truth sound more palatable. It is another definition that has been manufactured by the Bubble. While many observers recognize that the Market is a-moral, few want to admit that it is a-theistic as well, particularly when we are proclaiming that the Market is America.

The Market loved watching God lose, of course. Once the moral code is eradicated, human beings are completely free to accept the Market Code, where good is profit, truth is whatever works, beauty is efficiency, love is performance, courage is selfishness, and meaning is money. We are free to transform the law into an instrument of materialism and institutionalize the Market's will. This is the death of democracy, where the people rule, through their own individual moral action, and the emergence of *marketocracy,* where the Market rules. American democracy was founded on *spiritual* fundamentals: truth, justice, freedom, equality, principles that infuse the Constitution. By undermining their higher legitimacy, all the secularists did was trade one set of fundamentals for another: market fundamentals, the only thing left when the Judeo-Christian tradition was wheeled away—and not just in Alabama, but from schools and a courthouse in Ohio; the Elkhart, Indiana, Municipal Building; a public park in Plattsmouth, Nebraska; a public courtyard in Johnson County, Iowa; a courthouse in Kentucky; and many other targets of litigation, threatened or otherwise.

This same antispirit has now spread across the land. Secularism has so far distanced us from God that to mention the word in open debate is to incite embarrassment and dismissal. God is anathema to our media, our political commentators, and our academics, at least in public, and increasingly in private. It used to be that God was front and center, while sex and money were personal matters. Now those roles are reversed. God is a dirty word, while your sex life and your 401(k) plan are the common subject of cable TV shows. This transition is particularly apparent in the business world, for obvious reasons. Just imagine for a moment what would happen if you began your next business meeting with the simple ecumenical suggestion that everyone pause for a brief moment to say grace. Your cringing CEO would later apologize to everyone on your behalf. You might even be fired for it. And if you were, the Supreme Court would uphold your company's right to do so. It is amazing how the simplest references to man's spiritual life now inspire such discomfort and even revulsion in American society, and how our legal and political machinery has been marshaled against them—even though over 90 percent of Americans say they believe in God. Meanwhile, in Islamic countries, the muezzin is calling the entire society to prayer five times a day. Instead of "Remember God," our society is blaring "Remember the Market," a message communicated through the telemarketing calls that interrupt your dinner, the spam that clogs your computer, the junk mail that fills your mailbox, and the more extreme forms of advertising appearing now, from the beer logos pressed into the sand of the beach before you arrive to the mobile billboards circling our cities on the backs of trucks. If this were balanced by some higher message, all would be fine, but there is not a single higher message in sight, a situation that is clearly unhealthy, but that we accept as normal, even American, of all things.

There are many repercussions that follow removing God from a society, but perhaps the most inhuman is that it eradicates the spirit of life, which is love. This is pure market dynamics. Love is the *binding* force, the creator of *us,* while the market is the *dividing* force, *me vs. you.* That is what competition is all about. While individuals and businesses may cooperate, based on a legal contract, no one confuses that with love. Hence, as the power of the Market increases in a society, society fragments, and all kinds of love, joy, passion, and other sensibilities cool. At best, people become more "professional" with one another. Continue this trend, and you pass from indifference to hostility—as evinced by a rise in litigation—and ultimately, violence. In America, the home of the unbridled market, the over-the-counter assault weapon, and the largest legal army on Earth, even *The Wall Street Journal* has concluded that Americans have "a profoundly rationalistic vision of human relations which looks with suspicion on mystery, myth, and strange feelings . . . there has been a flattening of the sensibilities . . . pleasure and self-fulfillment, yes; passion, no."

At the same time, the Market's innate antipathy toward the soul, religion, and God is by no means an exclusively American problem. The entire modern age has given birth to an increasingly efficient economic system. The well-known pathologies of modernity—meaninglessness, purposelessness, loneliness, anxiety, depression, fear, heartlessness, boredom, alienation, indifference, desensitization—are all pathologies brought about by the hypermarket. They are the product of an imbalance between the spiritual and material sides of life and the social fragmentation that results. The Industrial Revolution bred them en masse. Such pathologies can be politically dangerous, as they tend to radicalize those adversely affected by them, to the point where they think the Market is the problem. Well, the unbalanced *hyper*market most assuredly *is* the problem. But a Market restrained by Judeo-Christian values, as codified in law and represented in democratic institutions, most certainly is not. It is, rather, a recipe for social success, the very recipe that made America. But like the "postmodern family" we are now in the process of changing that long-standing recipe. With great irony, we are trying to do what the Soviet Union tried to do: replace the religious core of our civilization with a materialistic ideology. It doesn't work. Our approach to the spiritual side of life may need significant rethinking, it may be antiquated, it may be represented by flawed institutions, but the eradication of religion and its replacement with the market system will only breed social chaos. Without God, anything is permissible, which is just what they want to hear on Wall Street.

## Economic Materialism

While secularism has gathered momentum, it has been assisted by a potent weapon, the social science of economics. The discipline of economics arose at a time when society was dominated by traditional values. Since these values were taken as a given, early economic philosophers like Adam Smith, Alfred Marshall, and David Ricardo implicitly assumed that the Market would be operating on top of a moral foundation. As the Market has intensified, however, it has corroded that very foundation in an effort to free it-self from restraint. It has created its own idealized market world, free of all morality, where everyone is merely a trader operating in his own self-interest—and nothing more. This is a useful intellectual exercise, but eco-nomics now tries to explain all of human behavior with this model, as if the boundaries of the economy were the boundaries of reality itself. The result is economic materialism.

The high priests of economic materialism are found in many places, but the Market's leading seminary is the Chicago School, so called because it emerged from the University of Chicago. To the Chicago School, life boils down to rational self-interest, a model applied to law, crime, family, sex, health, education—everything:

> Economics formerly observed what might be called "stopping points"—demarcations of subject areas where economic rationality was not con-sidered to operate. The Chicago [School], in essence, seeks to abolish all stopping points. For those who believe that there are things in life that are sacred and beyond the workings of self-interested rationality, the Chicago [School] sees such attitudes as part of a superficial ideological "cover" for the underlying true workings of economic forces.[6]

Naturally, this drives Chicago School economists to rather extreme lengths in their attempts to explain human life. For instance, to the Chicago School, marriage is not based on love, but is centered on a contract, in which the parties perform sexual and other services for each other; there is no moral distinction, therefore, between marriage and prostitution. This same ap-proach results in such ruminations as this from a paper on marital stability from *The Journal of Economic Theory*[7]:

> The *stable marriage problem* was first introduced by Gale and Shapley [2]. A stable marriage problem is a triplet $(M, W, P)$, where $M$ and $W$ are disjoint finite sets which we refer to as "men" and "women" and $P$ is a function that maps each $m \in M$ into a strict preference relation $P(m)$ over the set $\{m\} \cup W$ and each $w \in W$ into a strict preference relation $P(w)$ over the set $\{w\} \cup M$. We refer to $V \equiv M \cup W$ as the set of *agents*. We write $v' >_v v''$ when $P(v)$ ranks $v'$ higher than $v''$, and in this case

we say that *v* *prefers* *v'* to *v''*. The relations $<_v$, $\geq_v$, and $\leq_v$ are derived from $>_v$ in the standard way. We say that *v'* is *acceptable to v* if $v' >_v v$. A pair $(m, w) \in M \times W$ is called *acceptable* if *m* and *w* are acceptable to each other.

I think love was the only variable left out of that stable marriage.

Ultimately, the Chicago School aims to use this approach to explain all human life, thereby enthroning the Market as the king of all social reality. What we see here is the emergence of a completely flat religion, with the Market at its head, one maintained in the face of an Everest of evidence against it, from the individual who gives an old woman his seat on the subway to every love song ever written.

If you think this economic materialism is somehow restricted to Chicago, guess again. The Chicago School is the epicenter of modern economic thought, the core theology of the market society. It has consequently become an increasingly common paradigm outside the boundaries of economics itself. To show just how deeply it has penetrated, consider the sociology of religion. There it is now all the rage to apply the market paradigm to churches, transforming them, at least on paper, into the franchise operations of large multinationals. Acting as consultants, sociologists advise these retail outlets how to improve their product lines, service consumers, firm up their customer base, increase market share, and survive in a competitive marketplace. Needless to say, "a god whose message to the world is delivered entirely in a vocabulary of the workings of the forces of economic self-interest can hardly be the God of the Bible." [8]

One of the great dangers of such economic materialism is that it blinds us to the enormous role played by morality in society. For example, while corporate scandals are clearly a moral problem, and while they have wrought inestimable damage upon our economy in recent years, economists cannot explain why this failure has occurred, or why it has spread like a cancer throughout our system, other than telling us "the boom made us do it." The usual metrics just don't apply. Something has happened beyond the confines of the economic discipline, something that is deep in the fabric of our society, yet inextricably part of our economic well-being.

In an even larger sense, we talk about the triumph of "democratic capitalism" as if the successful recipe for a society were merely the right combination of politics and economics. Our secular minds have overlooked the central role that the moral code has played in virtually all healthy civilizations, including our own, where the essential recipe has been *Judeo-Christian* democratic capitalism. Man is not just a political and economic creature, he is primarily a spiritual creature, a creature in need of metaphysical explanations of where he came from, why he is here, and where he is going, answers built into the framework of a higher culture that provides his life with meaning and purpose, and extends his responsibilities beyond himself. The success of a nation, or a civilization, is a three-legged stool composed of economics, politics, *and* religion, the framework of a healthy culture. Unbalance any leg of that stool and the entire society begins to tilt.

## Market Idolatry

The widespread acceptance of economic materialism in our society, the flawed assumptions upon which it rests, and their noteworthy result are all epitomized by a difference of opinion that arose in 2003 about, of all things, the Thanksgiving turkey. In late November of that year, Jeff Jacoby, a columnist for *The Boston Globe,* published an article entitled "Giving Thanks for Capitalism," which suggested the following:

> Isn't there something wondrous—something almost inexplicable—in the way your Thanksgiving weekend is made possible by the skill and labor of vast numbers of total strangers? To bring that turkey to the dining room table, for example, required the efforts of thousands of people—the poultry farmers who raised the birds, of course, but also the feed distributors who supplied their nourishment and the truckers who brought it to the farm, not to mention the architect who designed the hatchery, the workmen who built it, and the technicians who keep it running. . . . No one rode herd on all those people, forcing them to cooperate for your benefit. And yet they did cooperate. When you arrived at the supermarket, your turkey was there. You didn't have to do anything but show up to buy it. If that isn't a miracle, what should we call it?

Adam Smith called it "the invisible hand"—the mysterious power that leads innumerable people, each working for his own gain, to promote ends that benefit many. Out of the seeming chaos of millions of uncoordinated private transactions emerges the spontaneous order of the market. Free human beings freely interact, and the result is an array of goods and services more immense than the human mind can comprehend. No dictator, no bureaucracy, no supercomputer plans it in advance. Indeed, the more an economy is planned, the more it is plagued by shortages, dislocation, and failure.

It is commonplace to speak of seeing God's signature in the intricacy of a spider's web or the animation of a beehive. But they pale in comparison to the kaleidoscopic energy and productivity of the free market. If it is a blessing from Heaven when seeds are transformed into grain, how much more of a blessing is it when our private, voluntary exchanges are transformed—without our ever intending it—into prosperity, innovation, and growth? The social order of freedom, like the wealth and the progress it makes possible, is an extraordinary gift from above. On this Thanksgiving Day and every day, may we be grateful.[9]

Where do we start? While it is true that the market system deserves credit for bringing the turkey from Point A to Point B, it doesn't deserve all the credit, for it is only half the story. The other, equally important half is the moral system, the internal side of the turkey delivery network. A small sampling includes the working conditions on turkey farms, including the pay and benefits given whatever unskilled, immigrant labor they employ; the tactics of the unions that impact the entire turkey industry; the occupational safety and health regulations pertaining to turkeys, including the use of growth-enhancing drugs; the honesty of the farmers in living up to those regulations; the integrity of the bureaucrats enforcing those regulations; the honesty of the distributors in dealing with the farmers, to include not stealing their product; and the conditions the animals themselves are raised in, the amount of pain they do or do not endure.

Ironically, three days prior to Jacoby's piece, an editorial appeared in the *Globe*'s sister paper, *The New York Times*, that hit this last point, by describing the life and death of the modern turkey. This process begins with artificial insemination, then hatching in an incubator. Once it has attained a certain size, the turkey's upper beak is snipped off so it can only guzzle fortified corn mash, and its toenails as well, so it won't hurt any other turkeys in the crowded conditions of its new home. This is a windowless barn, holding as many as ten thousand other birds, where the lights shine twenty-four hours a day, keeping them all awake and eating. Even if they feel tired, they are so tightly packed that they cannot move around or indulge their instinct to roost. They are like human beings forced to sleep upright. They spend their lives standing on a pile of wood chips so full of waste that the smell of ammonia stings the eyes. After years of market selection, these turkeys are all one genetic strain, the Broad Breasted White, developed for its ability to quickly produce large amounts of white meat. By their eighth week, each one is so large that it is unable to walk or have sex. Since their breeding has left their immune systems so weak, farmers add large amounts of antibiotics to their feed and wear masks for fear of infecting them. Finally, with what must come as a great relief, the bird is slaughtered. Because of their monotonous diet, however, their flesh is so bland that processors inject it with vegetable oils and saline solution, improving "mouthfeel," increasing shelf life, and adding weight. In 2003, 45 million of these birds were sold on Thanksgiving alone. Benjamin Franklin once suggested that the fast, spirited, and elusive turkey he knew in colonial times would be a better national symbol than the bald eagle. One has to wonder how he would have felt about the Broad Breasted White.[10]

Now you may, or may not, have sympathy for the plight of the turkey caught in this Brave New World. But if not, consider that the very efficiency that Jacoby praises in the turkey industry was once found in another industry, which likewise had a long and intricate production line, involving numerous participants, beginning in the forests of Africa, and ending up in places like my home town, Annapolis, Maryland, whose historic auction block for human beings, the aptly named Market House, operated for over a century and still stands by the city dock. Slavery should put to rest forever the idea that the Market is a moral system, or an immoral system. It is neither. It is purely amoral. It does what is productive, and slave labor can be very productive indeed.

The failure to recognize the spiritual side of society leads to the second misconception in Jacoby's piece, the common identification of the Market with Adam Smith's "invisible hand." In what has been called "one of the most often distorted passages in economic literature,"[11] Adam Smith stated, in *An Inquiry into the Nature and Causes of the Wealth of Nations,* published in the auspicious year 1776, that every individual "neither intends to promote the public interest, nor knows how much he is promoting it . . . he intends only his own gain, and he is in this, as in many other cases, led by an invisible hand to promote an end which was no part of his intention." Smith was no patron saint for the Chicago School. He was, first and foremost, a moral philosopher, the author of *The Theory of Moral Sentiments*. Like others of his time, he always assumed that the Market would be operating within a moral framework. Thus, Smith's "invisible hand" does not just arise from self-interest, but is, rather, the very principle that integrates *both* the moral and the productive, creating a single social outcome. This is God, not the Market.

> ### Some Moral Sentiment from Adam Smith
>
> *"People of the same trade seldom meet together but the conversation ends in a conspiracy against the public, or in some contrivance to raise prices."*
>
> *"Those exertions of the natural liberty of a few individuals, which might endanger the security of the whole society, are, and ought to be, restrained by the laws of all governments."*
>
> *"Our merchants and master manufacturers complain much of the bad effects of high wages in raising the price, and thereby lessening the sale of their goods both at home and abroad. They say nothing concerning the bad effects of high profits."*

The final misconception of the article arises from the other two. By failing to take into account the moral side of life, thereby collapsing reality to a single plane, the author not only equates the Market with the "invisible hand," but with all reality. In this way, the Market becomes God. This idea is implied by the entire article, which begins "Gratitude to the Almighty is the theme of Thanksgiving," recalls the original blessings to God by the Pilgrims, and then redirects those blessings to the "free market." It concludes by suggesting that the "free market" is the ultimate blessing from Heaven. This prompted one reader to question, in a letter to the editor entitled "Mistaking Man's Actions for God's," why it is that "genuflecting at the altar of the free market is an act worthy of religious reverence," while another rebuttal, this one by a Jesuit theologian, advised, "Let's not bow down in worship to the idol of free markets."[12] Here the true nature of free market ideology finally lies exposed. It is nothing but market idolatry, the worship of the Market.

# The Modern God

The idea that Americans think of the Market as God is a notion that has now been gathering steam since the end of the nineties. In 1997, Buddhist scholar David Loy wrote:

> Our present economic system should also be understood as our religion, because it has come to fulfill a religious function for us. The discipline of economics is less a science than the theology of that religion, and its god, the Market, has become a vicious circle of ever-increasing production and consumption by pretending to offer a secular salvation. The collapse of communism makes it more apparent that the Market is becoming the first truly world religion, binding all corners of the globe into a world-view and set of values whose religious role we overlook only because we insist on seeing them as "secular." [13]

A more popular exposition of this idea occurred in 1999, when *The Atlantic* published "The Market as God." Written by Harvard theologian Harvey Cox, the article soon spread across the Internet and became part of many a sermon. Among Cox's many insightful observations: "At the apex of any theological system, of course, is its doctrine of God. In the new theology this celestial pinnacle is occupied by The Market." [14] In 2002, Harvard Business School followed up with a four-way debate called "The Market as God, Science as God, Law as God, or God as God," aimed at identifying the seat of moral authority in the modern age. Surprisingly, Harvard was not an option.

In 2000, culture critic Thomas Frank published a scathing critique of extreme capitalism, *One Market Under God,* in which he painstakingly laid out how unthinking our allegiance to the Market had become. A year later the Reverend Bill Phipps, the outspoken head of the United Church of Canada, that country's second largest church, was quoted as saying that "the ideology of the so-called free market is obliterating all other criteria for the development of human society. The market has become our God." [15] On the other side of the Atlantic, another well-known minister, David Jenkins, retired

bishop of Durham and author of *Market Whys and Human Wherefores,*
struck the same note: "The market is a good that has been turned into a
god—and that is a problem." [16] Back in America, the academic journal
*Bridges,* an interdisciplinary study of theology, philosophy, history, and
science, devoted an entire issue to "The Market as God: Converting Creation into Commodities." That same year, two articles in the same vein
popped up in the British Green Party journal, *Sustainable Economics.* The
first suggested that:

> Our world has become almost completely dominated by a system of
> beliefs and doctrines that stem from something now described as
> "The Market". But few could offer a consistent explanation of what
> it is. . . . It's as if it's all pervasive, everywhere at all times—which
> sounds like a definition of God, or at least of a false god. Indeed, for
> its adherents, The Market is as much a religion as for any other sort
> of believer. [17]

The second article, by philosopher John McMurtry of Canada, author of
*Unequal Freedoms: The Global Market as an Ethical System,* stated that the
Market is by no means a metaphor, but is now considered by many to be "the
ultimate structure of reality." [18] In California, where nothing stays new for
long, they were already taking this for granted. "The deity of our new state religion," wrote Ernest Partridge, a professor at UC Riverside, "is, of course, 'the
free market.' " [19]

Meanwhile, back in a small college in Iowa, the idea that the Market was
the modern God had already been turned into performance art. In 2000,
using a combination of dance, theater, music, sound, text, puppetry, and
digital technologies, Paul Zmolek and his colleagues at Luther College
staged *In God We Trust,* a dynamic collage of ancient religious rites that "ex-
amines the metaphor of the Free Market as the omnipotent, omniscient,
and omnipresent godhead for a newly dominant global religion with a fully
developed theology." Zmolek explains, "I had the idea for this work over
ten years ago while riding an express bus into San Francisco's Financial District during rush hour. I was the only person on the bus who was not wearing
a power suit and carrying a briefcase. Feeling like an anthropologist ob-

serving a society that was completely foreign in its culture and values, I amused myself by speculating what kind of sacred ritual dance this culture would create."[20]

What these diverse and disconnected voices represent is the evidence for a transition that is remarkable not only for its magnitude, but for how quietly it has been unfolding. The rising power of the Market has slowly but surely been pulling America inside out, from an ancient, inward-focused, moral foundation, governed by God, to a modern, outward-focused, productive foundation, ruled by the Market. In effect, America is in the process of swapping gods, trading Heaven for Earth, a seismic shift that has passed by with hardly a blip of explanation and that has nothing to do with how good or bad the stock market happens to be doing today.

## Gross Domestic Happiness

The extent to which we have accepted the Market as God, and thus, the extent to which the Market's veil has fallen, can be seen in how we have subordinated the very idea of human happiness to the economy. You can see this in two widespread beliefs held by Americans, the first being that old saw, money buys happiness. Needless to say, this belief is a great boon to productivity, but all the evidence suggests that it is at best a half-truth. Studies reveal that money only makes people happy up to a certain point, the point at which one has lifted oneself out of poverty. But once you have clothes on your back, a roof over

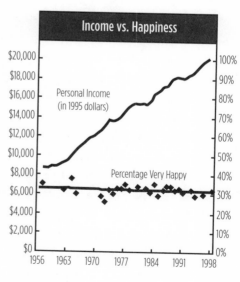

your head, and food on the table, multiple sources of evidence suggest that all the money in the world is not going to make you one bit happier. In the

United States, for instance, personal income has been rising steadily since the 1950s. But depending on your sources, happiness has either been flat or even trended downward slightly.[21] And if you think about it, this theory passes the commonsense test, too. Over the past two centuries the world has experienced tremendous economic growth. Between 1820 and 1992 the average world GDP per capita increased eight times.[22] But does this mean we should be eight times happier than Abe Lincoln?

Indeed, what is ironic about the statement "money buys happiness" is that, beyond the threshold point, it is actually the route to *unhappiness*. Once you have achieved a basic standard of material well-being, happiness comes from family and friends, marriage, leisure activities, and the nature of your work. These things are all negatively impacted by the excessive pursuit of money, which creates stress, steals family time, alters moods, breeds friction, and drains the meaning from life.

The second fallacy begins with the idea that a nation should be judged primarily by its economic performance. While there are many different indicators of that performance—the deflation rate, the balance of trade, the Index of Leading Economic Indicators, the various market indices—the main offender here is the GDP.

The Gross Domestic Product ostensibly measures the size and growth of the economy, but in the way we actually use it today, it is meant to represent the health of an entire nation, a fallacy that was eloquently debunked a long time ago. In his first major campaign speech on March 18, 1968, Robert Kennedy warned:

> Too much and too long, we seem to have surrendered community excellence and community values in the mere accumulation of material things. Our Gross National Product, now, is over eight hundred billion dollars a year, but that GNP—if we should judge America by that—counts air pollution and cigarette advertising and ambulances to clear our highways of carnage. It counts special locks for our doors and the jails for those who break them. It counts the destruction of our redwoods and the loss of our natural wonder in chaotic sprawl. It counts napalm and the cost of a nuclear warhead, and armored cars for police who fight riots in our streets. It counts . . . the television programs which glorify violence in order to sell toys to our children. Yet the Gross

National Product does not allow for the health of our children, the quality of their education, or the joy of their play. It does not include the beauty of our poetry or the strength of our marriages, the intelligence of our public debate or the integrity of our public officials. It measures neither our wit nor our courage, neither our wisdom nor our learning, neither our compassion nor our devotion to our country; it measures everything, in short, except that which makes life worthwhile. And it can tell us everything about America except why we are proud that we are Americans.[23]

Today, thirty-seven years later, the GDP is still measuring America, and just as senselessly. The subsequent breakdown of the American family, for instance, has been a great boon to the GDP, with divorces alone now adding over $60 billion a year.[24] While youth suicide has tripled in that time, the market for antidepressants and antianxiety drugs is fast approaching $20 billion a year.[25] We are still calling this progress. Interestingly, there have been several attempts to provide a more inclusive measure of American social progress, such as the Index of Social Health at Fordham University (since 1987), the Genuine Progress Indicator of Redefining Progress (since 1995), and the Index of Sustainable Economic Welfare—but you don't hear about them on the nightly news or in federal government reports. Unlike the GDP, which has shown strong growth since the 1950s, all three of these alternative indicators show that the overall health of American society has actually *declined* since the 1970s. This has led to the development of a "threshold hypothesis" for market economies:

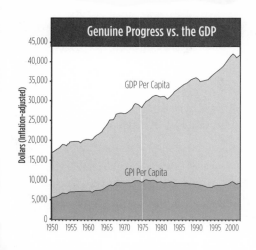

> For every society there appears to be a period in which economic growth (as conventionally measured) brings about an improvement in the quality of life, but only up to a point—the threshold point—beyond

which, if there is more economic growth, quality of life may begin to deteriorate.[26]

To this we should add: if a "bull market" is fueled by credit-card debt, fraudulent accounting, phony stock research, a lack of business fundamentals, and intense social pressure, who needs that kind of "productivity"?

The GDP is so obviously flawed, and those flaws have been pointed out in so many places for such a long time, that it is stark testimony to the grip the Market has on our minds. One must travel all the way to the tiny Himalayan kingdom of Bhutan, a country that has yet to enter the modern world, to find the simplest common sense being exercised on a national level. There the king has decreed that his nation's success will be measured by a standard of Gross National Happiness. Once you realize how obvious that standard should be to anyone, it reveals the premise our market society is really working under: instead of happiness being our priority, *all that matters is the money.* We have been deeply penetrated by the most basic notion of economic materialism.

## The Unholy Alliance

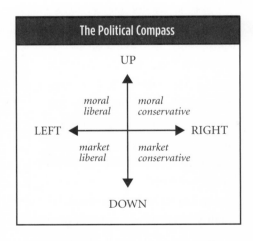

As our modern God has risen, it has increasingly exerted a gravitational attraction on the American political system. In addition to the classic opposition between left and right, liberal and conservative, progress and tradition, there is now a strong competing tension between up and down, spiritual and material, moral and economic. These two complementary axes divide the political landscape into four quadrants, as shown to the right.

In this new political landscape, left and right each have a market element and a moral element. On the left, the moral liberal (also known as the classical liberal) pursues moral progress, spawning such vitally important movements as environmentalism, human rights, corporate responsibility, and civil rights. The market side of liberalism (also known as "modern liberalism") is the newer, more virulent form bred by the hypermarket. Attacks on religion, the nuclear family, and America itself all spring from here. In fact, there is a one-for-one correspondence between the common elements of market liberalism and market philosophy. For example, the fracturing and fragmentation of society into race, class, and gender, and the creation of ideologies that legitimize family breakdown, are nothing but *atomization*, the reduction of human society to competitive particles. Likewise, moral relativism is the philosophical underpinning of the Market's amoral, "anything goes" mentality. The reduction of the moral to the purely political, the promotion of nihilism in the guise of "secularism," sanctioning individual moral judgment through political correctness, and promoting hyperindividualism all serve to advance the Market's self-centered, competitive, amoral agenda. The market liberal even attempts to erase all natural gender differences, as if men and women were not just equal, but interchangeable, thereby transforming human beings into a single class: "employee." In sum, the market liberal is the Market's stormtrooper. Unsatisfied with believing in nothing himself, he wants to proactively destroy the sources of meaning and purpose in society, leaving it wide open to the Market's advance. Not surprisingly, this attitude is the product of the Bubble. The market liberal's identity does not arise from within, but is programmed from without, by the fashion industry, the music industry, and a wave of advertising. Once again, this is the very opposite of freedom.

On the right we have a similar duality. The moral conservative is, like the moral liberal, an essential element of democracy, safeguarding its institutions, traditions, and values, political, religious, and familial. Market conservatism, however, exists to serve the Market. It is the voice of self-interested big business and also of free-market ideology. While market liberalism paves the way for market culture, market conservatism defends market doctrine, the blueprints of the market

| A Perfect Match | |
| --- | --- |
| Modern Liberalism ⟷ | Market Philosophy |
| hyperindividualism | selfishness |
| politicization | competition |
| moral relativism | amorality |
| hyperegalitarianism | homogenization |
| political correctness | enforcing amorality |
| race, class, gender | atomization |
| gender neutralization | commodification |
| secular | materialism |
| antiestablishment | nihilism |

economy. Together they form a two-piston engine: the former disseminates the ideology of Bubble life, while the latter promotes the ideology that builds the Bubble itself. Market conservatives are also the driving force in redefining the nature of America. Lacking any moral vision, they push the idea that the free market is "what we are about." In this way the business of America becomes business rather than democracy.

Both market liberalism and market conservatism are products of the hypermarket. They are distortions of the norm, the inversion of the two essential sides of our political life to serve the Market. Collectively, they form the material underworld of American life, the unholy alliance of Market America.

To this genus we add two species both known for their strident worship of the free market. The first is the libertarian, a strange amalgamation of left and right, both radical individual and free marketeer. "The market is supreme," trumpets the Ludwig van Mises Institute, which promotes libertarian economic theory. "The market alone puts the whole social system in order and provides it with sense and meaning."[27] A classic example of market idolatry.

The second are the acolytes of Ayn Rand, who exist in a world of confused metaphysics. Rand felt that capitalism was innately moral, a common misconception. Capitalism is the philosophy that brings the Market to life, and the Market is purely amoral, as we have seen. Indeed, amorality is its dominant characteristic. So to call capitalism moral is a contradiction in terms. To put it another way, the Market is a divisive, atomizing power. It is purely *me vs. you*, the principle of unbridled competition. Morality, on the other hand, reinforces *us*, the principle of unity. One is exterior, the other interior. By conflating these distinctions, Rand raised the bar of market idolatry, as the Market became a *moral* God. But as an atheist, she left herself no choice.

As a whole, Market Americans are now the dominant political force in America today. Since the 1960s, America has fought a cultural revolution, and it is generally accepted that the market liberals have won. The cultural storm troopers have spread secularization, dismantled moral judgment, established politically correct speech, and deconstructed truth itself. "Anything goes." Meanwhile, the market conservatives have won an equally important war over economic doctrine. The palace guard has successfully defended the unbridled Market, handing an enormous victory to corporate America and all those in the highest income bracket. In total, we have created one Market Nation, culturally and economically, in which the Market is our leader. We have bred a market society, in which the principles of democracy are increasingly subordinate to market principles: a marketocracy. We have created the first marketocracy.

## God vs. the Market

While the hypermarket has turned the American political landscape into four quadrants, the numbers of people involved in each create only two major voting blocs. Since market conservatives tend to be in the upper region of the economic pyramid, the largest numbers of conservative voters are actually moral conservatives, from the moderate to the so-called religious right. This middle-class branch of Moral America is strong in areas that the Market is relatively weak: rural areas and small towns and cities. The dominant liberal vote is not moral liberals, however, but market liberals, the product of our powerful market culture, whose growing numbers have changed the balance of liberalism since the 1960s. This branch of Market America is naturally strongest where the Market is strong: cities and their sprawl. Since America is a maritime nation, many of these market centers are found on the coasts and in the Great Lakes region. They include New York and Los Angeles, the twin turbochargers of the Bubble. In sum, the hypermarket has created a deep divide among the American population, with market liberals holding sway in metropolitan areas, and moral conservatives prevailing beyond. The former are the modern product of the hypermarket, of concrete canyons ruled by an economic power, while the latter are the legacy of America past, of wide-open spaces ruled by Jehovah. In other words, America is now split between God and the Market, the deepest of all possible divisions.

These are loose generalizations, as any characterization of 280 million people must be. But the election results of both 2000 and 2004 support this polarized reading. In each case, America was divided into the so-called Blue and Red states (a reference to their coloring on the election results map), the former being the bicoastal urbanized regions and the Great Lakes states, and the latter being the "heartland" states. Married people were more likely to vote Red than Blue, as were those who prioritized trust and character, or who attended church weekly. Ominously, the distribution of home-video porn movies eerily mirrors this same duality, with Blue states filling up on porn and Red states more likely to abstain.[28] Such results suggest the corrosive impact of the urban hypermarket on the human character. As Thomas Jefferson put it, "I view great cities as detrimental to the health, the morals, and the liberties of man," although he should have added "cities where all values are subordinate to market values." Not all are this way.

There is great danger when a country is divided along the most deeply held beliefs, and in a country that has already had one bloody civil war, a danger not to be overlooked. As the hypermarket continues its march, we can only expect this divide to deepen, as it is doing right now. There is currently, for instance, a well-funded media campaign called "Retro vs. Metro" that exemplifies the chasm the Market is creating. Here *metro* is a flag for the urban market liberal, while the disparaging *retro* is meant to consign the balance of America to the past. "Welcome to the Divided States of America," exclaims the national ad, which explains its perspective thus:

> Some Americans think our much discussed current divide is both unique and disturbing. It may be disturbing, but it is not unique. America is not a unified country with common traditions, needs, and desires. Rather, it is an amalgam of antithetical entities: two nations, each with its own history, traditions, needs, and aspirations. Throughout our history, these two nations have been joined constitutionally but have almost always been apart in culture, economics, politics, and increasingly, religion. In the beginning, the two nations were defined as the North and the South, which division lasted from the founding of the republic down through the Civil War and Reconstruction. As the nation expanded geographically, the division encompassed the new states, but from 1789 to the present, the agrarian South has remained the anchor of Retro America.[29]

What this divisive propaganda represents is the latest evidence of our ongoing social fragmentation. And lying at the bottom of it, beneath questions of geography, income, ethnicity, or social class, is the choice of deity among Americans. "The two Americas apparent in the 48%-48% 2000 election are two nations of different faiths," finds Michael Barone, publisher of *The Almanac of American Politics.* "One is observant, tradition-minded, moralistic. The other is unobservant, liberation-minded, relativist." [30] This is the divide between God and the Market, couched in politically acceptable terms. It is the difference between authentic spirituality and economic materialism.

Since the hypermarket has both liberal and conservative elements, its growing power has created massive contradictions on both sides of the aisle. On the left, the hypocrisy of liberals has been stunning. How many times have we heard the liberal railing against big business, against commercialism, against consumerism, when it is the liberal that has unleashed the Market upon all of us, by removing all moral limits from it? The liberal lashes out at the corruption at Enron, yet who were Enron's youthful executives but the product of the same universities that choke on the word *moral? The New York Times Magazine* devotes an entire issue to corporate corruption, then tops it off with a fashion spread on what to wear on the way to court. Hollywood is up in arms about the war in Iraq, meanwhile Hollywood is creating and distributing the decadent content that is offending all of Islam—for good reason. Liberals put the Darwin fish on the back of their cars, then rail against our social Darwinism, as if there were a higher reality to consider. And if Darwin is our guide, why do liberals willingly overlook the 2 million years of evolution that have shaped women to be mothers, in favor of day care?

Similar and equal hypocrisies are found in conservatism. Conservatives rightly bemoan the dumbing-down phenomenon in our society, yet conservatives promote the very unbridled Market that causes it. Likewise, conservatives attack the pornography industry, yet fail to connect the mainstreaming of porn to the market mechanism, even though the adage "sex sells" is far from new. Robert Bork wrote an insightful book on American decline, *Slouching Towards Gomorrah,* in which he detailed the deadly virus of modern liberalism—but failed to find any fault with capitalism. Conservatives talk about moral values, then vote down the majority of bills aimed at defeating sprawl and protecting the environment. What could be more moral than a healthy and beautiful world to live in? They moan about the decline of the family, when it is the unbridled Market that is pulling it apart.

By sowing these contradictions and intensifying polarization, the hypermarket has confused and degraded our political discourse. Instead of honest debate, Republicans fire volleys at Democrats, and Democrats fire back, and in the midst of the ensuing battle the Market escapes unscathed. This chaos has poisoned our political culture, as expressed in a new book, *Fat Man Fed Up*, by longtime journalist Jack Germond:

> I doubt there is any easy way—or, for that matter, any way at all—to fix the things that are wrong with American politics today. They are too deeply rooted. They are too much a part of a pattern of mindless behavior in our culture. We worship all the wrong gods—money, celebrity, and television, most notably. We listen to the loudest voices. We pay obeisance to false standards imposed on us by those with an axe to grind. We are too lazy intellectually to go beyond the glib language of politics.[31]

Here every last "deeply rooted" problem Germond cites—mindless behavior, the wrong gods, money, celebrity, television, loud voices, false standards, intellectual laziness, glib language—is a symptom of the hypermarket.

The great irony of Market America is the hidden dynamic that links its two sides together. Market conservatism actually *produces* market liberalism. The market liberal professes to want to be free from the very economic order the market creates—and in so doing, becomes part of that order, where "anything goes." So why does the Market create both a thesis and an antithesis like this? Why not create one uniform economy?

The answer lies in the nature of an economy itself. Every economy has two sides, production and consumption. Market conservatism is the philosophy of production, the engineering necessary to create the Bubble. Market liberalism is the philosophy of consumption, the consumer culture created by the Bubble. Collectively these two sides of the Market may appear to represent opposing principles, but their yin–yang relationship reflects the very nature of the economy. We have hammered our politics upon an economic template, another sure sign of marketocracy.

## The Two-Front War

Once we understand the nature of the San Andreas Fault that has opened up within America, the truth abroad reveals itself as well. Needless to say, the

Market is not an American phenomenon, nor does it operate differently elsewhere on Earth (the regulations imposed upon it being a separate matter). So as the Market spreads abroad and increases its power, all the market pathologies we have discussed will emerge: the same moral ozone holes, the same meltdown of the nuclear family, the same stress and burnout, the same marketecture, the same environmental damage, and the same decadent Bubble, jolting people with mindless sex and violence, and dumbing down even the strongest intellectual traditions. Most important, the Market will come into conflict with other religious traditions, just as it has the Judeo-Christian tradition. The hypermarket makes no distinction between religions: it is the moral absolutes it wants to erode. Ultimately, the Market wants to do away with the prevailing forms of civilization, each one of which has a religious tradition at its core. In their place, it wants one global market civilization, an entire planet that operates on market values. This is what the Market means by globalization, a process that is more accurately termed *marketization,* the conversion of human society to the market paradigm.

Naturally, this marketization is the recipe for conflict. Within the United States, that conflict has been mostly peaceful, as the tension between Red and Blue America, while manifesting itself in a "culture war," has so far been restrained by common bonds. But internationally those common bonds are lacking, particularly as one moves beyond the West. Moreover, there is an important distinction to be made in how different peoples view the damage wrought by the hypermarket. In America, the hypermarket is a domestic phenomenon, something we have bred and grown accustomed to. In non-Western countries, the scandals of American corporations, the soulless Chicago School economics of the market conservative, and the decadent Bubble of the market liberal are all the foreign products of Western, and particularly American, culture, imposed upon them from abroad, with devastating results. To make matters worse, this Market America is typically what other people see of us. It is the face of business and pop culture. The result is that while Moral America blames Market America for the excesses of the hypermarket at home, the rest of the world simply blames America itself, without discrimination. They equate the Market with America, and Moral America is lost.

When one puts our current conflict with Islamic civilization in this context, a simple dynamic becomes apparent beneath the surface complexities. The Market is not just targeting the Judeo-Christian tradition, it is targeting Islam, too. Muslims view this as an attack from America. In their eyes, America is a godless system, the Great Satan. A radical wing of Islam has decided to fight back. They have even struck down the global symbol of the Market, the World Trade Center. What we call "the war on terrorism" is thus fundamentally driven by the same conflict as our own "culture war" at home. It is the Market vs. God. The Market is simply fighting a two-front war.

## The National Storm Trooper

If you are wondering how this global Market War is proceeding, there is a clear signal now emanating from the National Cathedral in Washington, D.C. When the foundation of the National Cathedral was laid on September 29, 1907, it contained the following inscription from the Bible: "The Word was made flesh, and dwelt among us" (John 1:14a). By the time the building was finished in 1990, however, a very different Force was dwelling there: Darth Vader, the evil villain from the box-office smash hit *Star Wars.*

No, I am not kidding. In the 1980s, a contest was held to design gargoyles for the cathedral, and a thirteen-year-old won, after proposing a bust of Vader's head. The cathedral then placed the bust at its summit, the highest point in Washington. If you go to the cathedral's Web site (www.nationalcathedral.org), there is an entire Web page dedicated to this essential artifact of modern Christianity. It sits up there next to the other winning designs: a raccoon, a girl with pigtails and braces, and a man with large teeth and an umbrella. Perhaps Homer Simpson will be next.

Vader, of course, is the dark side of the Force, and a fine example of Mr. Hyde. He symbolizes the system as an inhuman machine, as his wheezing life support suggests. He invades foreign countries on false pretenses, tortures prisoners, tramples civil liberties, and alienates the galaxy. It is this distorted figure that now stares down at the capital of the United States from its highest point, the very summit of its National Cathedral. I guarantee you won't find anything like it in Mecca.

**National Bestseller, 1997.** This cover photo is both richly symbolic and eerily prescient. The twin towers of the World Trade Center have ascended into the heavens, where storm clouds are gathering. In addition to representing commerce, the perfectly straight, parallel towers are the embodiment of Euclidean geometry—the geometry of parallel lines that underlies Cartesian space, modern technology, and the entire mechanical, industrial worldview of the Market. This symbol further looms over the bell tower of a church, which by comparison is sinking into the city. Here the small cross symbol is held up in contrast to the dominant parallel lines. Unlike Euclidean geometry, the cross is commonly interpreted—in numerous religions—as the intersection of the spiritual and material sides of reality. Hence, what is sinking is this traditional view of reality itself, replaced by a purely one-sided, material view, a flat reality. This inversion of the natural order, the hallmark of the Modern Age, is captured in the title: the world has become the Underworld. Meanwhile, Nature watches and waits in the form of a lone bird. . . .

**Terrorist Attack, 2001.** Four years later an orthodox religious group attacks the World Trade Center, striking down the global symbol of the Market in its capital, New York. The group happens to be Muslim, but they worship the same God of Abraham as Christians and Jews. Like many orthodox Christians in America, the attackers consider American culture to be decadent and immoral. However, since they commonly experience only market America, not moral America, they identify America itself as the Great Satan, i.e., the leader of the Underworld. Religious fundamentalism attacks market fundamentalism, and America's domestic culture war goes international. Orthodox Christians respond to the attack by quoting Proverbs 14:34 to the media: "Living by God's principles promotes a nation to greatness, violating those principles brings a nation to shame."

From across the political and cultural spectrum, whether peacefully or violently, artistically or militarily, everyone here is criticizing the same thing: the modern worldview, which subordinates the human spirit to the Market, and hence, imprisons the soul. The central paradigm of our time is not a clash of civilizations or religions, it is God vs. the Market.

# 9. The Market Curve

Site prep, Annapolis.

Our thesis is that the idea of a self-adjusting market implied a stark utopia. Such an institution could not exist for any length of time without annihilating the human and natural substance of society; it would have physically destroyed man and transformed his surroundings into a wilderness.

—Karl Polanyi, *The Great Transformation*

Like a star condensing out of dust and gas, the market economy has coalesced into a powerful agent in our lives. This modern system is now exercising a profound gravitational attraction on our entire social space, warping its very fabric and dragging us all toward its burning core. If the ancients were here, they might profess that Earth has laid siege to Heaven. Based on what we have seen, we can now provide a more modern explanation.

As an active principle, the Market impacts all of society. That impact naturally lies along a curve, depending on how powerful the Market is. At one end of this curve lies a very weak Market, an *undermarket*. Here the Market does not have sufficient power to organize society along productive lines. This is bad for society, as it fails to adequately provide for its material well-being. The undermarket typically occurs when a society exerts too much control over the Market, such as by maintaining choking traditions or exerting governmental control over pricing, or when a critical mass of market values is absent.

At the other end of the curve we find a very strong Market, which is equally bad. This turbocharged condition is the *hypermarket*. Here the Market starts running society, and we all become subservient to it. This creates a diversity of symptoms, but in general, life becomes a meaningless rat race, society becomes increasingly Darwinian, and a host of social problems ensue, from the decline of the family to corporate corruption.

The optimal point, then, is the top of the curve, where the values of society exist in the proper balance. Here the Market is subject to moderation, like any other principle.

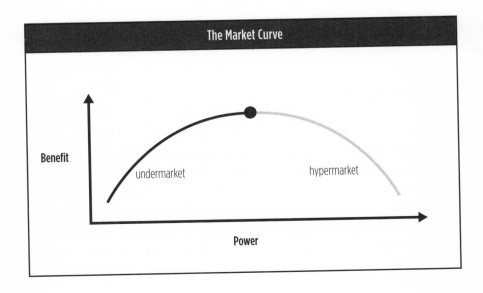

The American approach to capitalism has implicitly been to deny this logic. Instead of encouraging moderate capitalism, we have treated the Market as a virtually unlimited good. We have extolled "the wisdom of the marketplace," encouraged people to "let the market decide," and sought to spread this laissez-faire philosophy around the globe, as if it were an aspect of democracy. Implicit in this approach is the idea that the "free market" is somehow exempt from the laws of nature, in which all principles become an evil when pursued to excess.

As one might expect, this is a dangerous game. When you unbridle the Market, you start moving from one end of the Market Curve to another. It is like putting a turkey in the oven and turning the temperature knob all the way up. As the temperature rises, the impact is initially good. The bird starts to cook. Eventually the stove reaches 350 degrees, the optimum temperature. This is the top of the curve. At this point it seems like the laissez-faire approach is a big winner, because all the evidence points to it. But as the temperature continues to rise, the stove suddenly turns on you and becomes increasingly destructive. The bird starts to overcook, then blacken. If you aren't careful, the entire kitchen can go up in flames. Clearly, someone needs their hand on the knob.

An alternative metaphor arises from that classic symbol of the securities markets, the bull. With the proper harness on, the bull is the workhorse of the farm, plowing the fields night and day. But weaken that harness too much and the bull breaks free, trampling the crops.

## The American Hypermarket

These *market dynamics* explain what happened to American society in the latter half of the twentieth century. As technology advanced, the pace of life quickened, and competition increased. This heightened time demands and survival pressures, increasing stress levels and causing a host of physical and mental-health issues, such as rage, violence, depression, obesity, burnout, and substance abuse. Put on the defensive, people focused on themselves. A "me generation" arose, community ties weakened, and litigation exploded. Social pressures intensified, and consumption spiraled upward. The home-

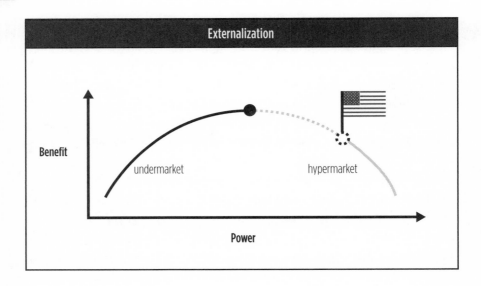

maker was industrialized, mothers were pulled into the workplace, the kids were sent to day care, and the nuclear family melted down, causing a raft of social problems: divorce, single mothers, teen suicide, latchkey kids. The corporate safety net disappeared, corporate loyalty followed, and corporate integrity plunged. A winner-take-all society broke out, fueling a widening income gap and causing an unprecedented, and unending, series of corporate scandals. Business became increasingly predatory. Incarceration levels rose to halt an advancing crime wave. Media penetration of daily life increased, particularly through television, and cultural space became saturated with commercial messages. The public was slowly withdrawn from reality and placed in the Market's Bubble, which broadcast 24/7. Programming devolved to measured jolts of sex and violence, and standards fell bar by bar. The dumbing down of content eroded the standards of journalism and literature alike. Reading itself declined. Vulgarity was championed as art. The humanities went into decline, while the sciences, the primary source of new technologies, boomed. The social hierarchy was pulled inside out: The authentic hero fell, the celebrity took his place, and the rich were placed on a pedestal, no matter how they got there. Entire professions—accounting, law, journalism, and increasingly medicine—replaced their standards with the

Market Code. The mall replaced the town square, and shopping became the national obsession. Savings rates plunged, while debt skyrocketed. Half of all people worked on vacation, when they went at all. Amid tremendous material prosperity, an equivalent spiritual poverty took hold. God fell, accelerated by a caustic "secularization" movement. The Market took His place, supported by a new economic theology. The ancient Sabbath disappeared with hardly a murmur. Society became increasingly Darwinian and predatory, targeting children, wielding health insurance as a weapon against the poor, and filling the ranks of the military with an economic draft. The political spectrum was realigned along a spiritual–material axis, creating a deep and dangerous divide in the nation. Public service declined, leaving the nation wide open to attack. Trust in government fell. Voter apathy grew. National unity fragmented into race, class, gender: every group for itself. The influence of special interests successfully pushed the Market's agenda. White-collar crime was slapped on the wrist, while critical environmental legislation was weakened or blocked. The market economy became an enormous alimentary canal, eating natural resources on one end and expelling trash on the other. Sprawl flourished, the ozone layer deteriorated, the global climate warmed, ecosystems declined, and 90 percent of the large fish in the sea disappeared. Anti-American sentiment rose across the world as people identified America as the cause of the Market's work. A deadly attack was launched at America by the militant wing of an orthodox faith, sparking a new era of intercivilizational conflict.

With the benefit of this hindsight, we can now see that the "free market" has betrayed us. Far from being an unlimited good, the Market has become the driving force of American decline, a decline that surfaced in the 1960s and has been going strong ever since. The Market has pitched us into a hypermarket and ripped through our society like a twister. Our long postwar expansion has certainly benefited our economy, but at tremendous human cost. Our lives are now spent in the service of the system, a marked difference from even our closest relatives. As the saying goes, Europeans work to live, but Americans live to work.

The reason why this has happened is deeply embedded in our history and character. When America was founded, it was a small nation of several million, unhindered by the cultural constraints of Europe, protected by two vast oceans, and with an enormous, wide-open frontier. This was a recipe that not only encouraged unlimited growth, but could absorb it. We naturally became a land of economic opportunity, and as such, attracted millions of people interested in improving their material well-being. In this early environment, when the national character was established, the idea of moderation did not play a strong role, and didn't have to. The unlimited ethos of "more" is not a problem when you don't have much, and there's lots of room for growth. But today our social environment is very different. The principles upon which America was based are all being challenged by market philosophy, and thus, no longer adequately describe who we are, or how we live. The system we live in has coalesced around us, grown in complexity, and become a very real power in our lives. We need a new vocabulary just to keep track of how it operates, and what it is doing to us. It doesn't just affect us, either, it affects people all over the world, people no longer held at bay by two enormous oceans. And it continues to accelerate. By 2050, it is estimated, America will be home to half a billion people. By then the sprawl along the East Coast will connect Washington, D.C. to Portland, Maine, forming a single megalopolis. Today America is like a can of soda that is slowly being shaken: the pressure is building.

Most deadly of all, as this great transformation has unfolded, we have fallen in love with the driving force behind it. Now, surrounded by evidence that something has gone drastically wrong with our society, we are like a proud parent who cannot admit that his A student has begun to steal. Even when the integrity of our society is shaking, when our popular culture is a catalog of grotesqueries, when our major institutions have lost their credibility, when American life is increasingly meaningless, when terrorism has erupted around the globe, and when the chief target of that terrorism is us, we resist all efforts to identify the culprit. Instead we throw up a thousand defense mechanisms around the Market, as if it were America itself, even as it continues to erode the very principles upon which our country was founded, and which once made us a light to the world.

In his famous defense of the free market, *The Road to Serfdom*, F. A. Hayek explained this phenomenon as follows:

> When the course of civilization takes an unexpected turn—when, instead of the continuous progress which we have come to expect, we

## Hypervocabulary

rat race
stress
burnout
type A
road rage
latchkey kid
time poverty
antidepressant
radical individualism
radical egalitarianism
political correctness
secularism
me generation
day care
self care
Inhibited Sexual Desire (ISD)
trophy wife
Type A personality
Home Meal Replacement (HMR)
Shaken Baby Syndrome
naming rights
branding
product placement
supermodel
metrosexual
dumbing-down
Celebrity Worship Syndrome
couch potato
sprawl
megalopolis
24/7
9/11
McMansion
bedroom community
mall
global warming
dead zone
Red and Blue America
Flyover Land
Genuine Progress Indicator (GPI)
market fundamentalism
clash of civilizations
Homeland Security

find ourselves threatened by evils associated by us with past ages of barbarism—we naturally blame anything but ourselves. . . . We are ready to accept almost any explanation of the present crisis of our civilization except one: that the present state of the world may be the result of genuine error on our own part and that the pursuit of our most cherished ideals has apparently produced results utterly different from those which we expected.[1]

So it is today. Unbridled capitalism now represents the gravest threat to our nation and the world, all the more so because it is the last thing we want to admit.

And the last thing the Bubble will tell you.

## Inversion

While the Market Curve explains our predicament, it is also great cause for hope. The Market Curve is no one-way street. Inversion can occur in either direction, at any time, creating historic cycles. While our society has experienced externalization, internalization is also possible, a process in which productivity becomes increasingly beholden to the Good.

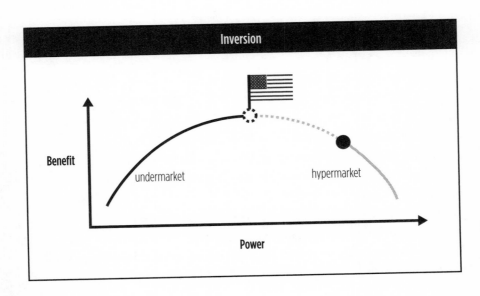

To understand the power of this transformation, just consider what would have happened if we had moderated the power of the Market in American life, and hit the top of the Market Curve. The pace of life would have hit a ceiling, competition would not have grown so intense, and the Market would not have become such a corrosive force. Other values—social, moral, cultural, religious—would have thrived rather than wilted beneath the onslaught. The deadly spiral of consumption would have been replaced by the natural ethos of sustainability. Stress levels would not have exploded. People today would be physically and psychologically healthier. Many people would be with us who are not. The nuclear family would not have melted down. The social and financial costs of crime, substance abuse, and health care would be much less. Community ties would be stronger, discouraging the need for lawyers to resolve our problems. Some of us who got divorced would not have; others would have grown up in an intact family. Moms could have afforded to spend time with their kids, rather than their desk. An "us" generation would have supported and strengthened our institutions and traditions. Fewer of us would have spent years behind bars. Companies would still be responsible to us, and we to them. We could expect to trust the people in charge to look after both their shareholders and the community. The income gap would have been flat. The corporation would have become not the seat of crime, but responsibility. Our cultural space would not be advertising space. Television would still be elevating our minds, on more than one network. So would art. The humanities would have marched forward on an equal basis with science. The authentic hero never would have left us, and the empty celebrity never would have risen. Professions would have upheld their standards, rather than shedding them. Life would be about more than how much we own. Our national unity would have taken preference over the selfish ambitions of factions. We would not have allowed sprawl from coast to coast, nor global climate change, nor the deep decline in ecosystems. We would have passed the legislation necessary to provide universal health insurance, to punish corporate criminals, and to protect the environment. We would not have inspired such hatred abroad, distanced ourselves from our allies, or eroded our civil liberties. We would now live in a society that supports us rather than preys on us with a wink and a nod.

There is absolutely no reason why we cannot create this balanced society today. The question is how to moderate the Market.

## The Anti-Market

Moderation is not a cause, but an effect. It arises from a spiritual awakening, an elevation of consciousness, an awareness of the way things truly are. This is the great missing piece of our social puzzle. After tremendous pain and suffering, on a global basis, mankind has finally crafted a universal economic solution (the free market) and a universal political solution (democracy). What we lack is a universal spiritual solution, a common understanding of the human interior, one rooted in the nature of reality, as we experience it. As a result, the modern world now sits on two legs of a three-legged stool—market democracy—and tilts accordingly.

While we have made tremendous advances in understanding the material side of human life, metaphysics, the study of the nature of reality, has withered since the Middle Ages, so long now that people treat the human interior as if it were unfathomable. When it comes to the nature of reality, we are like medieval scientists trying to explain the body without knowledge of evolution or genetics, the fruit of centuries of hard work and incremental discovery. Instead of making equivalent spiritual progress, we have fallen back on ancient traditions that, while the storehouse of tremendous wisdom, are also preventing us from moving forward to discover the missing global solution. This has not only left us ignorant, but weak. It has allowed an animal spirit to enter the temple of man and supplant the spiritual side of his life with, of all things, free-market theory, an ideology that is completely blind to the larger framework in which humanity resides.

We began this book by noting what a mystery "the market" is today. Hopefully by now some of that mystery has been revealed. At the same time, the Market only points the way to another, even greater mystery. As one reads through this book, one should feel the inhuman nature of the Market. When viewed in isolation, as we have purposefully done, the Market is relentless, exhausting, indifferent, and purely amoral. Like the economy it serves, it has all the warmth of an engineering diagram. At the same time, there is great value in studying the naked Market for this very reason: it reveals what is missing in the world, the other side of the story. In literary terms, the Market is a foil for another character. Once you know our economic yang, its complement, the missing yin, becomes rather obvious, and also, *necessary*. The Market is, after all, only the external side of life; otherwise our society would be very flat indeed and, with endless irony, completely unproductive. So if you are looking for hope, never forget that another, internal side of life must exist, just as particles necessitate a wave, and matter requires energy. There is an anti-Market, and its spirit is found in you.

# EPILOGUE: The Market Cross

The dedication of the Southgate Memorial Fountain, May 21, 1901. If you look closely, you can see the benediction being read from the platform.

The alarm is still ringing.

You haven't moved. You hear it, but this morning things are different. The very thought of the commute is enough to freeze your heart. Finally, you reach out and slap it off with unusual force. The List disintegrates in the silence. There is no question in your mind: you are taking the day off.

At some point as you are getting dressed it dawns on you where you are going. It pulls on your mind with a mysterious force, a place you know well. It is your little secret, though hardly private. An Alice's looking glass, if you know how to use it. And on a day like today, just what you need.

The trip downtown passes in silence. You park the car and wander the ancient streets awhile, as you have done so many times. This is your favorite spot in America, this little brick town poised on the edge of the Chesapeake Bay. There is a cheerful warmth here, an optimism, a quiet dignity that surrounds you. An elusive charm seeps from hundreds of eighteenth-century buildings, lovingly restored, with their handmade imperfections, their slight lean, their lidded windows; from the uneven sidewalks of brick and their wrought-iron lamps; from the entire town with its human scale huddled around its small harbor. It is like walking into the past.

Here even the geometry of the streets sings a bright tune. In 1694, while the modern grid was unfolding elsewhere, the governor of Maryland, who designed his new capital, embedded three starburst patterns in the streets, a Baroque style borrowed from European capitals and later found in only one other American city, Washington, D.C. Today these three suns are traffic circles, which spread their rays in all directions, each one marking a different sphere of society, and different forms of freedom as well.

One of these now passes beneath your feet. This is State Circle, so named because it surrounds the elegant Georgian edifice of the Maryland State House, its classical facade recalling the deepest roots of democracy. Beneath its resplendent white dome, the largest in colonial America, you find the Old Senate Chamber looking just as it did in 1783, when Annapolis served as the first peacetime capital of the United States. During that historic session of Congress, Thomas Jefferson established the U.S. currency system, and the Treaty of Paris was signed, formally ending the Revolutionary War. It was also here, in this very room, that an emotional George Washington stopped by on his way home to Mt. Vernon for Christmas to resign his commission in the Continental Army. Facing these same rows of frail and tiny desks, quill pens lodged in their inkwells, the commander of the most powerful military force in America chose to forgo the path of Napoleon, and instead became the father of a democratic country.

You look at him now, standing there in effigy, wishing he could speak.

Down the stone steps and through an elusive alleyway, and you pop out on the most beautiful Main Street in America: a red carpet of brick, flanked by charming shops, that slopes down to the City Dock, a harbor filled with sailboats, and the broad blue swath of the Chesapeake, shining in the distance. Midway down you pause at the site where Mann's Tavern, a popular colonial gathering place, once stood. It was here, in 1786, that James Madison assembled the Annapolis Convention to discuss what to do about the weak Articles of Confederation then holding the country together. As the historic marker reveals:

> Their call for another convention in
> Philadelphia to render the government "adequate to the exigencies
> of the Union"
> resulted in the creation of
> The Constitution of the United States of America

It was also here that Jefferson gave Washington a farewell party the night he resigned his commission. Two hundred people showed up, and the bar tab was $644. Jefferson did like his wine.

Continuing on down the hill, you dead-end on the second sunburst, which surrounds a flagpole. Here you find three levels of freedom flying above you, beginning at the bottom, with the flag of Annapolis, whose motto is *Vixi Liber et Moriar*—"I have lived free and will die so"; moving upward to the flag of Maryland, known as the Free State; and finally ending with the flag of the United States.

This lower sun marks the commercial center of colonial Annapolis, where sailing ships once docked to unload their cargoes. Here freedom meant the free market, a power that helped build the entire city, and created its golden age, marked by the mansions whose chimneys still rise above the town. This tremendous economic success was built on the backs of African slaves. Arriving in chains, they were auctioned off inside the aptly named Market House. It stands facing you now on the edge of the circle, full of restaurants, but still issuing a cry for freedom. In 1767, the British ship *Lord Ligonier* sold an African from Gambia here, a fact one of his ancestors discovered over two hundred years later. Standing before the new granite memorial, you read:

> To commemorate the arrival
>
> in this harbor of Kunta Kinte,
>
> immortalized by Alex Haley
>
> In *Roots,* and all others
>
> who came to these
>
> shores in bondage and who
>
> by their toil, character and
>
> ceaseless struggle for freedom
>
> have helped to make these
>
> United States

You raise your head, and the city takes on a different hue. Clearly, there must be a third sun, without which market freedom and political freedom are worthless. It lies at the top of Main Street.

The red carpet of brick passes beneath your feet. Ahead rises the brick temple of St. Anne's, as if transplanted from the English countryside. Its slate spire, complete with town clock, pierces the blue sky. A wrought-iron fence surrounds it, enclosing a tiny graveyard. The traffic circles merrily around. This is Church Circle.

The iron gate is open. You cross the threshold, the twin doors close behind you, and the city is suddenly gone. Silence descends, and an awareness of time with it. Ahead lie row after row of pews and an empty altar, light slanting in from stained-glass windows out of sight. As you stand at the head of that long aisle, your feet feel heavy, until you notice a bronze plaque on the wall:

> In Memory of
>
> The Four Marylanders Who
>
> "With A Firm Reliance On the Protection of Divine Providence"
>
> Signed
>
> The Declaration Of Independence
>
> July 4, 1776

The smooth bronze feels cold to your touch. That was a brave move, signing the Declaration. Paca, Carroll, Stone, Chase—these were wealthy men, with everything to lose. If the Crown had prevailed, they would have been hanged as traitors. Instead, three of their homes still stand nearby, open to the public.

You turn to the adjacent plaque, which honors a later member of the parish:

Francis Scott Key

1779–1843

Churchman and Patriot

Author of

"The Star Spangled Banner"

The silence is suddenly broken, at least in your own mind, as you hear that familiar refrain:

O say, does that star-spangled banner yet wave

O'er the land of the free and the home of the brave?

Yes, you realize, the plaques melding into one: "with a firm reliance on the protection of divine providence." There is no freedom without spiritual freedom.

Finally your eyes lower to a third and smaller plaque, the humblest of them all. It honors a man now lost to history, the Honorable J. Wirt Randall, without explaining why. But to you it is a signpost. It leads you outdoors, to your final destination. Just a few steps away, you find yourself facing Alice's looking glass.


May 21, 1901 was an extraordinary day in Annapolis. After days of rain, the sky had finally cleared, and the morning sun revealed several thousand people descending upon Church Circle. They were moved to witness the dedication of a new memorial, and to say good-bye to an old friend. The Southgate Memorial Fountain had been created in memory of the Reverend

William Scott Southgate, the beloved rector of St. Anne's, who had passed away after nearly thirty years of service. Funded by the local citizenry, the memorial stood on an island in the middle of the street, on land granted by the city, gleaming white.

The fountain was noteworthy for its intriguing design. It had a granite octagonal basin and a central square pedestal, from which arose a striking shaft of Indiana limestone twenty-three feet high, topped off by an ornate, equilateral cross. On the north and south sides of the shaft, water flowed into the basin from the mouths of two carved lion heads. As the local paper had noted in previous days, the monument had been designed "much after the style of the English market cross," without further explanation.

While ostensibly a Christian symbol, the market cross actually predates Christianity, and strikes a common chord with all mankind. It is an example of what religious scholars call an *axis mundi,* or "hub of the universe," a symbol of where Heaven and Earth meet, and thus, of reality itself. These sacred symbols are found throughout the world, and throughout recorded history, from Paleolithic caves to the present. They utilize various forms, including mountains, trees, pillars, temples, cities, and even people, to make the same metaphysical connection. A few well-known examples include Mt. Kailas in Tibet, which serves as the sacred mountain for half a billion Hindus and Buddhists; the mythological Mt. Meru of India; Harney Peak in South Dakota, the *axis mundi* of the Sioux; the tree of good and evil in the Garden of Eden; the pillar stones of Ireland; Yaxche, the Mayan tree at the center of all directions; the *sefiroth,* the tree of life in the Kabbalah; numerous mosques, where a square base is Earth and a dome Heaven; the Babylonian ziggurat, an artificial sacred mountain; Jacob's ladder in the Bible; the obelisks of ancient Egypt; the Star of David, whose interpenetrating triangles represent Heaven and Earth; ancient Chinese sages, who donned a round hat for Heaven and square shoes for Earth; the pope, a *pontifex,* or "bridgemaker," between Heaven and Earth; and various imperial cities, from premodern China (most notably old Beijing) to the pre-Columbian Americas (especially Tenochtitlán and Teotihuacán). You might also say that every church spire and headstone in America falls into this category, too.

The most common form of *axis mundi* is the simplest: a cross, often surrounded by a unifying circle. As Carl Jung noted, this is also the most common symbol of mankind. Today it is not only the *axis mundi* for two billion

Christians, but for all the world's Buddhists and Hindus as well, in the form of the famous mandala, or sacred circle, their symbol of reality.

In sum, the universal presence of this symbol throughout history adds a final level of meaning to it. *In every culture prior to the modern age*, people recognized that the material world, "Earth," was only half of reality, and the lesser half at that. "Earth" was subordinate to "Heaven," the spiritual side of reality. The idea that there is more to reality than the material world—the world of sensation, of observation, of science, of the entire material assembly line, and of the worldly power at its summit—is thus not just a religious notion, it is the single common legacy of the human race.

The market cross in the middle of Southgate Fountain was a particularly interesting example of that legacy, as it was actually two different *axis mundi* fused into one. The first market cross was a pagan symbol that evolved in pre-Christian Britain, most likely from simple standing stones. As with mosques, Earth was represented by a square base, implying the four compass directions, and Heaven by a sphere. A long shaft connected the two, forming a bridge between Heaven and Earth. The term *market cross* likely arose from the fact that these stone symbols were placed at crossroads, where markets naturally developed. In effect, the meeting of Heaven and Earth stood over the meeting of buyer and seller. When Christianity spread through the British Isles, this symbolism was reinforced by placing a cross on top of the sphere, or by replacing it with a cross, fusing one *axis mundi* with another. The latter version evolved into a popular Anglican symbol, and thus was a natural choice by which to remember a rector in the Episcopal church, the American branch of the Church of England.

The basin of the memorial had been an unfinished project of Reverend Southgate's, a public resource "for thirsting man and beast." This morning it was full of fresh-cut flowers, so many that the gathering crowd could smell them. Nearby stood a raised platform, draped with two large American flags. The crowd was noted for its diversity: All races and classes were present. In a rare move, an interracial choir had even been assembled from area churches. They took their seats on the platform along with the speakers. The Reverend Southgate had touched the entire community.

At the appointed hour, the public ceremony opened on a large scale. Five hundred schoolchildren began singing "Our Fathers God to Thee" within the nearby churchyard. This was followed by a reading from the Bible, an invocation of divine blessing, and the aforementioned choir singing Francis Scott Key's composition "Lord, Pour Thy Spirit from on High" from the platform. Then all eyes turned to the Honorable J. Wirt Randall, who took the stage. The mustachioed lawyer was the chairman of the committee that had overseen the funding, design, and construction of the memorial. It was his job to present the fountain to the city.

Randall arose at a seminal moment. The Reverend Southgate had died in the final year of the nineteenth century, a time of industrial revolution and faith in progress. Wandering the Great Exposition in Chicago a year later, the perceptive author Henry Adams had detected a profound new spirit at work. "As he grew accustomed to the great gallery of machines, he began to feel the forty-foot dynamos as a moral force, much as the early Christians felt the Cross." [1] Now the twentieth century was dawning, and it was anyone's guess where that shift in polarity would lead.

To Randall, however, the future only looked like so much of the past. Shortly after the American Revolution, the Annapolis harbor had become too shallow for large draft vessels, which moved on to Baltimore, taking the local economy with them. Progress had slowed to a halt. For over a century now, the city had stood frozen in time, its buildings cocooned by a lack of development. While Annapolis was still the state capital, and only a buggy ride from the nation's capital, no railroad had even been built to it. Some called it the Forgotten City, others the Finished City. But as these economic clouds gathered, they also produced, as they often do, a silver lining, one contained in that old adage "suffering breeds wisdom."

Randall looked down his pince-nez glasses and began:

This ceremony marks the completion of an undertaking that stands alone in the history of the city. Never before have our people united to honor by a public monument, erected by general contribution, the memory of one of our departed citizens—and never before has our City Government, acting in speaking for the whole community, inaugurated such a movement and set apart a portion of a public street as the site.

Annapolis has had many citizens who have attained to great honor. They have been distinguished on the bench and at the bar; in the pulpit and the halls of legislation; in high executive office at home and as representatives of their country abroad; in the field and on the quarterdeck; in the fierce light of public station and in the loving hearts of those whom they served through long laborious private lives. Many, many of those, in all these walks of life, we hold in deserved admiration, or in grateful recollection. But never before has the general public voice of our community unhesitatingly and promptly spoken and said: "Here was a life that must be publicly honored and commemorated by some lasting memorial."

The stranger, who may hereafter read the simple inscriptions on this monument, will naturally inquire: "Why was this memorial erected?" He will say: "It seems to have been the result of a sort of spontaneous movement on the part of a number of people, but what had this man done that he should have been so singled out for special honor?" It is an inquiry difficult to answer in a single sentence. . . .

Dr. Southgate does not stand out on the page of our country's history, associated also with the story of this town, as one of the many historic figures we are accustomed to venerate. There is no one act of his, known to us, and as mankind generally reckons such things, of phenomenal heroism or merit, which, in itself lifted him up, as it were, upon a pedestal, to be admired of all.

The current of his long life here was not broken by any amazing whirlpool of circumstance or cataract of incident. True, but it reflected, as nearly as is given into the stream of human life, many of the beauties and glories of the heaven above. History makes haste to record great deeds, but often neglects good ones. There was nothing spectacular in the preaching, or in the life, or in the character of Dr. Southgate. His character was one of those that wear well, and require time in trials to be thoroughly appreciated, and his long ministry of 30 years in Annapolis endeared him to our people, as perhaps no one has ever been endeared before. There was a daily beauty in his life, that became more and more manifest and generally recognized as time passed by. His popularity was not a sentiment suddenly acquired, but it was all the more enduring because of that fact. This community learned to know him as having inflexible spirit, and yet a most tender heart; as being an indefatigable toiler along the path of every heavenward duty; as being filled with the true spirit of Christian humility and benevolence, and as having, with it all, a certain simple rugged manly strength of bearing and of soul that inspired respect and confidence in all, and that made him a shelter in the storms of trouble, and a haven of rest, alike for men and for women, for the old and for the young. . . .

This monument, then, is peculiar and—it stands alone—not only here in Annapolis, but elsewhere, so far as we know, in this: it is a public testimonial of public admiration and affection for a quiet, beneficent, truly good, private life.

Gentlemen of the City Government—We do not ask you, therefore, to accept this memorial merely for the sake of perpetuating the memory of an earnest Christian; and, most emphatically, we do not ask you to maintain it in this most conspicuous position, because his particular religious views have received, or have merited, your commendation, but we do ask you to receive it as the public property of the city, to care for it and to cherish it; so that it may keep fresh in the minds of all who knew him and may teach those who are to walk the streets after we are dead and gone, the lesson of his life, the continuing influence of a noble private character; and that it may be a witness between us, and you; and our generations after us; that we honor and bless an unselfish, useful life. Let it stand as the public expression of belief in purity and serenity of life; in public spirit and good citizenship; in tenderness for the suffering and distressed; in devotion to duty and principle.[2]

When the speeches were done, the choir sang "It Is Not Death to Die," the crowd dispersed, and a committee of ladies carried the flowers from the basin to the adjacent churchyard, where they were laid on the Reverend Southgate's grave.

You stand leaning on the fountain, staring through it. No, none of that would ever happen today. Character is no longer the highest value. The local rector would never be a celebrity. The city would never grant public land for a "religious" memorial. If they did, they would be taken to court, and the market cross found "unconstitutional." Heaven had collapsed to Earth. Blinded by an unnamed power, no one even knew what this symbol meant anymore. To many it was a superstition, all that was left when the meaning went away. Hundreds of people drove past it every day, depositing another layer of exhaust upon it, without even remembering it was there. They had their own symbol now, the very ornament that graced their hoods. The hub of the universe, traded in for a logo. The singular legacy of the human race, exchanged for a brand. Meanwhile the market cross stood watching in resignation, like the last pillar of an ancient civilization, shrouded by the Market's veil.

You step into the empty basin, and lean forward to study the words chiseled into the stone base:

Erected By

The Citizens

Of Annapolis

And By His Old

Parishioners

To Keep In

Remembrance

A Noble Life.

Your fingers lightly trace the words in stone. *A noble life.* There was a time; yes, there really was. . . .

# APPENDIX A:
# The American Hypermarket, 1950–2000

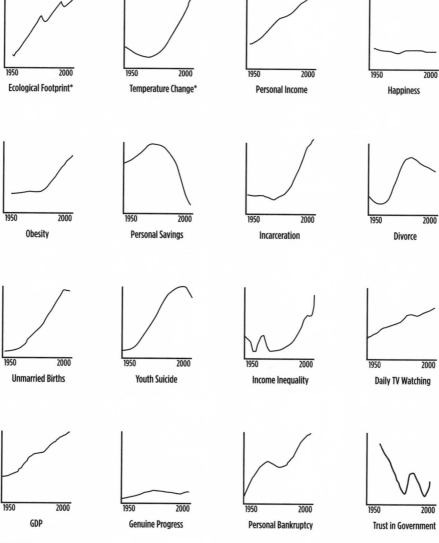

| Ecological Footprint* | Temperature Change* | Personal Income | Happiness |

| Obesity | Personal Savings | Incarceration | Divorce |

| Unmarried Births | Youth Suicide | Income Inequality | Daily TV Watching |

| GDP | Genuine Progress | Personal Bankruptcy | Trust in Government |

* global indicator

# APPENDIX B: Society in the Balance

The following is a brief synopsis of the philosophy underlying this book:

The market economy is shaped upon a material template, in which every individual is a particle interacting with other particles out of self-interest—i.e. a trader. Here the central operating principle is necessarily *me vs. you*—i.e. competition. Capitalism and free markets reinforce this natural order by granting traders property rights and allowing them to interact freely. The result is a flat reality: the external, productive side of society, a material universe ruled by the Market.

The other side of society is its internal, spiritual side, as manifested in the culture. This is a very different template, in which the selfish particle becomes part of a larger whole, *us*. This higher sensibility dampens the potentially unlimited aggression of pure competition and lifts the trader above the beast. He becomes a full-fledged human being. The central operating principle of this side is moral rather than productive—i.e. the Good. This Good expresses itself in a variety of values, be they cultural, familial, aesthetic, institutional, or social. It is the apex of a moral universe.

Society, at all levels—from the individual, to the institution, to the nation—contains *both* of these sides, internal and external, neither of which can exist on its own. Pure competition is anarchy unless controlled by moral sensibility. What we experience in ourselves and our lives is thus the critical *balance* between them. Deadly philosophies arise when one side is conflated with another (e.g. "capitalism is moral") or confused with the larger society ("the GDP measures America"). While a person can buy and sell, the trader in us is never a complete person, nor is the marketplace ever a complete society.

So how should our two sides relate to each other? For society to be healthy, the Good must clearly control the Productive—and hence, the spiritual the material, the internal the external, the moral the amoral, the human the animal. As long as this is the case, society cannot be anything *but* good, de facto. If the reverse is true, society is turned inside out—i.e. corrupted. The Market rules, and amorality spreads. Society becomes tyrannized by quantity, the measure of the material world, and by the market price. Institutions become predatory. The social system becomes senseless and chaotic. Life loses its meaning, purpose, and seriousness, becoming a kind of joke.

The primary cause of this imbalance is an overemphasis on quantitative thinking, which sets the entire material assembly line in motion, while blinding its operatives to the qualitative side of life. Materialism follows. Materialism rests on the notion that society only has one side—the external, material side—and hence that all is economics, that free-market capitalism defines all reality, and that the Market is God. The physical universe becomes the Universe itself. A deadly veil falls, as fully half of reality is lost. Society is hammered upon the material template, where we are all nothing but particles, in order to make it more efficient. This causes the deepest of all possible damage: it is the death of the soul.

The defense against materialism is education in all spheres: the family, the school, the religion, the society at large. However, such efforts are destined to fail if not rooted in an understanding of the nature of reality itself, which gives them shape and legitimacy. The problem we are facing today is thus primarily metaphysical. We have cut ourselves off from the truth. Beware of those who put the word in quotation marks.

# APPENDIX C:   A Market Lexicon

**the Market:** 1) the active economic principle; 2) the governing power arising naturally from free trade; 3) the economic system as an independent whole.

**market(place):** a virtual or physical location in which traders exchange goods.

**free market:** a market in which all individuals are free to participate, and the Market is free to govern. Also called the unbridled, untrammeled, or unfettered market.

**market economy:** an economy managed by the Market. Also called a market system.

**capitalism:** 1) the economic philosophy arising from the principle of me vs. you; 2) the natural philosophy of the material world.

**market mechanism:** the feedback loop between traders and the Market.

**market paradigm:** the summation of all the ways in which the Market manifests itself in society (market principles, market values, market forces, etc.).

**market principles:** the principles upon which the market economy operates; e.g. competition.

**market forces:** forces created by the Market within the economic system; e.g. supply and demand.

**market value:** economic value assessed by the Market.

**market price:** the price of a commodity.

**material assembly line:** the stages involved in the production of market value: scientific research, technology development, manufacturing, distribution.

**the Bubble:** the alternate reality created by commercial media.

**market pressures:** the psychological pressures created by the Market, including:

**social pressure:** pressure to move up in the market hierarchy.

**survival pressure:** pressure that arises from running out of money.

**time pressure:** pressure to do more in the same amount of time or less.

**competitive pressure:** pressure from others seeking to win at your expense.

**economic pressure:** direct financial pressure; e.g. a mortgage.

**environmental pressure:** pressure generated by the speed, complexity, and congestion of the market environment.

**market stress:** the human response to market pressures.

**marketism:** bias toward the Market.

**the Market Code:** the antithesis of morality, in which

- Good is **Profit**
- Truth is **Effectiveness**
- Beauty is **Efficiency**
- Love is **Performance**
- Courage is **Selfishness**
- Justice is **Power**
- Meaning is **Money**

**market people:** people who live by the Market Code.

**market hierarchy:** a social hierarchy based primarily on net worth.

**market values:** individual values that serve productive ends (not to be confused with market *value*).

**market status:** one's place in the market hierarchy.

**money:** as the means of increasing one's status.

**material possessions:** as the means of demonstrating one's status.

**power:** in order to command the means of production.

**market character:** the antithetical nature of market people—amoral, aspiritual, acultural—that serves their market values.

**vanity:** inflated sense of self; reinforces market hierarchy.

**greed:** unlimited desire for money; provides motivation.

**aggressiveness:** pushing to make things happen; drives productivity.

**selfishness:** self-interest at the expense of moral principle; flattens the person into a trader.

**disloyalty:** breaking of human bonds; furthers atomization for efficiency.

**cowardice:** disconnection of self from higher responsibilities; enables pure selfishness.

**market feminism:** feminism that primarily serves a productive end.

**marketsexual:** an individual whose gender identification has been confused by the Bubble.

**market culture:** a culture whose content is defined by whatever sells (i.e. it is acultural).

**market conservative:** a political conservative who prioritizes the Productive over the Good.

**market liberal:** a political liberal who prioritizes the Productive over the Good.

**market correctness:** social pressure not to make a moral judgment.

**marketocracy:** a political democracy controlled by the Market.

**pro-con:** the Market's one-sided view of a human being: a producer and consumer in one.

**market vortex:** an upward spiral of social pressure to produce and consume.

**market society:** a society in the service of the Market.

**market environment:** the entire external environment created by the Market.

**market temperature:** the perceived intensity of the market environment.

**marketecture:** architecture built exclusively to maximize profit.

**marketscape:** a landscape shaped by the Market.

**the Market's veil:** the Market's ability to blind people to any reality beyond the economy.

**market fundamentalism:** the idea that free-market theory is Scripture.

**market idolatry:** the idea that the Market is God.

**Market America:** the element of American society in the service of the Market.

**market dynamics:** the action of the Market on society, including:

> **inversion:** a change in the orientation of society from interior to exterior, or vice versa.

> **externalization:** a negative inversion: the collapse of the interior, moral side of society, or one of its elements, and the simultaneous inflation of the productive, economic side.

> **market selection:** the Market's ability to promote or demote, to the point of eradication, all aspects of society, primarily via the market price. The economic version of natural selection.

> **atomization:** the breakdown of society into its smallest constituent parts in order to make it more efficient.

> **marketization:** the conversion of society, or any of its elements, to the market paradigm.

> **commodification:** the transformation of the natural world into commodities.

> **quantification:** a by-product of commodification, whereby the market price quantifies reality.

**the Market Curve:** the relationship between the power of the Market and its benefit to society.

**undermarket:** the spectrum of the Market Curve where the Market is too weak to maximize its benefit to society.

**hypermarket:** the spectrum of the Market Curve where the Market is too strong to maximize its benefit to society.

**the anti-Market:** the power that moderates the Market.

**market philosophy:** the complete description of the external side of society, including all of the above definitions.

# APPENDIX D: Market Metaphysics

1. A principle is the union of opposites, positive and negative:

Principle

2. The relationship between two different principles creates a *thesis* and an *antithesis*. This is symbolized by placing the two principles perpendicular to each other, creating a cross:

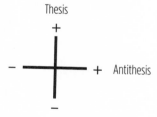

3. The integration of thesis and antithesis into a higher unity is a *synthesis*, as symbolized by a circle. This creates a wheel, the most common symbol of reality:

4. The moral principle has two poles, good and evil:

5. The economic principle has two poles, profit and loss:

6. The synthesis of these antithetical principles creates our social reality, an ongoing struggle between morality and productivity. When expressed as the struggle between positive poles, this is Good vs. Profit, or (depending on your theology) God vs. the Market.

# Notes

## Introduction

1. Walter Williams, "What or Who Is the Market?" *Capitalism Magazine*, August 14, 2002.
2. Even Darwin did it. In *The Origin of Species* he refers to "the works of Nature."
3. James G. Carrier, ed., *Meanings of the Market: The Free Market in Western Culture* (Oxford: Berg Publishers Ltd., 1997).
4. Bill Williams and Justine Williams, *Trading Chaos: Maximize Profits with Proven Technical Techniques,* 2nd ed. (New York: Marketplace Books, 2004), 3.

## Chapter One

1. See the Executive Summary of *The Global Burden of Disease and Injury Series,* sections 3, 4, and 6, http://www.hsph.harvard.edu/organizations/bdu/GBDseries.html. Supplemented by an interview with Christopher Murray, director, Burden of Disease Unit, Center for Population Studies, Harvard School of Public Health, December 9, 2003.
2. G. Andrews et al., "Why Does the Burden of Disease Persist?" *Bulletin of the World Health Organization* 78, no. 4 (2000): 446.
3. Simon Szreter, "The Population Health Approach in Historical Perspective," *American Journal of Public Health,* March 2003: 421.
4. James Gleick, *Faster: The Acceleration of Just About Everything* (New York: Pantheon, 1999).
5. Juliet Schor, "The (Even More) Overworked American," in John de Graaf, ed., *Take Back Your Time* (San Francisco: Berrett-Koehler, 2003), 6.
6. Stephen S. Roach, "The Productivity Paradox," *New York Times,* Op-Ed, November 30, 2003.
7. See http://www.simpleliving.net/timeday/pdf/TimeDayHandbookFlyer.pdf. Also John de Graaf, "Workweek Woes," *New York Times,* April 12, 2003, A13.
8. "What's Behind the Low U.S. Personal Saving Rate?" *FRBSF Economic Letter,* No. 2002-09, March 29, 2002.
9. Ichiro Kawachi and Bruce P. Kennedy, *The Health of Nations: Why Inequality Is Harmful to Your Health* (New York: The New Press, 2002), 80.
10. Ibid., 79.
11. Tamara Draut and Javier Silva, "Borrowing to Make Ends Meet: The Growth of Credit Card Debt in the '90s," *Demos* (2003).
12. Lyndsey Layton, "Beyond the Beltway, Gridlock Is Growing; Traffic Worsens on I-66, B-W Parkway," *Washington Post,* October 17, 2002, A1.

13. Survey by Pitney Bowes, in Carol Hymowitz and Rachel Emma Silverman, "Stressed Out: Can Workplace Stress Get Worse?" *Wall Street Journal,* January 16, 2001, B1.

14. Wayne Weiten and Margaret Lloyd, *Psychology Applied to Modern Life* (Lawrenceville: Thomson Wadsworth, 2003).

15. Jerry Mander, as quoted in Stephen Bertman, "Hyperculture," *Futurist* 32, no. 9 (December 1998): 18–24.

16. Michelle Weil and Larry Rosen, *Technostress: Coping with Technology @ Work @ Home @ Play* (New York: John Wiley, 1997).

17. "Is America Suffering from 'Desk Rage'?" *PR Newswire,* November 29, 2000.

18. *Psychology Today,* September/October 2000.

19. "The Rat Race," *Wilson Quarterly,* Spring 1991, 15.

20. Suzanne Schweikert, "An Hour a Day (Could Keep the Doctor Away)," in John de Graaf, ed., *Take Back Your Time* (San Francisco: Berrett-Koehler, 2003), 78.

21. "The Rat Race," 15.

22. Michele Marchetti, "High Anxiety," *Potentials,* March 2003, 10.

23. Mary Duenwald, "More Americans Seeking Help for Depression," *New York Times,* June 18, 2003, A1.

24. As quoted in Robert E. Lane, *The Loss of Happiness in Market Democracies* (New Haven: Yale University Press, 2000), 347.

25. Martin Seligman, "Boomer Blues: With Too Great Expectations, the Baby-Boomers Are Sliding into Individualistic Melancholy," *Psychology Today,* October 1988.

26. Lane, 21–23.

27. Carin Gorrell, "Wall Street Warriors," *Psychology Today,* January/February 2001.

28. See Seligman.

29. Josh White, "Musician Raged, Too, Charged Motorist Says," *Washington Post,* July 7, 2001, B02.

30. Scott Bowles and Paul Overberg, "Aggressive Driving: A Road Well-Traveled, *USA Today,* November 23, 1998.

31. Ibid.

32. Louis Jacobson, "Focus on Anger May Help to Curb 'Road Rage,' " *Washington Post,* January 21, 2002, A06. Overall, the United States is doing extremely well in reducing traffic fatalities. In 2001, the fatality rate per 100 million vehicle miles of travel reached a new historic low of 1.51. However, these gains have been attributed to increased seat-belt usage and the success of anti–drunk-driving measures.

33. Ronald Burns and Michael Katovich, "Examining Road Rage/Aggressive Driving," *Environment and Behavior,* September 2003, 621–36.

34. Nancy Haggerty, "Moving to Stop Road Rage," *New York Times,* August 11, 2002, 14.

35. See Bowles and Overberg.

36. Ibid.

37. "Driven to Despair by Recent Surge in Road Rage," *Washington Post,* December 18, 2003.

38. "Is America Suffering from 'Desk Rage'?"

39. Jerry L. Deffenbacher et al., "Characteristics and Treatment of High-Anger Drivers," *Journal of Counseling Psychology,* March 2000, 5–17.

40. "Hostility Predicts Heart Disease," http://my.webmd.com/content/article/53/61366.htm.

41. Mary Eberstadt, "The Child-Fat Problem," *Policy Review,* February/March 2003, 4.

42. Hara Estroff Marano, "Stress and Eating," *Psychology Today,* November 21, 2003.

43. "Is America Suffering from 'Desk Rage'?"

44. "HHS Report Shows 7 in 10 Adults Are Not Active Regularly," National Center for Health Statistics Press Release, April 7, 2002.

45. Eric Schlosser, *Fast Food Nation* (New York: HarperCollins, 2002), 119–29.

46. "You Want Fries with That?" *New York Times Book Review,* January 12, 2003. See also Greg Critser, *Fat Land: How Americans Became the Fattest People in the World* (Boston: Houghton Mifflin, 2003), 6.

47. "Overweight and Obesity Threaten U.S. Health Gains," *HHS News,* December 13, 2001.

48. See "You Want Fries with That?"

49. "Overweight and Obesity Threaten U.S. Health Gains."

50. Hippocrates, "On Airs, Waters, and Places," part 24, trans. Francis Adams (http://classics.mit.edu/Hippocrates/airwatpl.24.24.html).

51. Robert Pear, "Health Spending Rises to Record 15% of Economy," *New York Times,* January 9, 2004.

52. Stephen Bezruchka, "Is Our Society Making You Sick?" *Newsweek,* February 26, 2001, 14.

53. "Society at a Glance: OECD Social Indicators," OECD, 2001, 86.

54. Stephen Bezruchka, "The (Bigger) Picture of Health," in John de Graaf, ed., *Take Back Your Time* (San Francisco: Berrett-Koehler, 2003), 6.

55. John Komlos and Marieluise Baur, "From the Tallest in the World to (One of) the Fattest: The Enigmatic Fate of the Size of the American Population in the 20th Century," *Economics and Human Biology* 1 (2004), in preparation.

56. See both Bezruchka and Kawachi and Kennedy.

57. Robert Pear, "New Study Finds 60 Million Uninsured During a Year," *New York Times,* May 13, 2003.

58. "NIDA Community Drug Alert Bulletin—Stress and Drug Abuse," National Institute on Drug Abuse, NIH (http://www.nida.nih.gov/drugpages/stress.html).

59. Shannon Henry and Christopher Stern, "Ex-WorldCom Head Sidgmore Dies at 52," *Washington Post,* December 12, 2003, E01; Barnaby J. Feder, "John Sidgmore, 52, Dies; Headed WorldCom," *New York Times,* December 12, 2003, A41.

## Chapter 2

1. Alice Kessler-Harris, *Out to Work: A History of Wage-Earning Women in the United States* (New York: Oxford University Press, 1982), 300. Labor statistics from U.S. Department of Labor, Wage and Labor Standards Administration, *Background Facts on Women Workers in the United States* (1968), 14; Howard Huyghe, "Families and the Rise of Working Women—An Overview," *Monthly Labor Review,* May 1976, 13.

2. Jesse Bernard, *The Future of Marriage* (New Haven: Yale University Press, 1982) 128, in Brian Robertson, *Day Care Deception* (San Francisco: Encounter Books, 2003), 110.

3. Kessler-Harris, *Out to Work,* 301.

4. The Future of Services, *American Demographics* 17, no. 11 (November 1995): 30.

5. 2003 Restaurant Industry Forecast, National Restaurant Association, Washington, D.C.

6. Karen Benezra, "Short-cut Chef," *Brandweek* 38, no. 5 (February 3, 1997): 36.

7. Shannon Dortch, "Maids Clean Up," *American Demographics,* November 1996, 4.

8. Robertson, 37.

9. Mark Dolliver, "The New Motherly Mantra: Ask Me to Work When My Kids Are Grown," *Adweek,* March 3, 2003, 44.

10. Deborah Stone, "Work and the Moral Woman," *American Prospect,* November/December 1997, 78–86.

11. Carol Iaciofano, " 'Two-Income Trap' Has Financial Advice for a Struggling Middle Class," *Boston Globe,* November 19, 2003, C7.

12. Ibid.

13. Sue Shellenbarger, "More Couples Try to Time Childbirth to Accommodate Jobs," *Wall Street Journal,* October 27, 1999, B1.

14. Barbara Reskin and Irene Padavic, *Women and Men at Work* (Thousand Oaks, CA: Pine Forge Press, 1994), in Ichiro Kawachi and Bruce Kennedy, *The Health of Nations: Why Inequality Is Harmful to Your Health* (New York: The New Press, 2002), 199.

15. Julian Barling, Stephen Bluen, and Verne Moss, "Type A Behavior and Marital Dissatisfaction: Disentangling the Effects of Achievement Striving and Impatience-Irritability," *Journal of Psychology* 124, no. 3 (1990): 312.

16. Juliet Schor, *The Overworked American* (New York: Basic Books, 1992), 12.

17. David Gelman et al., "Not Tonight, Dear," *Newsweek,* October 26, 1987, 64.

18. Murray A. Straus, Richard J. Gelles, and Suzanne K. Steinmetz, *Behind Closed Doors: Violence in the American Family* (Garden City, NY: Anchor Books, 1981), 185. Here we show wife abuse, but there was also a direct correlation with husband abuse as well.

19. Julian Barling and Alan Rosenbaum, "Work Stressors and Wife Abuse," *Journal of Applied Psychology* 71, no. 2 (May 1986): 346–48.

20. Helen Tauchen and Ann Dryden Witte, "The Dynamics of Domestic Violence," *American Economic Review* 85, no. 2 (1995): 414.

21. *The Economist: Pocket World of Figures* (London: Profile Books, 2004).

22. "Cohabitation, Marriage, Divorce, and Remarriage in the United States," U.S. Centers for Disease Control, National Center for Health Statistics, July 2002. The overall divorce rate is derived from the fact that the divorce rate in 2002 was 4.0/1000, while the marriage rate was 7.8/1000. See also National Vital Statistics Reports, "Births, Marriages, Divorces, and Deaths," June 17, 2003 (http://www.cdc.gov/nchs/data/nvsr/nvsr51/nvsr51_10.pdf).

23. "Cohabitation, Marriage, Divorce, and Remarriage in the United States."

24. Nicholas Eberstadt, "Prosperous Paupers and Affluent Savages," *Society,* January 1998.

25. "Nonmarital Childbearing in the United States, 1940–1999," U.S. Centers for Disease Control, National Vital Statistics Reports, October 18, 2000 (revised), 3.

26. "U.S. Birth Rate Reaches Record Low," U.S. Department of Health and Human Services News Release, June 25, 2003.

27. Drawn mainly from "Cohabitation, Marriage, Divorce, and Remarriage in the United States."

28. "Cohabitation, Marriage, Divorce, and Remarriage in the United States."

29. Lynn White and Stacy Rogers, "Economic Circumstances and Family Outcomes," *Journal of Marriage and the Family,* November 2000, 1042.

30. Robert E. Lane, "Diminishing Returns to Income, Companionship and Happiness," *Journal of Happiness Studies* 1 (2000): 104.

31. Gary Becker, *A Treatise on the Family* (Cambridge, MA: Harvard University Press, 1991), 119.

32. Alessandra Stanley, "Contestants, Meet the King of the Jungle," *New York Times,* January 8, 2004.

33. Suniya Luthar, "The Culture of Affluence: Psychological Costs of Material Wealth," *Child Development,* November/December 2003, 1584.

34. Ronald L. Simons and Les B. Whitbeck, "Economic Pressure and Harsh Parenting," in Rand D. Conger, Glen H. Elder, and Frederick O. Lorenz, eds., *Families in Troubled Times: Adapting to Change in Rural America* (New York: Aldine de Gruyter, 1994), 219–220.

35. Camille Chatterjee, "Stressing Your Kids Out," *Psychology Today,* March/April 2000.

36. Drawn mainly from "Cohabitation, Marriage, Divorce, and Remarriage in the United States."

37. Patricia Dalton, "Life Isn't Just Getting into College. Really," *Washington Post,* March 28, 2004, B4.

38. Suniya Luthar, "The Culture of Affluence: Psychological Costs of Material Wealth," *Child Development,* November/December 2003, 1583–84.

39. David Popenoe, "American Family Decline, 1960–1990," *Journal of Marriage and the Family,* August 1993, 527.

40. "U.S. Birth Rate Reaches Record Low," *HHS News,* National Center for Health Statistics, June 25, 2003.

41. Sharon Vandivere, Kathryn Tout, Jeffery Capizzano, and Martha Zaslow, "Left Unsupervised: A Look at the Most Vulnerable Children," Child Trends Research Brief, April 2003.

42. See Robertson, 7, 37.

43. Ibid, 112–13, 121, 164.

44. Ibid, 66–67.

45. Study was done at the University of Minnesota. See Kathy Tout et al., "Social Behavior Correlates of Cortisol Activity in Child Care," *Child Development* 69 (1998): 1247–62. From Robertson, 80.

46. Ibid, 79, 81, 144–47. See also UNC–Frances Parker Study reported by R. Haskins, "Public School

Aggression Amongst Children with Varying Day Care Experience," *Child Development* 56, 1985, 689–703.

47. Robertson, 39, 63. 122–23.

48. Aldous Huxley, *Brave New World* (New York: HarperCollins, 1989; originally published in 1932), 23.

49. Robert Blum and Colleagues, "Lost Children or Lost Parents of Rockdale County?" http://www.pbs .org/wgbh/pages/frontline/shows/georgia/isolated/blum.html.

50. "The Lost Children of Rockdale County: Discussion: Teens and Parents," http://www.pbs.org/ wgbh/pages/frontline/shows/georgia/talk/b.html.

51. Interview with Dr. Kathleen Toomey, "The Lost Children of Rockdale County," http://www.pbs .org/wgbh/pages/frontline/shows/georgia/interviews/toomey.html.

52. Interview with Claire Sterk, "The Lost Children of Rockdale County," http://www.pbs.org/ wgbh/pages/frontline/shows/georgia/interviews/sterk.html. Italics added.

53. Kevin Sack, "One Month After Littleton Massacre, 6 Are Shot at Georgia School," *New York Times*, May 21, 1999.

54. Nicholas Eberstadt, "Prosperous Paupers and Affluent Savages," *Society*, January 1998.

55. Joseph Campbell, *The Power of Myth*, Interview with Bill Moyers.

## Chapter 3

1. Urie Bronfenbrenner, Peter McClelland, Elaine Wethington, Phyllis Moen, and Stephen J. Ceci, *The State of Americans* (New York: The Free Press, 1996). See William Bennett, *The Index of Leading Cultural Indicators, 2001*, available at www.empower.org.

2. From *Publisher's Weekly* review of Leslie Savan, *The Sponsored Life* (New Orleans: Temple University Press, 1994).

3. Richard Sandomir, "At (Your Name Here) Arena, Money Talks," *New York Times*, May 30, 2004.

4. Ibid.

5. Caroline Mayer, "A Growing Marketing Strategy: Get 'Em While They're Young," *Washington Post*, June 3, 2003.

6. Ginia Bellafante, "Poor Little Rich Girls, Throbbing to Shop," *New York Times*, August 17, 2003.

7. Virginia Heffernan, "A Gas-Guzzling Revenge Plot Meets Souped-Up Sales Pitch," *New York Times*, June 2, 2004.

8. Michael Snider, "Watch out for Adver-tainment, *Maclean's*, May 17, 2004.

9. Karen Karbo, "Goodbye to All That Feng Shui," *New York Times Book Review*, May 11, 2003, 7.

10. Stephanie Kang, "Naming the Baby: Parents Brand Their Tot with What's Hot," *Wall Street Journal*, December 26, 2003.

11. James F. Tracy, "Between Discourse and Being: The Commodification of Pharmaceuticals in Late Capitalism," *Communication Review* 7 (2004):15–34.

12. Ibid.

13. Sally Satel, "Antidepressants: Two Countries, Two Views," *New York Times*, May 25, 2004.

14. See Tracy.

15. Elizabeth Armstrong, "Debate Grows over Antidepressant Use Among Preschoolers," *Christian Science Monitor*, April 8, 2004, 1.

16. See Tracy.

17. Editorial, "Depressing News on Depression," *New York Times*, April 23, 2004, A22.

18. Marc Kaufman, "FDA Cautions on Antidepressants and Youth," *Washington Post*, October 28, 2003, A2.

19. Leonard Downie Jr. and Robert Kaiser, *The News About the News: American Journalism in Peril* (New York: Vintage, 2003). See also "Does 9/11 Make a Difference?" *Columbia Journalism Review*, March/April 2002.

20. Television survey by the Center for Media and Public Affairs, August 1997.

21. "Fear & Favor 2000: How Power Shapes the News," Fairness and Action in Reporting, http:// www.fair.org/ff2000.html.

22. Leonard Downie Jr. and Robert G. Kaiser, "Network Anchors See a Diminished World," *Columbia Journalism Review,* March/April 2002.

23. Ibid.

24. Robert Samuelson, "Snob Journalism," *Washington Post,* April 23, 2003, A35.

25. Downie Jr. and Kaiser, "Network Anchors See a Diminished World."

26. Wilhelm Ropke, *A Humane Economy: The Social Framework of the Free Market* (Chicago: H. Regnery Co., 1960), 89.

27. John Kenneth Galbraith, "The Commitment to Innocent Fraud," *Challenge,* September/October 1999, 16.

28. Simon Szreter, "The Population Health Approach in Historical Perspective," *American Journal of Public Health,* March 2003, 421.

29. Michael P. McCauley, "The Contested Meaning of Public Service in American Television," *Communication Review* 5, no. 3 (2002): 207.

30. Keturah Gray, "Celebrity Worship Syndrome: Is America's Obsession with Stardom Becoming Unhealthy?" ABC News, September 23, 2003.

31. Frank Rich, "Bullies Are Not What Ails Hollywood," *New York Times,* January 11, 2004.

## Chapter 4

1. Alexis de Tocqueville, *Democracy in America* (New York: Knopf, 1948; originally published in 1835, 1840, as *De la démocratie en Amérique*), 145.

2. George Soros, "The Capitalist Threat," *The Atlantic Monthly,* February 1997, 52.

3. John Kavanaugh, SJ, "Idols of the Marketplace," *Media & Values,* Fall 1986.

4. Interview with Dr. Kathleen Toomey, "The Lost Children of Rockdale County," http://www.pbs .org/wgbh/pages/frontline/shows/georgia/interviews/toomey.html.

5. Michael Brick and Corey Kilcannon, "Rapper Slain in Queens; Linked to Label in Inquiry," *New York Times,* September 6, 2003.

6. Jeff Leeds, "From Behind Bars, a Rapper Aims at the Top of the Chart," *New York Times,* August 8, 2004.

7. April Witt, "Acquiring Minds: Inside America's All-Consuming Passion," *Washington Post Magazine,* December 14, 2003.

8. Jennifer Barrett, "No Time for Wrinkles," *Newsweek,* May 10, 2004, 82.

9. Alex Kuczynski, "A Nip and Tuck with That Crown?" *New York Times,* May 16, 2004.

10. Alex Kuczynski, "A Lovelier You, with Off-the-Shelf Parts," *New York Times,* May 2, 2004.

11. Riad Dikes and Vincent Gallon, "Understanding the Male Cosmetics Market," E-Beauty News, http://www.beauty-on-line.com/ebn/newsletter.asp?eid=92.

12. National Public Radio, "Setting the Beauty Agenda," June 15, 2004.

13. "Acquiring Minds: Inside America's All-Consuming Passion."

14. Keturah Gray, "Celebrity Worship Syndrome: Is America's Obsession with Stardom Becoming Unhealthy?" ABC News, September 23, 2003, http://abcnews.go.com/sections/entertainment/ Living/celebrityworship030923.html.

15. "Worshipping Celebrities 'Brings Success,' " BBC News, August 13, 2003.

16. Robin Givhan, "How Does Courtney Plead? Grungy," *Washington Post,* May 28, 2004, C1.

17. Dana Priest, William Booth, Susan Schmidt, "A Broken Body, A Broken Story, Pieced Together," *Washington Post,* June 17, 2003, 1.

18. Ichiro Kawachi and Bruce P. Kennedy, *The Health of Nations: Why Inequality Is Harmful to Your Health* (New York: The New Press, 2002), 80.

19. Stephanie Strom, "Some Alumni Balk over Harvard's Pay to Top Managers," *New York Times,* June 4, 2004, 1.

20. Bruce Weber, "Fewer Noses Stuck in Books in America, Survey Finds," *New York Times,* July 8, 2004.

21. Annenberg Public Policy Center, University of Pennsylvania, "Media in the Home 2000: The Fifth Annual National Survey of Parents and Children."

22. "Readers Embrace Ghetto Lit Genre," *Morning Edition,* NPR, January 20, 2004.
23. Harold Bloom, "Dumbing Down American Readers," *Los Angeles Times,* September 24, 2003.

## Chapter 5

1. Percy Bysshe Shelley, *Defence of Poetry: Part First (1821)* § 26.
2. Morris Wolfe, *Essays: New & Selected* (Toronto: Grub Street Books, 2004).
3. "Measuring 'Jolts Per Minute,' " *Media & Values,* Spring 1993.
4. Robert Kubey and Mihaly Csikszentmihalyi, "Television Addiction Is No Mere Metaphor," *Scientific American,* February 2002.
5. Charles Johnston, MD, "Addicted to Violence: Has the American Dream Become a Nightmare?" *Media & Values,* Spring 1993.
6. See Kubey and Csikszentmihalyi.
7. Ibid.
8. Ibid.
9. Pamela Paul, "The Porn Factor," *Time,* January 19, 2004.
10. Norman Lear, "The Culture of Capitalism," *Media & Values,* Summer 1989.
11. The Parents Television Council, *What a Difference a Decade Makes: A Comparison of Prime Time Sex, Language, and Violence in 1989 and '99,* March 30, 2000.
12. The Parents Television Council, *TV Bloodbath: Violence on Prime Time Broadcast TV,* December 2003.
13. The Parents Television Council, *Sex Loses Its Appeal,* May 2003.
14. Stefan Fatsis, "Smash-Mouth: Sick of the Term? Sorry, There's No Stopping It—Blame the XFL If You'd Like, but It's Old and Seems to Fit the Popular Culture Well," *Wall Street Journal,* February 16, 2001, A1.
15. William Booth, "In Los Angeles, Actors with a Proven Record; Need a Gang for Your Next Movie? Manny Can Help," *Washington Post,* May 26, 2004.
16. Sharon Waxman, "Sparing No One, a Journalist's Account of War," *New York Times,* June 10, 2004.
17. Joel Achenbach, "Numb Nation; When What Once Shocked Elicits Only a Shrug, Haul Out the Sledgehammer," *Washington Post,* April 1, 2004.
18. Sharon Waxman, "Study Finds Film Ratings Are Growing More Lenient," *New York Times,* July 14, 2004.
19. Daniel Patrick Moynihan, "Defining Deviancy Down," *American Scholar,* Winter 1993.
20. Arthur S. De Vany and W. David Walls, "Does Hollywood Make Too Many R-Rated Movies?: Risk, Stochastic Dominance, and the Illusion of Expectation," June 5, 2000. Available through Social Science Research Network.
21. "Profitability Study of MPAA Rated Movies Released during 1988–1997," Seidman School of Business, December 1, 1998, commissioned by the Dove Foundation. See Index of Leading Cultural Indicators.
22. Randall Rothenberg, "Media Infatuation with 'Sex' Clouds Reality of Viewership," *Advertising Age,* March 1, 2004, 15.
23. "Key Facts: TV Violence," Kaiser Family Foundation, Spring 2003, 4.
24. Edward Wyatt, "Sex, Sex, Sex: Up Front in Bookstores Near You," *New York Times,* August 24, 2004.
25. Libby Copeland, "Naughty Takes Off; the Stripper Aesthetic Sheds Some Sleaze, and a Few Pounds," *Washington Post,* November 30, 2003.
26. Pamela Paul, "The Porn Factor," *Time,* January 19, 2004.
27. Guy Trebay, "Sex, Art, and Videotape," *New York Times Magazine,* June 13, 2004.
28. Martin Edlund, "Hip-Hop's Crossover to the Adult Aisle," *New York Times,* March 7, 2004.
29. Stephen Baker and Kimberly Weisul, "This Virgin Has a Kinky Side," *BusinessWeek,* December 15, 2003.
30. See Paul.

31. Jeremy Caplan, "Pornography for Preppies," *Time,* March 1, 2004.

32. Barbara Kantrowitz, "Dropping the H Bomb," *Newsweek,* June 7, 2004.

33. See Copeland.

34. See Trebay.

35. Sonya Coelho Rasquinha, "Sex and the Conservative Halls of Academia," *Times* [of India] News Network, May 24, 2004.

36. See Paul.

37. Frank Rich, "My Hero, Janet Jackson," *New York Times,* February 15, 2004.

38. Ibid.

39. See Johnston.

## Chapter 6

1. UN Development Program, UN Environment Program, World Bank, World Resources Institute, *World Resources 2000–2001: The Fraying Web of Life: People and Ecosystems* (Washington, DC: World Resources Institute, 2000). See Introduction.

2. Ibid., 6.

3. Jonathan Loh, ed., *Living Planet Report 2002* (Cambridge, England: World Wildlife Fund, 2002).

4. Jason Venetoulis, MD, Dahlia Chazan, and Christopher Gaudet, *Ecological Footprint of Nations,* Redefining Progress, March 2004. See also Loh.

5. See the EPA Web site, http://yosemite.epa.gov/oar/globalwarming.nsf/content/index.html. Also see the statement from the American Geophysical Union, "Human Impacts on Climate," adopted December 2003.

6. The Union of Concerned Scientists, http://www.grida.no/climate/vital/index.htm.

7. United Nations Environment Program, Vital Climate Graphics, "Potential Impacts of Climate Change," http://www.grida.no/climate/vital/impacts.htm.

8. Arthur von Wiesenberger, "Reading Between the Lines of Bottled Water Labels," www.bottledwaterweb.com/articles/avw-0002.htm.

9. Verlyn Klinkenborg, "Be Afraid. Be Very Afraid," *New York Times Book Review,* May 30, 2004.

10. Rafe Pomerance, "Coral Bleaching, Coral Mortality, and Global Climate Change," Bureau of Oceans and International Environmental and Scientific Affairs, U.S. Department of State, March 5, 1999.

11. "Bleached Bond," http://greeningearthsociety.org/wca/2004/wca_19a.html.

12. John Browne, "Beyond Kyoto," *Foreign Affairs,* July/August 2004.

13. The United Nations Environment Program (1997) quoted in Richard Eckersley, "The Mixed Blessings of Material Progress: Diminishing Returns in the Pursuit of Happiness," *Journal of Happiness Studies* 1, no. 3 (2000).

14. See Klinkenborg.

15. James Howard Kuntsler, "Home from Nowhere," *The Atlantic Monthly* 278, September 1996, 43–66.

16. Robert Wassmer, "An Economic Perspective on Urban Sprawl," California Senate Office of Research, September 2002, 3.

17. Sierra Club.

18. Paco Underhill, *The Call of the Mall* (New York: Simon & Schuster, 2004).

19. Michael L. McKinney, "There Goes the Neighborhood," *Forum for Applied Research and Public Policy* 15, no. 3 (2000): 23.

20. Julie Iovine, "Building a Bad Reputation: Sloppy American Construction," *New York Times,* August 8, 2004.

21. Bethany Warner, "Suburban Sprawl Spreads Incivility, Book Author Says," *Washington Times,* April 25, 2001, 2.

22. Iver Peterson, "War on Sprawl in New Jersey Hits a Wall," *New York Times,* October 21, 2003.

23. See http://www.aacounty.org/RecParks/Parks/quiet_waters_park/index.cfm.

24. Florence Williams, "Obscurity Becomes It," *New York Times,* June 24, 2004.

## Chapter 7

1. Material adapted from my previous book, *Riding the Bull: My Year in the Madness at Merrill Lynch* (New York: Times Books, 1998), 106–08.
2. John Schwartz, "Up From the Ashes, One Firm Rebuilds," *New York Times*, September 16, 2001, 14.
3. "Howard Lutnick's Second Life," www.newyorkmetro.com/nymetro/news/sept11/features/5486.
4. Rob Walker, "The Morning After," *New York Times Book Review*, February 2, 2003, 26. (Review of Tom Barbash, *On Top of the World* [New York: HarperCollins, 2003].)
5. "From Devastation to Determination," *New York Times*, September 10, 2002, C1.
6. "British Judge Splits Ruling on Suit by Cantor Fitzgerald," *New York Times*, July 30, 2002, W1.
7. Peter A. McKay, "Former Unit Files Complaint Alleging Cantor Breached Deal," *Wall Street Journal*, October 9, 2002, C12.
8. "Please Be Kinder While Trading," *New York Times*, August 3, 2003, 35.
9. "Trading Firm Pursues Return to Downtown," *New York Times*, October 18, 2003.
10. Landon Thomas, "If Only for a Night, Wall St. Fallen Idol Is One of the Boys," *New York Times*, February 6, 2004.
11. Editorial, "Enron's Awesome Cynicism," *New York Times*, June 6, 2004.
12. Gary Weiss, *Born to Steal: When the Mafia Hit Wall Street* (New York: Warner Books, 2003).
13. Todd Zaun, "Japan Shuts Unit of Citibank, Citing Violations," *New York Times*, September 18, 2004.
14. Kurt Andersen, "City of Schemes," *New York Times Magazine*, October 6, 2002, 76–77.
15. Sources: The Corporate Library, Citizenworks, *Washington Post*, *New York Times*, CNN, CBS Marketwatch, Forbes.com.
16. Some additional examples include the Hollinger scandal, in which 95 percent of corporate profits were looted by a few individuals led by Conrad Black; the money laundering necessitating the sale of Riggs Bank, the so-called bankers to the world, in Washington, D.C.; the widespread price rigging discovered in the insurance industry; and the $9 billion accounting scandal at Fannie Mae.
17. Arthur Levitt, *Take on the Street* (New York: Pantheon, 2002).
18. *Washington Post*, Friday, June 13, 2003.
19. Editorial, "The Spirit of the Fourth," *New York Times*, July 4, 2004.
20. Allan Bloom, *The Closing of the American Mind* (New York: Simon & Schuster, 1987), 218.
21. Thomas Merton, *The Way of Chuang Tzu* (New York: New Directions, 1965), 147.
22. Matthew Boyle and Christopher Tkaczyk, "When Will They Stop?" *Fortune*, May 3, 2004.
23. Alex Berenson, "From Coffee to Jets, Perks for Executives Come Out in Court," *New York Times*, February 22, 2004.
24. Deborah Solomon, "Life After Whistle-Blowing," *New York Times Magazine*, June 6, 2004.
25. David Pogue, "Checking Your Bill for a New Charge Called 'Oops,' " *New York Times*, December 4, 2003.
26. "Rebates Motivate Consumer Choices," *USA Today*, March 1, 2004.
27. Kimberly Brinson, "The Check's in the Mail? Rebate Realities," *PC World*, March 2004.
28. David Callahan, *The Cheating Culture* (New York: Harcourt, 2004), 19–25.
29. Josephson Institute of Ethics, Los Angeles.
30. ABC News *Prime Time* Investigation, "Caught Cheating," April 29, 2004.
31. Timothy L. O'Brien, "U.S. Investigates Payments to Equatorial Guinea," *New York Times*, August 6, 2004.

## Chapter 8

1. Matthew 6:24 and Luke 16:13.
2. Jeremy Rifkin, *The European Dream* (New York: Tarcher/Penguin, 2004) 117–18. Italics added.
3. Chris Hedges, "Path to Riches (But No Coveting); Seeking, After Rough Stretch, to Unlock the Inner Tycoon," *New York Times*, December 24, 2002.
4. Harvey Cox, "The Market as God," *The Atlantic Monthly*, March 1999, 18–23.

5. Library of Congress Exhibit, *Religion and the Founding of the American Republic,* Section 1: "America as a Religious Refuge." See www.loc.gov.

6. Robert H. Nelson, "Economic Religion Versus Christian Values," *Markets and Morality,* October 1998.

7. Josef Blum and Uriel G. Rothblum, " 'Timing Is Everything' and Marital Bliss," *Journal of Economic Theory,* April 2002, 429.

8. See Nelson.

9. Jeff Jacoby, "Giving Thanks for Capitalism," *Boston Globe,* November 27, 2003, A23.

10. Patrick Martins, "About a Bird," *New York Times,* November 24, 2003, A23.

11. Jonathan Schlefer, "Today's Most Mischievous Misquotation," *The Atlantic Monthly,* March 1998, 16.

12. "The Negative Side of Capitalism" and "Mistaking Man's Actions for God's," Letters to the Editor, *Boston Globe,* December 2, 2003.

13. David Loy, "Religion and the Market," *Journal of the American Association of Religion,* 1997, http://www.religiousconsultation.org/loy.htm.

14. See George Soros, "The Capitalist Threat," *The Atlantic Monthly,* February 1997, 45, and Cox.

15. In Martin E. Marty, "Testing Faith in the Market God," *Sightings,* University of Chicago Divinity School, November 5, 2001.

16. Rajni Bakshi, "The Market as God," *The Hindu,* March 18, 2001.

17. Bill Daly, "The Market Is a Convenient Excuse," *Sustainable Economics* 10, no. 4 (July 2002): 26.

18. John McMurtry, "The Invisible Hand: Magical Thinking in Market Theory," *Sustainable Economics* 10, no. 4 (July 2002): 28. McMurtry is also the author of a short paper, "The Global Market Doctrine: A Study in Fundamentalist Theology," http://arts.uwaterloo.ca/ECON/needhdata/McMurtry-2.html.

19. Ernest Partridge, "The State Religion," *The Democratic Underground,* January 10, 2002.

20. See http://www.rkdn.org/jhm/IGWTnotes.htm.

21. See, for instance, "The Yearning for Balance" poll commissioned by the Merck Family Fund in 1995; also General Social Surveys data.

22. Richard Eckersley, "The Mixed Blessings of Material Progress: Diminishing Returns in the Pursuit of Happiness," *Journal of Happiness Studies* 1, no. 3 (2000): 268.

23. Edwin O. Guthman and C. Richard Allen, eds., *RFK: Collected Speeches* (New York: Viking, 1993), 330.

24. The Genuine Progress Indicator, 1998 Update, 14; see Redefining Progress, www.rprogress.org.

25. Jeanne Sahadi, "The Cost of Stress," CNN/Money, March 21, 2003, http://money.cnn.com/2003/03/20/commentary/everyday.sahadi/.

26. Manfred Max-Neef, "Economic Growth and Quality of Life: A Threshold Hypothesis," *Ecological Economics* 15 (1995): 115–18.

27. See http://www.mises.org/humanaction/chap15sec1.asp.

28. Pete du Pont, "Gore Carries the Porn Belt," *Wall Street Journal,* November 10, 2000.

29. John Sperling, *The Great Divide: Retro vs. Metro America* (Sausalito, CA: Polipoint Press, 2004).

30. Ibid., 13.

31. Jonathan Yardley, "Heck, Blame It on the Press," *Washington Post Book Review,* July 8, 2004.

## Chapter 9

1. F. A. Hayek, *The Road to Serfdom* (Chicago: University of Chicago Press, 1994), 13. Hayek was trying to free the Market from collectivist tendencies that had weakened it.

## Epilogue

1. See Chapter 25, "The Dynamo and the Virgin," of Henry Adams's *The Education of Henry Adams* (1907), www.bartleby.com.

2. "Granite and Roses Commemorate," *The Annapolis Capital,* May 21, 1901.

# List of Illustrations

## List of Photographs

*Page 1    The Commute (Courtesy Stock.xchng)*

*Page 13*    The Market as ethereal boundary: a huge glass cylinder symbolizes the "market center" at the Tokyo Stock Exchange. *(Courtesy: Tokyo Stock Exchange.)*

*Page 20*    The Market as moving quantity: the NASDAQ's MarketSite Broadcast Center. *(© Copyright 2004, The NASDAQ Stock Market, Inc.)*

*Page 21*    The Market as mind. TOP: The analysis of brain waves (the "eggs" are human heads). BOTTOM: The analysis of "market waves." *(TOP: Courtesy of Laboratory for Advanced Brain Signal Processing, Riken, Japan. BOTTOM: Courtesy of the author.)*

*Page 22*    The Market as financial Matrix: Smartmoney's interactive "Map of the Market" (http://www.smartmoney.com/marketmap/). The map shows the performance of the top companies in the U.S. stock market, updated every fifteen minutes. Each tile represents a single company, its size being proportional to its market capitalization. The color of the tile reflects the change in the company's stock price over a set time period: red is declining, green is increasing, black is flat. The stronger the color, the stronger the price movement. Companies are further arranged in eleven major industry sectors. Neighborhoods within each sector contain similarly performing companies. By scrolling over a company, one can access another level of quantitative data. *(© SmartMoney.com 2005. Used with permission. All rights reserved. SmartMoney is a joint venture of Hearst SM Partnership and Dow Jones & Company, Inc.)*

*Page 27*    The Market as Beast: the bull and the bear sparring over time. *(Courtesy Westland Giftware.)*

*Page 29*    "In general, you will find the forms and dispositions of mankind to correspond with the nature of the country."—Hippocrates *(Photo by the author.)*

*Page 55*    America's Family: The Bradys (1970–74) vs. The Osbournes (2001–present). *(Brady Bunch is courtesy Everett Collection; Osbournes are "MTV/courtesy Everett Collection.")*

*Page 81*   Product Placement: Nicole Kidman in *The Stepford Wives,* 2004. *(Paramount/courtesy Everett Collection.)*

*Page 91*   Made in the Middle East. *(Photo by the author.)*

*Page 105*   A Hummer Limousine: $1,000 per night. *(Photo by the author.)*

*Page 123*   LEFT: *The Creature from the Black Lagoon,* 1954; RIGHT: *Friday the 13th,* 1980. *(Black Lagoon credit is "courtesy of Everett Collection"; Friday 13th credit is "Paramount/courtesy Everett Collection.")*

*Page 135*   The staff of *H Bomb,* Harvard's first student-run porn magazine, pose for the centerfold of their debut issue. *(Concept: Andy Pasquesi; photograph: Christopher Anderson; copyright* H Bomb *magazine, 2004.)*

*Page 141*   Tract homes, Delaware. *(Photo by the author.)*

*Page 163*   Annapolis, MD: 18th and 19th century; Annapolis, MD: 20th century. *(Photos by the author.)*

*Page 173*   Car dealer, Maryland. *(Photo by the author.)*

*Page 207*   The statue of Darth Vader at the summit of the National Cathedral, Washington D.C. *(Photo by C. Harrison Conroy Co., Inc. This image is for sale in the National Cathedral gift shop.)*

*Page 237*   LEFT: National Bestseller, 1997. RIGHT: Terrorist Attack, 2001. *(Underworld: "Reprinted with the permission of Scribner, an imprint of Simon and Schuster Adult Publishing Group, from* Underworld *by Don DeLillo, Copyright © 1997 by Simon & Schuster, Inc." 9/11 Attack: "© Reuters Pictures.")*

*Page 239*   *Site prep, Annapolis. (Photo by the author.)*

*Page 250*   The dedication of the Southgate Memorial Fountain, May 21, 1901. *If you look closely, you can see the benediction being read from the platform. (Courtesy St. Anne's Parish.)*

## List of Charts and Graphs

# ACKNOWLEDGMENTS

This book began ten years ago, when I was working on a bond-trading desk. It was there that I began to think of the Market as a higher power of some kind, since virtually everyone around me was clearly serving it. And since, as noted earlier, the trading floor is like a crucible, burning away all principles but market principles, I also had the opportunity to look the beast in the eye, so to speak, an image that never left my mind.

After that experience, I began to investigate the nature of this mysterious power, and to assemble a comprehensive picture of its many diverse facets. I also began applying what I learned well beyond the trading floor, to the larger society in which I lived, yielding insights and explanations well beyond my expectations. This book is the fruit of all that thought and research, which was known to very few people, and supported by only one.

More recently, however, I have incurred several debts. My sincere thanks go out to Richard Curtis, who was relentless in selling this book; to my editor, Marion Maneker, who understood exactly what I was saying (when few others did) and had the guts to take the risk; to Edwin Tan, who helped me navigate the rapids of the production process with great skill; and to Gretchen Crary, my ace publicist.

Throughout the writing process, my two young sons, Curtis and Alex, have been a constant dose of perspective, a reminder of how to look at the world.

Most importantly, I would like to thank my wife, Sarah, whose endless love and patience continue to make all things possible. The Market has finally met its match.

# Index